The
MYTH
of the PERFECT
MOTHER

D0380408

The MYTH *of the* PERFECT MOTHER

Parenting Without Guilt

JANE SWIGART, PH.D.

CB
CONTEMPORARY BOOKS

Library of Congress Cataloging-in-Publication Data

Swigart, Jane.
    The myth of the perfect mother : parenting without guilt / Jane Swigart.
      p.   cm.
    Rev. ed. of: The myth of the bad mother. 1st ed. 1991.
    ISBN 0-8092-2938-2
      1. Mothers—United States—Psychology.   2. Motherhood—United
States—Psychological aspects.   3. Mother and child—United States.
4. Mothers in literature.   I. Swigart, Jane. Myth of the bad mother.   II. Title.
HQ759.S95   1998
306.874'3—dc21
                            98-24864
                            CIP

Excerpts from "Daddy" by Sylvia Plath, copyright © 1963 by Ted Hughes; "Magi" by Sylvia Plath, copyright © 1961 by Ted Hughes; "Brasilia" by Sylvia Plath, copyright © 1961 by Ted Hughes; "The Night Dances" by Sylvia Plath, copyright © 1961 by Ted Hughes; "Child" by Sylvia Plath, copyright © 1972 by Ted Hughes; "Nick and the Candlestick" by Sylvia Plath, copyright © 1966 by Ted Hughes; "Death & Co." by Sylvia Plath, copyright © 1963 by Ted Hughes; "Morning Song" by Sylvia Plath, copyright © 1962 by Ted Hughes; "Lesbos" by Sylvia Plath, copyright © 1966 by Ted Hughes; "Balloons" by Sylvia Plath, copyright © 1963 by Ted Hughes. All the above poems are from *The Collected Poems* by Sylvia Plath, copyright © 1960, 1965, 1971, 1981 by the Estate of Sylvia Plath. Reprinted in the United States by permission of Harper & Row Publishers, Inc. and elsewhere in the world by permission of Olwyn Hughes. Excerpts from "The Disquieting Man" and "The Colossus" from *The Colossus* by Sylvia Plath. Copyright © 1962 by the Estate of Sylvia Plath. Reprinted by permission of Alfred A. Knopf Inc. and elsewhere in the world by permission of Olwyn Hughes. Excerpts from "Pain for a Daughter," "A Little Uncomplicated Man," "Little Girl, My String Bean, My Lovely Woman," and "Those Times" from *Live or Die* by Anne Sexton, copyright © 1966 by Anne Sexton. Reprinted by permission of Houghton Mifflin Company. Excerpts from "That Moment," "Looking at Them Asleep," and "The Signs" from *The Gold Cell*. Copyright © 1987 by Sharon Olds. Reprinted by permission of Alfred A. Knopf Inc. Excerpts from "Dutch Graves in Buck County" by Wallace Stevens from *The Collected Poems of Wallace Stevens*. Copyright © 1954 by Wallace Stevens. Reprinted by permission of Alfred A. Knopf Inc.

Cover design by Mary Lockwood
Cover illustration: Gustave Klimt, *The Three Ages of Woman* (detail). Gallery of Modern Art, Rome/E.T. Archive, London/SuperStock.
Photograph copyright © SuperStock.
An earlier version of this book was published as *The Myth of the Bad Mother: Parenting Without Guilt.*
Published by arrangement with Doubleday, a division of Bantam Doubleday Dell Publishing Group, Inc.

Published by Contemporary Books
A division of NTC/Contemporary Publishing Group, Inc.
4255 West Touhy Avenue, Lincolnwood (Chicago), Illinois 60646-1975 U.S.A.
Copyright © 1998, 1991 by Jane Swigart
All rights reserved. No part of this book may be reproduced, stored in a retrieval system, or transmitted in any form or by any means, electronic, mechanical, photocopying, recording, or otherwise, without the prior permission of NTC/Contemporary Publishing Group, Inc.
Printed in the United States of America
International Standard Book Number: 0-8092-2938-2
18   17   16   15   14   13   12   11   10   9   8   7   6   5   4   3   2   1

This book is dedicated to
Saramanda and Tess,
who taught me
how to love.

ACKNOWLEDGMENTS

I wish to express profound gratitude for the help and support of Dr. Leslie Fiedler, Dr. William Sylvester, Dr. Christina Wendel, Dr. Stephen Seligman, Dr. Arietta Slade, Sue Auchincloss, Lyn Ballard, Robert Bicks, Gayle Brown, Jack Bugas, Robyn Bugas, Dina Flaherety, Michael Flaherety, Luella Flaherety, Dori Gores, Joe Gores, Patti Harris, Barbara Kinsey, Diana Mandell, Tish O'Dowd, and Cindy Wilber.

Table of CONTENTS

Chapter Five

**ON FATHERS AND MALE MOTHERS:
THE MYTH OF THE BAD FATHER** 110

*The Myth of the Bad Father . . . ▪ The Importance of the
Father During Early Childhood . . . ▪ Forms of Paternal
Caring . . . ▪ Exclusion of the Father . . . ▪ Aversion to
Children . . . ▪ Child Care and Regression . . .
▪ Effects of Paternal Distance . . . ▪ Sylvia Plath's
Father Poems . . . ▪ Sophie's Choice: The Metaphor of
Sacrifice . . . ▪ Children and Moral Visibility*

Part Three

LOVE AND RELINQUISHMENT 141

Chapter Six

THE WORK OF SEPARATION 143

*Devotion at a Distance . . . ▪ Emotional Realities of
Caring for School-Age Children . . . ▪ Maternal Clinging
and Compulsive Flight . . . ▪ The Refusal to Be
Dominated by Children . . . ▪ Voluntary Bondage . . . ▪ Maternal Individuation*

Chapter Seven

ADOLESCENCE AND THE END OF CHILDHOOD 169

*Unintended Feelings . . . ▪ Forewarnings of Loss . . .
▪ Defenses Against Attachment . . . ▪ Unrequited Love
. . . ▪ Relinquishment*

THE MYTH OF

THE PERFECT

MOTHER

The relationship to the mother is the first and most intense. Therefore, it must perish.

—Sigmund Freud,
Female Sexuality

Psychoanalytic theory has thus been unable to conceptualize the mother as a separate subject . . . we may wish to take some distance from a paradigm that grants the mother so much responsibility and so little concern for the conditions of her own subjectivity.

—Jessica Benjamin,
Like Subjects, Love Objects

If a community values its children, it must cherish its mothers.
—John Bowlby,
World Health Organization Monograph, 1951

Journal Entry: December, 1983

• *Last night I told N, a child psychiatrist, about the women I'd finally found who wrote honestly about the experience of mothering. He said, "They were angry, unhappy women. How could they be trusted to give an accurate account of what it's like to be a mother? Women who are happy as mothers don't talk about it."*

I couldn't sleep, wondering what in our culture makes it possible for a man as intelligent and learned as N to think in this way. Has he never spent a long period of time with a cranky child? Has he never experienced the guilt of knowing he has made a mistake with a child (has been insensitive or done the wrong thing)? I felt incensed, as though I'd been silenced—as though all mothers who were not angry or desperate had been rendered mute by this attitude.

But perhaps N is right, and many of the writers I have discovered (Tillie Olsen, Doris Lessing, Sylvia Plath, Anne Sexton, Grace Paley) were driven by rage or sadness to break the silence and explore the experience of mothering. Yet it's clear from their work that they loved their children. Maybe there's no way to be honest without sounding angry and resentful, like a "bad mother." Yet most mothers I know are neither blissful nor miserable, but live in a gray area we haven't really looked at closely. It's difficult now for all mothers who love their children not to be torn, anxious, guilt-ridden, pulled in many different directions at once.

The mother's need to be heard, cared for, understood is certainly as important as that of the child. Most children cannot be helped if mothers are not helped and supported as well. Yet why is it so hard to talk about what happens to us during all those days, weeks, years we spend with our children—the emotional realities of mothering that occur on an hourly, minute-to-minute basis?

Revised Introduction: January, 1998

> Myth: " . . . an unproved collective belief that is accepted uncritically and is used to justify a social institution."

What began as a personal journal exploring my experiences as a mother led this past decade to extensive research into the literature and psychology of nurturing. During my explorations I became both fascinated and threatened by what I learned about the processes of the human psyche during the activity of day-to-day child care—the deepest feelings and conflicts that child rearing evokes in us, and their meaning in our lives. As I examined all that is involved in nurturing children, I discovered how precarious the nature of altruistic love is, yet how the experience of child rearing can humanize us as nothing else can.

Where I grew up in the Midwest, during the 1940s and '50s, raising children was considered women's work. Families were large; mothers were always pregnant. Four children was the average number. Even in white middle-class neighborhoods, mothers often looked exhausted and overburdened. Child rearing seemed to make them mindless and irritable.

Fathers appeared brisk and clean-shaven in the early morning, then disappeared like escape artists until late evening and sometimes for days or weeks at a time on business trips. The center of their lives was elsewhere. Elsewhere they did important work and thought about things other than children and tedious domestic chores. The sense of importance the men exuded reminded me of peacocks with brilliant plumage.

The women, trapped in the close, humid world of small bodies with constant demands for food and attention, seemed as drab as clucking hens. Warm bundles of vibrant flesh would always be climbing on the women's laps to nestle inside their arms. Then these bundles of flesh would crawl down, run off and away, each day a little farther away. . . . That these mothers might be weathering violent emotional storms, experiencing a kaleidoscope of conflicting passions, I had not an inkling. That there might be enjoyment involved in the care of children (pleasures, I was later to discover, almost too exquisite and enviable to voice above a whisper), I could not then imagine.

Until I had children of my own, relatively late for my generation (my first was born when I was thirty-three), I had little sympathy for those flesh-tied mothers of my youth, my own mother least of all—I struggled too hard to escape the reach of her oppressive arms. Now, as I try to describe the inner world of the mother, I find that the brilliant plumage of the masculine intellect, where I had sought and found refuge from my mother's need-choked world, is of limited use. In fact, whenever I try to use those intellectual traditions now, I keep running into a charming young boy: it's Huck Finn, and he's got one foot out the door, ready to light out for "the Territory."

Huckleberry Finn is the embodiment of the desire to run away from the cloying world of the care-giver toward independence. The mother figure in Twain's novel represents, among other things, our more or less slavish tie to someone who curbs, thwarts, and makes demands that curtail our autonomy. In exchange we get basic needs met: food, clothing, approval, the safety of a warm bed, a roof over our heads. The price we pay is freedom. How I longed as a child to emulate Huck, to get away from the maternal circuit and onto the raft with Jim, floating down the river toward liberation.

But Huck is a boy, unfettered and childless. As I grew into a woman, his attraction paled. I cannot remember exactly when the freedom of Huck seemed more like a compulsion to run, another form of entrapment. I think it was when I began to long for children.

When I became a mother, my children ran from me. And then back again, clinging to me briefly (to make sure I was still there) only to run farther away the next time—one minute demanding, the next minute blithely skipping out the door. One day they needed those wonderful hugs, body warmth, a heart-to-heart talk—a profound connection; the next day they needed to be left completely alone with their friends or simply to experience the world in their own separate way. In this book I explore the fate of those who must nurture and thwart and make demands until the child can creep, crawl, walk, and finally run away.

Man's thinking is tainted by his desire to escape the mother, woman's by her inability to do so. Our first reality *is* the mother. It is this reality Western thought has been running from until it is exhausted, spent. It is this fusional universe we once experienced with our primary care-giver that we run from yet yearn for. We hide this yearning and our desire to escape it by devaluing the mother and keeping away from our consciousness *our own experiences as mothers, our own feelings as care-givers.* When we become parents, our own mother rises up in us—sometimes as Madonna, sometimes as Witch. This is the person we once felt closer to than any other human being—and now we have assumed her role.

What is it like *not* to light out for the Territory? To be the one who stays home and participates in the daily, hourly care of our children? To remain with small children often means being stuck in small cramped places, sitting or standing, often idle. To remain with a child means assuming responsibilities so heavy and awesome they must be repressed or denied: it means keeping the infant alive and safe from the perils to which she is exposed each day. (Babies creep, crawl, totter, and fall off sofas and jungle gyms and slides. They eat dirt, shoe polish, dog manure—anything if you don't stop them. They can choke on pebbles, drown in two feet of water.) It means keeping the children thriving, both emotionally and physically, and socializing them into a culture that spends billions of dollars each year trying to exploit them.

Before the birth of my first child, I had little curiosity about what mothers actually experienced when they took care of their children. I vaguely believed women were either perfect mothers who made their children happy or bad mothers who made them miserable. The bad mothers had many names: the Castrating Mother; the Smothering, Intrusive Mother; the Cold, Rejecting Mother. Perfect mothers, on the other hand, seemed pretty much the same: they loved their children unconditionally and worked constantly to provide what was best for them.

It was not until I became a mother that I realized how much we use these myths of good and bad mothers to obscure the chaotic, sometimes overwhelming experiences that child rearing inevitably stirs up in us. There is something about the extreme vulnerability of children that makes it difficult to look closely at what is involved in caring for them. Our resistance is even greater when it comes to acknowledging what child rearing *feels* like on a constant basis.

As we approach the intimate relationship between mother and child, our attention tends to swerve away from ourselves toward the child. The closer we look at the child, the further the care-giver recedes into a hazy background, looming large but indistinct as Madonna or Witch. Yet failures in nurturing are often caused by our reluctance to examine mixed, often contrary feelings we harbor toward our children.

Because we live in a society that simultaneously idealizes and devalues the mother, I have been compelled to look far beneath the myth of the bad mother, responsible for her children's emotional problems and unhappiness, and the perfect mother, selflessly devoted to her children's well-being. What I have discovered is an area of darkness in our culture that we have only begun to examine.

The Myth

Imagine a woman who wants only what is best for her children, whose needs she intuits effortlessly. This mother adores her offspring and finds them fascinating. She is exquisitely attuned to her children and is so resourceful she is immune to boredom. Nurturing comes as naturally as breathing, and child rearing is a source of pleasure that does not require discipline or self-sacrifice. She is the Perfect Mother.

Now imagine the opposite: a woman easily bored by her children, indifferent to their well-being; a mother so self-absorbed that she cannot discern what is in the best interests of her children. Insensitive to their needs, she is unable to empathize with them and often uses them for her own gratification. This woman damages her children without knowing it. Unable to learn from the suffering she causes, she is incapable of change. She is the Bad Mother.

However much we may yearn to resemble the mythical Perfect Mother, we know from the daily experiences of child rearing and the difficult moments we have with our children that we are not her and never will be. There are no perfect mothers on this earth. We hear of disturbed individuals who resemble the second mythical figure. The media reports stories of vicious or psychotic people who do horrible things to their children without guilt or remorse. But I am making a wide distinction between those isolated cases and the majority of us, parents who love our children and want to nurture them as best we can.

In theory, it is easy for us to imagine a woman capable of loving the way we think children should be loved. In practice, however, the emotional realities of child rearing expose us to our most destructive urges as well as our deepest hopes, longings, and capacities for love. With our offspring, we so want to be our best selves—full of love and genuine concern. Yet the absolute dependency and helplessness of young children require every care-giver to give, at times, without getting anything immediate or tangible in return. Even under the best of circumstances, this altruism is difficult to sustain. There are times when we all catch ourselves being inauthentic in our love, failing to meet our children's legitimate needs, becoming hurtful of their feelings. We love our children dearly yet in flawed ways that are painful to contemplate.

Child rearing evokes our most generous impulses—and our basest: cruelty, indifference, possessiveness, envy, and resentment not only of the child's right to be cared for, but also of the tedious, repetitive tasks of feeding and tending.

To ward off disturbing feelings that constant, intimate contact with children stirs up in us, we search for a scapegoat, the source of emotional pain. As a society, we point a collective finger at "bad mothers," silencing all mothers about the realities of child care for fear they might *be* the source of their children's problems and suffering. The myth of the bad mother is a photographic negative of the other myth, that of the perfect, all-giving mother. These myths encourage us to believe that mothers—either loving and gratifying or completely selfish and withholding—are solely responsible for how their children turn out.

The truth is that child rearing is a collective endeavor in which fathers, extended families, and the whole society play a role, as much by failure to act as by acting. The myth of the bad mother hides this crucial fact: the early years of a human life are the most important and formative. They should be the concern and responsibility of more than one isolated, devalued, unsupported person. Our tendency either to blame or idealize the mother blinds us to what we are and screens us from a close examination of the tremendous complexities of nurturing children. Without knowledge of the needs and feelings of care-givers, we are failing on a nationwide scale to provide optimum care for our children.

Mothering in the Light of Recent Infant Research

A number of years have passed since I finished working on this book. During that time, child rearing in this country has become even more fraught with conflict. Amid storms of controversy about what mothers should or should not do, it has become more and more threatening to examine the emotional realities of care giving. In too many instances, conditions have worsened for mothers and their children. Yet during the past two decades, advances in infant research have yielded important new information about the crucial attachment formed by infant and care-giver.

Scientific studies on the world of the infant clearly establish that the rich relationship between newborn and mother—not only the gratifications of feeding and being fed, but the eye-to-eye contact, smiles and coos, touching, holding, and rocking as well—is a truly *mutual* exchange. Clinical professor of psychiatry and leading infant clinician Dr. Stephen Seligman says the "magic of babies"—their power to hold us spellbound—lies in the fierce yet uniquely individual way they evoke responses in us and their vigorous capacity to initiate, maintain, and even terminate reactions. New studies indicate how competent and socially interactive infants are preprogrammed to be, refuting the belief that babies are born blind, "normally autistic," and highly disorganized. In fact, they can differentiate their mothers at birth, seek out stimulation as early as three days, and show distinct preferences for their mother's voice, face, and even smell. Most important is the discovery that babies need *attachment*—a *relationship*—as well as social bonding. Even the physical growth and intricate architecture of the brain depend on the infant's social interactions. Being spoken to, played with, and responded to greatly enriches an infant's mental apparatus. This need for a consistent, ongoing *connection* with a loving Other is as crucial as their need for nourishment.

Very early on, infants search out our emotional reactions to organize and to regulate their behavior and resolve uncertainties. We may intuit these things on a gut level—especially how greatly infants vary in such things as activity level, sensitivity to stimuli, mobility, curiosity, and the capacity to be soothed. Yet how easily swayed we are by trends, customs, fads, and advice from "experts," all of which are now amplified by the media.

It is sad and ironic that important scientific research about our children has come at a moment in history when conditions for nurturing are so stressful. Whether women work outside the home or take daily care of their children, they are given insufficient support. Yet mothers are held accountable for the well-being of their children and stand accused if anything goes wrong. This lack of support makes most women vulnerable to any information that makes them feel blamed or under attack.

Despite what we now know about infants, our society shows such indifference to the well-being of mothers and children in some segments of the population that the "magic of babies" has lost its power to affect those who bear and care for them. Caring for infants has become so difficult in our inner cities and other impoverished areas of our society that irreparable damage is being done to too many children. Yet most mothers' daily lives are so full of conflict, few have the equanimity or energy to consider the larger social issues that affect our nation's children.

Those precious times when mothers *are* able to experience the exquisite joys and tenderness of the mother-child bond should be protected and cherished by all of us. We must all work to create the environment of support and compassion mothers need to experience intimacy and connection with their children, and to expose what I see as the brutal effects of a society that deprives its children, penalizes women for being mothers, and denigrates the work of child care.

The New Morality

Society imposes the role of "Mother" on all women who bear children. Whether this role is accepted and lived or relegated to someone else (nurse, child-care center, relative, adoptive parents) depends upon socioeconomic factors, such as the need of a mother to provide financial support, cultural attitudes, the emotional capacities of the mother, and the current fashions in child rearing. In books such as *Centuries of Childhood* by Phillippe Aries, *Mother Love* by Elizabeth Badingter, and *Inventing Motherhood* by Anne Daly, we see such varying maternal attitudes toward children it is hard to say which is more shocking: the indifference toward infants in previous centuries or the more recent focus—almost obsession—

on children today. What is new, according to Badingter, is that the responsibility for the child's day-to-day well-being is now placed solely on the mother. Also new is the underlying ethical dimension that now pervades our attitudes about child rearing.

No longer do we see the birth of an infant as a biological event that serves the species. We now understand that what we *do* with our children, how we *feel* and *behave* when we are with them, has profound ramifications on their lives. We know now how easy it is to use children for purely selfish ends—for purposes of self-aggrandizement, to fill up an empty life, or to rescue a faltering self. One of the highest ethical achievements in Western thought may be this new awareness of how easy it is to hurt a child.

Yet interest in the child has taken such precedence over interest in the mother that we know next to nothing about ourselves as caregivers. Instead of pushing us to explore what is involved in the precarious task of emotional giving, this new morality has ended up postulating impossible ideals of parenthood and blaming mothers if they do not live up to these ideals. Intrinsic to the myth of the Perfect Mother is the assumption that the intuitive powers needed to successfully launch a child out into the world are effortless or somehow unworthy of consideration. The care of children is seen as a sacred trust, yet it is one in which women are unsupported. Thus, mothers cannot possibly fulfill this trust. Our society assumes that nurturing the young is an easy task that comes naturally to women but not to men. We cling to an image of mothers as born nurturers who do not want for themselves, only for their children.

Because there is so little interest in what care-givers actually experience, mothers deny or hide much of what is real and vital about the complexities of the tasks. Women are as reluctant to speak of the deep pleasures and gratifications of mothering as they are of the conflicts their children evoke. This cultural silence about the emotional realities of child rearing creates such anxiety that it is too threatening for many people to examine their subjective states as they care for their children.

Mothers and the Workforce

It was once thought that only men could be pulled away or distracted from the care of their children. Now most women are torn between work outside the home and the responsibilities of child care. Our experiences with our children are profoundly influenced by financial pressures, the organization of production, marketing, and the revved-up consumerism that now dominates our lives. In addition to giving us an extraordinarily high standard of living, our market economy has had a deleterious effect on the family.

In his last book, *Women and the Common Life*, Christopher Lasch claims that many now look upon the traditional family as obsolete, replaced like some outmoded technology by a family structure in which both parents work outside the home. To be the equal of men in the workforce, most mothers must spend long hours away from their children. Lasch asserts that professional women who "allow their children to slow them down lose out in the race for success." Mothers who choose to stay on the competitive edge in their careers and those who stay home to care for their children both pay a different but heavy price. Many mothers I interviewed in the workforce were tormented with fatigue, guilt, and legitimate concern over poor child care. Those I talked to who stay home to take care of their children sometimes feel like outcasts and are pressured to enter the workforce as much from loneliness and isolation as from financial concerns and public opinion.

In her recent study of an "enlightened" corporation, Arlie Hochschild found that for many mothers work had become a refuge from "the emotional tangles at home." Some mothers left their children ten to twelve hours a day at the corporation's on-site daycare center and did not even take "their full vacation allotment." In her provocative book *The Time Bind: When Work Becomes Home and Home Becomes Work*, Hochschild states that exhausted parents flee "a world of unresolved quarrels and unwashed laundry for the reliable orderliness, harmony, and managed cheer of work." Similarly, Stephanie Coontz, in *The Way We Really Are*, suggests that mothers "would not give up the satisfactions of their jobs even if they could afford to quit."

What is most alarming is how tenuous emotional ties are in our society, how quickly relationships can deteriorate. One in two marriages ends in divorce. Most families consist of single mothers. Given these statistics, Hochschild's most disturbing findings suggest many mothers, given the choice, focus on concerns at work rather than the chaotic demands of their growing children.

Now that we can no longer deny the importance of attachment in early childhood, we must summon the courage to ask disturbing questions: Has our avid consumerism created a kind of brainwashing that leads us to believe our children's need for human relatedness—*for loving relationships*—is less important than our stockpiles of material goods? Are the slender emotional attachments that our economy fosters doomed to be repeated in the next generation? How do we alleviate the pressures on parents that drive them to leave their children during early infancy, given what we now know about how critical these stages of development are to the ultimate formation of each child's brain and character? *How can we raise these questions without adding to the crushing burden of guilt so many mothers already experience?*

We must designate some common ground, free of condemnation and blame, to explore these issues. We must suspend judgment and rise above our tendency to accuse and moralize so that we can examine the elusive complexities of care giving. For unless we are able to explore what nurturing gives and demands of us, make it as important a discourse as the study of politics, economics, and environmentalism, we will not be able to bring forth and sustain the kind of altruism required to care for our children as well as the earth.

Understanding the Nurturer

What is it like to take care of a child? As a society, we tend to identify with the child rather than with the parent or care-giver.

Though we are great lovers of children in theory, in practice our country's child-care policies rank low among the developed nations. Child psychologists now believe that we will not know how to improve conditions for nurturing our children until those who care for them are able to speak openly about their experiences.

During an informal interview, one psychoanalyst told me this:

> I was unable to genuinely empathize with my female patients who were mothers of young children until my wife was called away and I spent two and a half weeks taking care of my three-year-old son. I'd never really experienced a one-to-one relationship before that was so one-sided—where I was doing all the giving. It literally changed my life. I realized I hadn't really known anything about children or what mothers go through; only by caring for them day after day, hour after hour, can you know both their world and how it collides with the adult world. It's frightening how much I just hadn't understood about myself, my patients, even my own son.

It is this kind of honesty that will help us learn what supports and maintains altruistic behavior and what it is that makes nurturing difficult for anyone.

What is it that makes child care so problematic? Whether we are male or female, parents or childless, the care of children reawakens our buried selves. For better or worse, child care pulls us in two directions: outward toward the children we tend and inward toward our own earliest experiences of being cared for. Our first, most intense relationship with our mother often remains unconscious and inaccessible until we have children, at which point all the longings and ambivalence we felt toward her rise up in us again.

In addition to evoking our early relationships with our parents, child care sometimes seems like what Thornstein Veblen described as "servile attendance on the needs of others." Part of the discipline of mothering is learning behavior we associate with being a servant—the drudge work of feeding, cleaning, *one-sided* tending.

By becoming more conscious of the feelings and conflicts our children generate in us as we care for them, we gain access to some of the emotions our parents might have felt toward us. Often it is after we have children that we are able to become more tolerant and forgiving and can achieve that crucial, humanizing integration that diminishes our tendency to blame others.

In an article entitled "Ghosts in the Nursery," child analyst Selma Fraiberg shows how a psychotherapist's compassionate understanding of a mother's traumatic experiences in early childhood can repair and restore a loving, life-giving relationship between that mother and her child. Fraiberg's other work, *Every Child's Birthright: In Defense of Mothering*, exemplified how our culture, in its refusal to acknowledge and conceptualize the subjectivity of the mother, contributes to the guilt mothers feel, making them reluctant to speak honestly. Asserting the importance of the mother's presence to an infant, *Every Child's Birthright* was a disturbing book to many mothers forced to work outside the home soon after the birth of their children. Selma Fraiberg's work at the end of her life (setting up a treatment center for troubled, high-risk mothers of infants and working closely with them) confirms the truths that she and many professionals have finally come to: that the *mother's* need to be heard, cared for, and compassionately understood is as important as that of her child and that most children cannot be helped if mothers are not helped and supported as well.

If no one is sympathetic to the mother, if no one is there to listen, understand, or respond to her pain and frustration, she cannot help but feel invisible, devalued, silenced, and ignored. This excruciating experience for mothers, of feeling unimportant and unseen, is much like the experience of infants whom no one loves, cares for, or mirrors. If no one is there to validate a child's deepest emotions and inner life, that child will not receive the feedback necessary for a sense of reality and a strong sense of self. The same is true of mothers. It is as though our culture has robbed mothers of their subjectivity, thereby putting the future of our children in jeopardy.

Mother-Infant Ecology

We must create for mothers a nurturing, supportive "holding environment" to counter a society that is in many respects inimical to the well-being of both children and their care-givers. As British psychoanalyst D. W. Winnicott's term suggests, the holding environment of the infant extends beyond the mother's arms to include all cultural influences that affect the mother in her role as care-giver. If a mother is not given a protective, compassionate holding environment for herself as she tries to provide for her infant, her relationship to the new life can become painful and traumatic. What is traumatic for the mother is traumatic for her child. By not attending to the needs of mothers, societies contribute to destructive ways of relating that get handed down through generations.

We know now that how we treat our children determines how the earth will be treated; how we feel toward them influences foreign policy, the weapons we build, the wars we send them to fight. If I concentrate on the darker side of maternal experience, it is because too little has been written on the impact of emotional *deprivation* in parents and how this influences caregiving. Part of our work as parents is to bring to consciousness tendencies that may be lethal to our children so that we do not hand down a legacy of self-destruction.

The birth of an infant is a transformational experience. At no other time in our lives are we as open, emotionally flexible, and subject to growth and change. Because of each infant's capacity to respond to, evoke, and thus amplify sensitive care giving, children offer us a new chance—a kind of rebirth—during which we can "right the wrongs" of past generations. Our tendency to repeat with our children what may have been traumatic in our own childhood is counteracted by our desire to "do a better job" than our parents did. This window of opportunity is a gift each new generation gives to its parents.

The mother is the baby's ecology. We now know how to enhance this ecology. What recent developments in infant-parent psychotherapy show us is how quickly babies and parents of all social classes respond to support, guidance, and the nonjudgmental use of interpretation. In writing about his work with troubled families, Dr. Steven Seligman says that "the provision of a supportive and emotionally secure background allows new parents to reflect on and gain insight about emotionally painful issues." Such understanding can detoxify and profoundly alter constrictive ways of relating and enrich the mother-infant ecology so that *both* can blossom and thrive.

Methods of Exploration

In this book, I mingle different methods of discovery: journal entries and formal works of art, informal interviews with parents and health care professionals and psychoanalytic case histories, personal confessions and philosophical statements. Purposely I move in this book from the detached, impersonal voice of the scientist, historian, and literary critic to the intimate human voice, undefended by any academic discipline or the heavy iron doors of the intellect.

Until recently, our culture has shown little interest in the mother's painful and frustrating experiences with her children. For this reason, I rely in some chapters on the craft, skill, and vision of women who through their fiction and poetry transform the raw experience of mother-child relationships into works of art. Through their compassion for the care-giver, these writers transfigure and monumentalize the complex emotions of mothers as they care for their children.

We now know that persistent difficulties in nurturing can cause irreversible damage to the child. This is especially true during the earliest years. Our deep identification with the helplessness of children makes it painful to examine disturbed relationships between children and adults. We are so troubled by injustice toward children that understanding of the distressed care-giver is frequently beyond us. Often we feel the urge to rescue the child and to punish whoever is doing the harm. In this way we bypass a thorough understanding of the conditions that created the tragic situation.

Some chapters in this book are meditations on issues that our culture tends to avoid or deny: our enigmatic longing for children; compulsive pregnancies when there is neither the desire nor the resources to nurture a child; the refusal of so many men to take a consistent part in the daily care of their children; and the deeper meanings of maternal failure. Though certain chapters deal with distinct phases in the mother-child relationship—infancy, the school-age years, and adolescence—other chapters focus on efforts to unravel areas of mystery, drawing on intuition and anecdote.

Part I, "The Complexities of Nurturing," considers all that nurturing involves and the subjective experience of the mother during the earliest years of her children's lives, and what motivates us to procreate. Part II, "The Reluctance to Know; the Reluctance to Care," examines our resistance to knowing what mothers experience, the devaluation of the care-giver, and what prevents so many people from involving themselves in the care of their children. Part III, "Love and Relinquishment," explores the nature of the gradual separation of the mother from her growing child. Part IV, "The Meaning of Maternal Failure," looks at postindustrial society's "holding environment" for mothers and the ways in which child rearing can be a transformative experience, leading to higher levels of consciousness and humanization.

I hope that understanding the deeper issues that underlie the experience of child rearing will elevate, as well as honor, one of our most critical tasks.

Part One

THE

COMPLEXITIES
OF NURTURING

Chapter One

MATERNAL LOVE AND MATERNAL IMPOTENCE

At the beginning love can only be expressed effectively in terms of infant and child care, which means for us the provision of a facilitating or good-enough environment, and which means for the infant a chance to evolve in a personal way according to the steady gradation of the maturational process . . .

—D. W. Winnicott,
The Maturational Process and the Facilitating Environment

I do not deny that the intangibles, such as the joys of watching children grow up, also influence behavior. But who is to say that the joys of watching ten children grow up to be carhops is greater than the joy of watching one grow up to be a surgeon? Or that it is more rewarding for a woman to rear one surgeon than to be one herself and rear none?

—Marvin Harris,
Cannibals and Kings

Notes from Interviews with Mothers

• *Nothing will be able to take the place of my children. If I were not too old, I would have another child. What disturbs me is the world—the nuclear arms race . . . It's not child rearing that is hard for me. It's the fact that no matter how good a job I do raising my four children, I'm powerless to change the world—all the bombs, wars, violence. It's the horrible, polluted air my children have to breathe each day, and the nuclear waste dumps.*

It's so bad now; what's it going to be like for my kids when they are my age and starting families of their own? If I had to choose a profession, I'd become a politician—something which would give me the power to reverse the destruction so that my children will have a good life. (Marion, forty-six, mother of four)

• *My mother taught me how to achieve, not how to nurture an infant. I've never had any intention of staying at home and taking care of a child. You might say my work as a child psychologist is care-giving, but a disturbed child presents me with a series of fascinating, complex problems which I must first understand and then try to solve. I translate this understanding into the psychotherapeutic process, which is an intellectual process as well as an intuitive, emotional one. None of this helped me as a mother. After my son was born, I found the grind of child care incredibly boring. My Ph.D. in Child Development didn't help, nor did my eight years of private practice. I had much more difficulty figuring out what to do with my son all day Sunday than two years of treatment with my most difficult patient. I have a better understanding of what mothers go through now. I'm convinced you can't help a child if you don't feel compassion for the mother (no matter how hard this sometimes is). But nothing has made it easier to be a mother, except the fact that on Monday I can go back to work. Maybe it's like a kind of impotence—maternal impotence. I can give only so much to my son during the day. Then I feel exhausted and want to get back to my own life, my own work, which replenishes me. (Tanya, thirty-five, mother of one)*

The birth of a child draws upon the emotional and material resources of every society. The absolute vulnerability and dependency of children makes each birth a kind of request or demand. Whether it is met with joy or indifference, love or resentment, the care of children forces us to confront issues of giving. When an entire culture ceases to care about nurturing and protecting human life—as I believe ours has—we must examine the deeper meanings of caring and not caring, our individual capacities and failures to love our children and ourselves.

Research into the nature of maternal love led me to hypothesize two distinct states of mind: one in which we feel concern for others and are capable of caring for them in an altruistic way, a state I call *maternal love;* and the other in which we are incapable of caring for others, a withdrawal I call *maternal impotence.*

Defining Maternal Love and Maternal Impotence

On an individual level, emotional withdrawal is normal, even necessary to be productive in our society. There are times when we cannot consider the well-being of anyone else, child or adult. Often we are engrossed in aims, thoughts, and feelings that have nothing to do with concern for others or nurturing of any kind. To pursue excellence or achievement outside the home, it is often necessary to withdraw from our children. Most work that we are paid to do in this society demands maternal impotence: that we do not consider the well-being of others (for example, inventing certain products, devising ways to manufacture them, and imagining ways to make these products seductive and marketable). When we are forced to work at something that frustrates or bores us, or are engaged in fierce competition with others, we have little time or inclination to care altruistically for a child whose immediate best interests (to be cleaned, fed, comforted, toilet-trained, etc.) seem quite remote from our own personal ambitions. Yet as I began to interview parents and those who work with children, I discovered one of our deepest fears is that we might be unwilling or unable to care for our children, even for a brief period of time.

What is maternal love? It does not seem necessary to define it. We recognize it in the madonnas of Raphael and Leonardo da Vinci and the paintings of Renoir and Mary Cassatt, whose portraits of mothers convey a sense of devotion to children, delight in their well-being, and pleasure in the acts of nurturing. Maternal love suggests an ability to intuit an individual child's needs and unique course of development, a capacity for genuine concern and actual physical care, and a willingness to use subjective experience, empathic identification, even symbiotic fusion to understand and care for the young.

Maternal love requires many different skills and behaviors. In addition to physical care, infants need a warm, loving "holding environment"; ideally, toddlers require freedom to explore an environment that is safe, and, after venturing forth with as little interference as possible, someone to return to for reassurance or "refueling." All children need certainty that the care-giver will not abandon them as they begin to enjoy more autonomy. Children of all ages need firm limits set on their behavior as well as protection from real dangers. Feelings of maternal impotence arise when we do not have the patience, desire, ego strength, time, money, or energy to fulfill these needs.

The empathy and self-sacrifice involved in this kind of altruistic behavior are precarious human achievements, the last to arrive in the maturational process, and the first to go when circumstances become difficult. Our society expects mothers to love and care for their children in an unselfish way, yet notions of maternal love and good child-rearing practices often conflict with what it is possible for a parent to feel and provide.

Most of us, men and women alike, experience both maternal love and maternal impotence off and on throughout our lives. I use the term *maternal* love because it more readily suggests the constant giving of care and protection that infancy and early childhood demand; giving without asking anything in return (except perhaps the wonderful hugs and smiles of devotion). Paternal love, in our culture, suggests a more distant, detached relationship, formed later and associated with one who guides, teaches, and encourages performance and achievement. The child "gives back" through her actual accomplishments.

Just as men tend to cover up feelings of sexual impotence by claims of exaggerated sexual prowess or "macho" behavior, women sometimes conceal feelings of maternal impotence beneath inordinate claims of nurturing abilities, assertions of how good we are at it, how close and wonderful our relationships with our children are, and so on. For a mother who loves her children, nothing is more devastating than the inability to provide loving care for those children, whatever the reason. Claims of potency stem from the fear of being a loser in the competitions fostered by our culture's sexual stereotypes, from feelings of inadequacy, shame, or powerlessness.

Because our society tends to lose sight of the crucial issue of emotional giving—the giving of time, understanding, concern, and care—I emphasize the *emotional* aspect of giving to a child what that child needs. Material well-being is too frequently confused in our culture with emotional well-being. Yet emotional deprivation can be as devastating as financial deprivation; often the two are directly related. Mothers coming home exhausted from work outside the home may be too depleted to give emotionally to their children. Financial deprivation and the consequent need to work can rob a mother of the time and energy to meet her infant's needs.

We do not understand the relationship between emotional deprivation and economic deprivation. Too many situations exist where feelings of maternal impotence are actually caused by things such as low wages, poor job opportunities, unfair hiring, and so on. However, even in situations where there is plenty of food, adequate housing, money to spare, and many luxuries, we find impoverished, unhappy, or destructive relationships between adults and children. Few cultures have known our society's great material abundance. This affluence does not prevent large numbers of people from experiencing inexplicable feelings of emptiness, boredom, or violence. Most people believe that if only they had more money they would be better parents, more capable of loving and giving to their children. Unfortunately, this is often not the case.

It is difficult to maintain altruistic capacities in a society that looks upon care-givers and children primarily as markets, sources of income for food and clothing industries and toy manufacturers. The manipulation and exploitation of parents and children by business is only one manifestation of the devaluation of child care and the impoverishment of the relationships between children and adults in our society. It is not good for our economy for people to think in a loving, nurturing way. The myth of the Perfect Mother has obscured from view the ruthless attitudes of society toward mothers and children. In a culture that accepts and condones the manipulation and exploitation of those close to you—even children—the demands of caring for the young overwhelm and exceed the emotional resources of many mothers.

The Emotional Realities of Nurturing

The birth of a child confronts every mother with profound and crucial issues. Will she be able to form and sustain the intense attachment to her infant and then slowly let go of it as the child grows up? And if, for whatever reason, she can't make this attachment, does the mother have the financial means and/or emotional maturity to find a good surrogate care-giver for her child?

Though child rearing is a discipline which teaches us an enormous amount about ourselves and the world, it is not really seen as such in our culture. We have no traditions that elevate caring for children and all that it involves, making it a way of achieving intellectual or spiritual enlightenment. It is not given the respect it deserves, and *child rearing without respect, practical help, and emotional support can create terrible deprivations in the mother or care-giver, making her a victim of her own unfulfilled needs as well as her children's demands.* For some, the constant tasks involved in the daily care of young children allow little time or energy for the sublimation of competitive strivings or creative self-expression. This puts the care-giver at a disadvantage in relation to other members of society.

Child rearing can elicit maturation and wisdom in those mothers who strive to raise their children as best they can. At the same time, there is a strong tendency in all care-givers to become or behave like the children they care for. We cannot help but identify with and feel whatever a particular child feels; to need love as much as the young life we care for needs it; to become dependent, angry, rebellious, insatiable—all the emotions children feel as they pass through that long, tortuous journey from infancy through adolescence to maturity. It is through our identification with them that we are able to empathize and thus learn much about ourselves. Children can humanize us, impelling us into a constant series of mini-epiphanies as they pass through the stages of childhood. Yet they can also arouse our propensity to be blind to the needs and differences of others. Paradoxically the painful evocation of narcissism, sensuality, cruelty, and indifference is itself part of the humanizing process. Child rearing often provokes exactly that which we must learn to master, control, or overcome in ourselves in order not to hurt our children.

In *The Way of All Women,* Jungian analyst Ester Harding claims the outstanding characteristic of mother love is

> *the desire for the conservation of life . . . a child may be quite*
> *different from what the mother would have chosen, he may even be*
> *physically or mentally defective, but she cannot discard this mate-*
> *rial for a better kind.*

According to Harding, the mother's primary task is nurturing a
child who inevitably frustrates, disappoints, becomes someone different from what she wanted the child to be. Harding also speaks of the

> *external discipline of maternity . . . the disturbed nights, the ever-*
> *recurrent duties of bathing, tending, mending, the anxiety which*
> *even trivial illness occasions, the sacrifice of intellectual and social*
> *recreation through many years, the long-continued submission of*
> *personal wishes to childish needs.*

To Harding, the most difficult and important duties of the mother
are to keep her children from living out her unconscious needs,
wishes, feelings, and impulses. According to Jungian thought, each
child can and will live out her parents' strivings, ambitions, pain,
guilt, depression unless these states are made conscious—that is,
lived and felt by the parent and thus kept separate from the child.

A child can easily become a symbol for the parents—a representa-
tion of parts of themselves or significant others in their lives. A child
can become a part of oneself that one hates or that is unfulfilled.
Children can become a source of gratification that the parent does
not want to relinquish. As the child becomes older, it can represent a
sibling, even a parent, who in the past created feelings of deprivation
or rivalry. A child can come to symbolize, for a parent, a beloved
brother, idealized father, envied sister, the nurturing mother experienced only in fantasy, or the intrusive grasping mother who reap-
pears in horror films disguised as a vampire or ghoul. In short, a child
can become anything for the parent, and this can make the child's
identity—his or her uniqueness or "true self"—a precarious thing.
How easily the sins of the parents can be visited upon their children

—it is in this vague, threatening area that Freudian and Jungian analysts agree. Parents must protect their child from their own internal conflicts, thereby preserving the freedom for the child to be whatever she truly is in all her uniqueness.

Equally crucial to every child's development—though elusive to our understanding—is the need for parents to act at times as containers for frightening or overwhelming emotions with which children cannot cope by themselves: night terrors, feelings of rage, guilt, sadness, and vengefulness toward those they love. Children are often frightened by irrational fears of retaliation or abandonment, and are unable to distinguish between their anger and actually hurting someone. All normal children have a strong need for a loving presence, for someone simply to *be there* to hold them when these intense emotions threaten to overwhelm them.

At a symposium on forms of nonverbal communication, psychoanalysts of differing schools explored the ways in which children communicate with their parents before they have acquired language. M. Chayes said that parents frequently need to understand the *feeling* states that are painful or disturbing to the child.

> *A small child has no words with which to communicate. He can communicate only by inducing a certain affective (emotional) response. If this affect is picked up by the mother and understood by her, she can give words to what she thinks the child is experiencing . . . If the mother is someone who does not accept her greed, her ambivalence, her hate, or some other aspect of herself, she is not going to react empathically to the messages from the child, and the child is going to feel misunderstood and lonely.*

This task—intuiting and responding to a child's "unacceptable" emotions—requires a kind of strength that we often underestimate. It is difficult to acknowledge, tolerate, and contain our children's hatred and aggression, their many fantasies of destruction. If, as children, we were not held and did not feel our "bad" feelings contained by a strong, loving, constant presence, we will find this task extremely difficult to perform with our own children.

Frequently in interviews I have heard women say things like: "My mother never held me when I was a kid. So I've made it a point to cuddle my child whenever she's feeling sad." Men usually said something like: "My dad never spent much time with me. I make a special effort to give my children those experiences I missed." It was not easy for these well-meaning, devoted parents to give their children what they had never received from their own parents. One loving father said,

• Taking my son on a fishing trip turned out to be one of the most difficult things I've ever done. I mean here I'd planned it all out so carefully, the camping and the cooking out, had bought all new fishing gear. But what turned out to be hard was how long the days were and how impatient I found myself getting. Just being alone with him was a challenge. It's hard to talk with a seven-year-old all day. And I didn't have any experiences like that with my own father to fall back on. There was no way I could use my dad as a model.

It is difficult to endure the pain of such altruism—giving what you have not received. You must *feel* the deficit or deprivation; sometimes you feel anger and resentment for never having gotten what you needed or wanted; it is even possible to feel envy toward the children you are giving to (and who will probably take this generosity for granted). For a parent, this can be excruciating as well as healing.

No matter how well intentioned a mother might be, there is sometimes a tendency to withdraw rather than to accept and respond to a child's intense emotions. If, when we were children, our parents did not contain and mirror back our feelings with acceptance and empathy—and in that way modify them—we will tend to be intolerant and critical of these feelings in our children. It will take tremendous effort and awareness *not* to pass this intolerance on to them. By nature we are all riddled with greed and ambivalence, but children do not hide these traits. To teach a child to accept and control such feelings is indeed a monumental task, requiring compassion for ourselves as well as our children.

Some care-givers are so driven by their own intense rage, fear, and longing that they unwittingly use children as containers for their needs and emotions. The most extreme example of this is sending the young to fight in wars about which they know little or nothing. Other examples are using our children to satisfy *our* needs for nurturing or self-aggrandizement, or treating them as though they were adults capable of containing our feelings of frustration or sadness. Acting out our own problems and conflicts through our children, perhaps the most common form of maternal impotence, is a threatening and elusive area of our lives which we need to explore. We know little about it and resist contemplating it. An examination of this phenomenon is crucial to understanding how destructive tendencies are passed on from one generation to another.

Current Maternal Conflicts

The incessant intimate tasks of child rearing and the emotions they evoke in us are indeed so trying and complex that many people, if they have a choice, do not participate in the full-time care of their children: most men, for instance. For centuries, the upper classes in Europe hired wet nurses, tutors, servants, or nannies to raise their children and were, at best, part-time parents. Wealthy people, who have always had the option of hiring surrogates, often spare themselves the tedious, physically draining, and intensely emotional work of daily child care. There is a kind of safety in any work that keeps people away from the needs and demands of young children because it spares adults the constant exposure to the stresses of altruistic giving and the temptation to neglect, exploit, or live vicariously through someone who is so dependent and vulnerable.

Yet few women are willing to forego the experience of becoming a mother. Most women now want to work *and* to care for their children. Though some mothers feel no conflict about relegating the full-time care of their children to others, most women I interviewed felt shame and doubt about handing their children over to surrogates for most of the day. Some expressed relief that they *had* to work outside the home for economic reasons, because they felt society secretly condemns women for choosing to leave their children unless financially pressed. Many mothers were driven by *emotional* necessity to work outside the home. They frequently expressed guilt about their personal ambitions and the fact that they could not nurture their children all day, that the nurturing attitude they thought they were supposed to feel (because they were women) seemed defective or grossly deficient.

Only recently has it become acceptable for a woman to acknowledge and act on her own ambitions for worldly success, which are as intense as a man's. It is difficult to nurture a child when your energies are being consumed elsewhere. This still does not allow many working mothers to give up the idea that they should be able to care for a child easily and well.

It is extremely difficult for mothers to admit they do not want to spend time caring for their children, and that nurturing seriously interferes with their personal ambitions. Being aware that you don't want to care for your own child (except when you feel like it) strikes many women at the core of their gender identity. It seems to be as mortifying for a woman to admit she often feels no desire to nurture her child as it is for a man to admit he cannot maintain an erection. What *is* a mother if in fact child rearing is tedious to her? What does it mean that she would rather do something else?

The Silent Collusion: Freud's Analysis of Helene Deutsch

Helene Deutsch was both a pupil and patient of Freud's. She eventually became a well-known psychoanalyst herself and wrote two volumes on the psychology of women. During her analysis with Freud, she never mentioned her painful conflicts as a mother.

Because most working mothers are silent about the tensions their children evoke in them, we have few models of honest self-examination. Examples of truthfulness, such as Helene Deutsch's autobiography *Confrontations with Myself*, both shock and enlighten. Though Deutsch did not set out to examine the feelings evoked in mothers when they must turn their children over to others, her sensitive memoir does describe the conflicts many mothers experience. One of the questions stimulated, and in part answered, by this moving autobiography is: Why is it so difficult for career women, torn between motherhood and meaningful, important work out in the world, to speak openly when it would clearly help themselves, their children, and other women?

Though Helene Deutsch hired a nurse, Paula, as a mother-substitute, she never talked about this woman when she was Freud's patient. Nor did she speak of the abdication of her motherhood to this nurse, who stipulated that Deutsch "was to appear and disappear like an affectionate visitor" to her baby:

> While trying to cope with the heavy professional workload caused by the war, I always had the painful suspicion that I was depriving both my son, Martin, and myself of a rich source of happiness—the mother-child closeness that is most significant to a baby during the first two years. I loved my child deeply, but the two of us could only occasionally experience the blessing of the mother-child bond with all its tenderness and care . . .

To succeed in her work, Deutsch had to give up something she considered precious, in a way most men are not called upon. As is frequently the case now, to nurture an infant means to give up being powerful out in the world. Conceivably, Freud was reluctant to contemplate the cost to Deutsch of not examining that part of her psyche.

Had Deutsch become a mother after her analysis with Freud, she might have claimed a more fulfilling relationship with her son. What was so radically new about Freud's method of treatment was the disinterested and curative listening, the benign and tolerant *attending to* another, the incipient creation of a safe place in which a patient's "true self" could emerge, unfold, and develop. Ideally, this is what we want to provide for our children. Whether we call this altruistic giving, empathic understanding, or mothering, it is hard for both parents and mental health professionals to give it for any length of time. "The capacity to give one's attention," said philosopher Simone Weil, "is a very rare and difficult thing. It is almost a miracle; it is a miracle." Compassion is miraculous because of our blindnesses and limitations that make truly knowing another so difficult. Freud's collusion with Deutsch's silence about her conflicts as a mother was perhaps due to his unconscious aversion to exploring the intimate maternal realm. Psychoanalyst Jessica Benjamin attributes this refusal to explore the mother's subjectivity to "unprocessed feelings of envy and fear of maternal sexuality, overstimulation, and abandonment." As Deutsch's memoir poignantly suggests, this aversion to examining the maternal realm is not exclusive to men.

Though Deutsch was trying to please Freud by not talking about her experiences as a mother, she was probably reticent for the same reasons we all are regarding this aspect of our lives:

> *My analysis was a didactic one, and thus a part of my professional training. I think that this feature allowed me to give in to my natural resistance and avoid mentioning conflicts with my mother-*

hood, which included Paula. After all, it was my silent agreement
with this woman that made my professional activity possible: I
could work on condition that I abdicate my role of mother in her
favor.

We must examine this "natural resistance" to mentioning conflicts surrounding motherhood and career. Most of the women I
interviewed, even those who were seeing a psychotherapist, said
they still find it extremely difficult to talk about *not* being able to
give to a child what they think that child needs and the guilt they
feel when they must relegate child care to someone else.

Our reluctance to acknowledge the difficulties we have in caring
for our children may have another source. Perhaps we do not want
to know how hard it was for our own mothers to mother us — how
much *they* might have needed help. We would prefer to think it was
easy to love us and that it did not take extraordinary discipline and
self-sacrifice. To admit how difficult it is to care for a child is a kind
of testament to how much trouble and effort we may have caused
our mothers. We may secretly fear that as children we drained our
mothers dry by our needs. Perhaps this is behind our need to idealize all mothers. To truly understand their experience as care-givers
might arouse too much guilt.

Had Helene Deutsch been more open in her analysis about the
complex feelings her child aroused, she might not have parroted
back, in her volume on motherhood, Freud's erroneous, misogynis-
tic ideas. If she had been able to speak freely of her conflicts and difficulties as a working mother, both she and Freud might have
considered the stresses of nurturing children. It might not have
taken so long for psychoanalytic thinkers, such as D. W. Winnicott,
Selma Fraiberg, Daniel Stern, Nancy Chodorow, Jessica Benjamin,
and Stephen Seligman, to begin exploring the mother's real feelings
as she cares for her children.We would have more knowledge about
the altruism required and why so many men avoid care giving or do
so little of it. Perhaps more fathers would examine the conflicts

stirred up by the demands of nurturing. What's clear is that both men and women are reluctant to explore this threatening area, and therefore both conspire in our society's refusal to acknowledge the needs of care-givers.

Most men do not want to know about women's feelings of guilt, shame, and failure around the nurturing of their children. To pursue their own goals without worrying excessively about the well-being of their children, men need to see their wives as loving mothers, for whom care giving comes easily. A loving mother is not supposed to be driven to distraction by the demands of child care.

Women hide their feelings about nurturing for a multitude of reasons. The desire to please a cherished husband keeps some women quiet. Some wives are afraid to confront their husbands with how much help they really need. One mother, an avowed feminist who worked full time yet was responsible for the care of her three children, said, "I'm afraid he'd split if I told him the truth. It would have meant he'd have to do more of the child care and I don't think he could stand it." Other women feel that speaking openly about their difficulties in caring for a child is an admission of inferiority.

If men interpret listening empathically to their wives as a demand to help out, this in itself might diminish their interest in becoming conscious or aware. A father's inability or refusal to participate in child care sometimes becomes a carefully guarded secret in which the whole family conspires for fear of alienating him or overtaxing his energies.

The Needs of Care-Givers

Deutsch's conflicts between motherhood and career are understandable in light of her autobiography's exploration of childhood relationships, the struggle to free herself from emotional oppression, and her participation in the psychoanalytic movement in Vienna and Berlin before World War II. In fact, the exciting life she led as a pupil of Freud's, a medical doctor, and psychoanalytic thinker informs us—perhaps more than anything else—of one of the most difficult aspects of being a mother today: the many possibilities for personal fulfillment outside the role of care-giver and the immense gratifications of other kinds of achievements.

Written at the end of her life, Deutsch's book illuminates how success in the world and the enjoyment of that success can draw us away from our children and may force us to choose in favor of our own goals:

> I later regretted that my son, then seven years old, paid the heaviest price for my professional progress during this year. My only qualm about going to Berlin was that it would mean a temporary separation of our family. As a compromise, we decided that Martin would spend half of the year with me in Berlin, and half with Felix in Vienna. While he was in Berlin, separated from his father and in a sense neglected by his mother, he had to put up with the strict educational methods of a German governess. Meanwhile, his mother was furthering her desire to be the director of a top-ranking training institute.

Yet earlier in the book she observes,

> . . . whenever the door to sublimation was open to me, I was much happier as a wife and mother. And vice versa: when something in my personal life interfered with my scientific productivity, I was less happy and more aggressive in my whole attitude toward my environment.

We see here that the line between maternal love and maternal impotence is indeed a thin one, having to do with creating a balance between self-interest and concern for others.

In some cases, psychoanalysis exacts a kind of discipline from its more ardent followers, a kind of honesty which persists after the treatment has stopped. Because of this dedication to truthfulness, Deutsch at the end of her life could uncover and admit "missed" insights which came to her long after her analysis with Freud. Because of her candor, we see a woman's experience as a mother as neither evil nor destructive. Deutsch shows us how these conflicts can be confronted, understood, talked about. It is our silence about feelings of maternal impotence that produces the greatest harm to both ourselves and our children.

We need to speak out to rise above maternal impotence. The guilt, fear, and blame that surround and invade child rearing inhibit us from achieving the kind of honesty that can, in fact, transform feelings of maternal impotence into feelings of maternal love. We must acknowledge women's competitive strivings, their desire for recognition and esteem, and their need for creative self-expression. We must be reminded that there are times when the needs of the care-giver are more important than the needs of the child. We must consider the care-giver's need for refueling—for care, nurturance, support—to counteract the insidious myth that mothers are an endless source of love and emotional sustenance. If we decide that our own goals are more important than anything else, we must know the impact this will have on ourselves and our children. Otherwise we lose the possibility of understanding and correcting errors.

The more we love our children, the more disturbed we are likely to be at the ways we are distracted from the love and concern they need. The more inadequate we feel about the care of our children, the less willing we are to explore the connections between inner conflicts and the external world. Yet for us to know the extent and possibilities of our love, we must explore our difficulties in caring for others. Only by confronting how hard it is to place the best interests of another before our own can we begin to accomplish the precarious task of nurturing our children in the best way possible.

Chapter Two

THE SUBJECTIVE
EXPERIENCE OF
THE MOTHER

There is a mind in the flesh. A mind quick as lightning.
—Antonin Artaud,
Art and Death

. . . I believe that the mother neither looks at nor manipulates the girl in the same way as the boy. Her gaze summarizes expectations and wishes that order and define the sexual profile of each. The boy is very early separated by his mother from closeness with her body and desire. The girl instead is held in that closeness . . . The maternal circuit . . . will be her world for a long time . . .
—Raquel Zak de Goldstein,
"The Dark Continent and Its Enigmas"

Journal Entries: 1974–78

• *My baby is a miracle of perfection. Everything about her is exquisite. Happiness is being with her, caring for her. I have never known such joy.*

• *One minute I feel if I don't get away from this prison of a house, the demands of this baby, I'll go mad. Yet often when I am away from her I want only to return and can't wait to see her. When I return and see her smile, I feel rapture . . . What is the meaning of this?*

• *I was unnerved today in the grocery store. The baby began screaming in pain. I held her for a long time among the Cheerios and oatmeal until finally, after a large bowel movement (part of which went all over my shirt), she stopped and began smiling. I did not recover so quickly. Couldn't decide whether to change her diapers on the floor, take her home and forget about shopping, or continue buying food as though nothing had happened. These kinds of decisions now preoccupy my days.*

• *Few mothers will talk honestly. Why? What is it that we have to lose? Is there something about the nature of child care that trivializes? Makes one prone to gossip and one-up-manship? Shrinks one's vision to the rivers of snot that run down children's noses and whatever will keep them from crying, whining, fighting, and grabbing each other's toys? If such work could be elevated, was seen as important, given higher meaning—the respect and esteem it deserves—would that make the daily grind easier to take?*

• *My grandmother was too busy surviving to consider the feelings stirred up in her by her ten children. My own mother was too miserable to become conscious of what child rearing did to her.*

Children only increased the chaos of her life. I know mothers who cannot be separated from their children and mothers who can't wait to get away from their kids; but neither show any desire to explore what they are clinging to or running from. Working mothers are usually too busy, guilt-ridden, or exhausted to consider such things. I too become reluctant to look too closely at all the feelings child rearing has unleashed . . . Whenever I try, I seem to be able to go only so far. Then I too suffer profound confusion, also a failure of nerve.

The earliest experiences we have with our children are so overwhelming, it is difficult to think clearly about them. The birth and care of an infant confounds the rational parts of ourselves, jolting us out of ordinary perceptions, catapulting us in and out of altered states. During their earliest years, children live out our most subversive longings, continually confronting us with aspects of the human psyche we have worked hard to master and conceal, hampering any fantasies we might harbor of self-transcendence. In addition to their psychological impact, babies are sensory stimulants, modifying our sensibilities and conscious perceptions, expanding our awareness.

After giving birth to my children, I began to live in two contradictory worlds: one was intuitive, fusional, enmeshed in body life. Though it felt wild and uncontained and completely beyond my control, it told me what was *real*. The other world—more or less rational but driven by the need to understand clearly, with precision —began to seem paper-thin, defensive, irrelevant.

The feather weight of my daughter's body, the softness of her skin, my intense need to hold her close—this is what became most real. The sight of her wispy hair and alert little eyes; her delightful cooing and bloodcurdling screams; the scent of breast milk and baby oil; feces and Desitin; her constantly changing facial expressions that seemed to recapitulate the entire spectrum of human emotion—

During this heightened time, I had to learn how to read my daughter's every sound and gesture: I had to learn when she was hungry and when she wanted to play; I had to learn whether she screamed from gas pains or wanted to be comforted from fear. By holding her, I discovered when she needed soothing and when she wanted to sleep. Conscious thought could not tell me what she needed. I became immersed in her world. Theories and abstractions paled; reasoning stopped. At times I became lost in my daughter's world, trying to figure out why she was crying, the reasons for her fussiness, what it was she wanted. At other times, just seeing her smile evoked rapture. Her delight in the sound of a cricket, her joy in following the flight of a dove, became a rediscovery of the pleasures of the senses.

The first part of this chapter explores that intuitive state of fusion with another, which a mother experiences after the birth of an infant. The chapter then looks at what happens when this intimate phase of the mother-child relationship comes to an end—the beginnings of that complex, highly charged process of separation/individuation.

Carnality and Selflessness

In a culture in which so many of our experiences are mediated by technological inventions and human relationships replaced by interactions with machines, the intense physicality of birth and early nurturing can come as a disturbing shock. Few women are prepared for the intense carnality of early child care. Pleasurable sensations of the flesh are often associated in our culture only with adult sexuality. The mother-infant relationship is often romanticized, as though the love a mother feels for her baby is a spiritual, ethereal emotion. The media constantly project saccharine images of idealized mother-child relationships—in commercials for Pampers or Similac, on television sitcoms, and in films for children and adults. Such images obscure the extreme physicality of the experience of nurturing infants.

In addition to the earthy sensuality of babies, mothers are confronted with a kind of intimacy never before experienced. During infancy, the mother can identify with her suckling child, feel gloriously at one with it. Through the giving of milk, nurturance, care, a mother can reexperience the exclusive tenderness she had with her own mother. When you give birth to an infant, you create someone who loves you unconditionally. It is the kind of love a part of us longs for yet can never quite find in another adult, except perhaps during the brief infatuation stage of a relationship. One mother compared the intensity of early infant care to the beginning of a love affair:

• When Elena went to nurse her son in the middle of the night, she said she felt as though she was going to a lover. She even bathed and made herself beautiful before going in to nurse him. After giving birth to her first child at twenty-seven, Elena fell passionately in love with him. She felt exactly the same way after her daughter was born. The best part of mothering for Elena was the delicious closeness as she rocked and nursed her babies late at night when her husband was asleep in another room.

Yet for some mothers the carnality of infant care comes too close to the erotic. Sensual feelings stirred up by the breast-feeding experience overwhelmed one mother:

• When Gretchen had her first child at twenty-three, she became so sexually aroused when she nursed her baby, she almost had an orgasm. After breast-feeding for two weeks, she stopped in total confusion, thinking she had become a pervert. Fortunately during her third pregnancy, Gretchen had many discussions with a member of the Nursing Mother's Counsel, who reassured her that it is not abnormal for women to have sensuous feelings when they are nursing their babies. These talks made it possible for Gretchen to breast-feed her third child without becoming too anxious or overwhelmed.

For other women the delicious exclusivity of the mother-infant relationship—especially during the first year—is more gratifying than any other. This can put a strain on the marriage, causing the husband to feel left out and neglected. Though many new mothers feel torn between their attachment to the baby and their love for their husbands, they choose the all-encompassing involvement with their child:

• Jeanette, a twenty-eight-year-old nurse, said that after her daughter was born, she wanted only to be left alone to hold and snuggle with her baby. Returning to work part-time when the baby was a month old, Jeanette had decided not to breast-feed. But bottle-feeding did not diminish the warmth and closeness she felt toward her daughter. When Jeanette came home from working the night shift, she would sing to and play with her daughter for hours. It was her husband's demands, especially his sexual overtures, that Jeanette came to resent. "I didn't want him to even touch me. I just wanted him to leave me alone so I could cuddle with my baby. I can't tell you how much I hungered just to hold her in my arms. That's all I thought about at work." It took her over a year to even think of sex with her husband and she continuously had to fight the urge to tell him to go away.

Jeanette did not regain interest in her husband or their sex life until the baby was over a year old. "I guess I'm lucky he didn't run off with someone else," she said. It was around this time they finally got away together, leaving the baby with grandparents for a week.

After the experience of closeness and unity with their infants, some mothers feel bereft when this exquisite intimacy comes to an end. After breast-feeding stops, exaggerated feelings of aloneness and emptiness can lead some women to want to become pregnant again right away:

> • Sitting in her kitchen in a small Wyoming town, twenty-nine-year-old Lorraine, mother of six, tells me of the "baby hunger" she feels now that her youngest, thirteen months old, has just been weaned. In fact, the desire for another baby is so overpowering, Lorraine is considering a seventh child, despite the fact they are having trouble paying their bills each month. Though her religious beliefs encourage large families and support mothers who have a lot of children, Lorraine says it isn't just those things that make her want to have another child. The longing for an infant is so strong, she says, sometimes she can't stand not having a baby to hold and suckle.

The mother-infant relationship is for some women intensely gratifying, especially in a society as cold and ruthless as our own. Yet the joys of caring for children are as taboo a subject as hostile, negative feelings toward them. Few speak of the exquisite sensuality of suckling an infant, which brings some women to orgasm. And what of the helpless dependency of the small baby, which soon turns into devotion? A baby loves and needs its mother more than any adult ever has or will. To be so urgently needed and to satisfy an infant's demands for love can bring a woman a sense of fulfillment that no other relationship provides.

For some women the pleasures of the early bonding phase are so exquisite they are difficult to relinquish. Yet the care of an infant is physically exhausting, demanding a kind of self-sacrifice that can feel like masochistic surrender, especially if a baby is colicky or ill for days. The emotional realities many mothers must grapple with at this time can fluctuate oddly between profound gratification and self-sacrifice, pleasurable sensations that seem almost self-indulgent, and feelings of depletion that accompany periods of self-denial.

Despite the ecstasy of giving birth and the pleasures of an infant's love, some women find taking care of babies so disturbing and depleting that they will do anything to avoid it. The excessive neediness of the infant, the care and nurturing it must have to survive, arouses in some women desperate feelings of panic, deficit, and rage. It is difficult to be conscious of anger toward an infant simply for its normal behavior. Unacceptable rage toward an infant frequently gets turned inward, becoming depression and self-doubt. Sometimes we transform intolerable feelings of anger into excessive fears that something will harm the infant. One mother said she spent nights hovering around her son's crib, checking his breathing, making sure he had not died of crib death.

For other mothers, the forced intimacy stirs up such feelings of emptiness and deprivation that the mother flees into work, career, an affair, another marriage—something, *anything* else. If a mother experienced deprivation during her own infancy and early childhood, the incessant work of nurturing as well as the physical closeness it involves can bring back feelings of loss and impoverishment. A good friend of mine confided that taking care of her baby made her feel unbearably deprived, reminding her of how much she had wanted to be held as a child, and how cold and withholding her own mother had been. Another mother confessed she could not handle her small children's demands and that this was why she went back to work full time: "I would have gone crazy if I'd stayed home to take care of them. The short time I did, until they were one and two, I lost twenty pounds and was sick continuously. I didn't feel right until I started my old job again."

Feeding an infant tends to evoke our own deepest hungers for love and care. Our infant's hunger can create unexpected and distressing responses in us, feelings of failure, inadequacy, the fear of being devoured, even disgust:

• Vickie, a twenty-five-year-old social worker, said her first six months as a mother were excruciating. Vickie spent the last months of her pregnancy preparing to breast-feed and looked forward to this experience. But her milk dried up a week after her baby was born. "I felt like such a failure. I just couldn't do it, the milk just wouldn't flow. I can't tell you how inadequate I felt. Every day I'd cry for hours."

Vickie went through a brief period when she felt so ashamed, she couldn't bring herself to go out of the house. It took several months of counseling for her to stop seeing herself as a bad mother and finally begin to enjoy her daughter.

• A vice president of a San Francisco bank, Anne took a three-month leave of absence from work after the birth of her first child. Having waited until her mid-thirties before becoming a mother, Anne planned to breast-feed her baby. She had read many books that said this was the best thing to do to "give him a good start in life." But during the first week of her son's life, Anne was overcome with anxieties. "I couldn't stand it," she said. "He seemed so greedy. I kept feeling that he was going to eat me alive! And then he'd bite my breast with his hard little gums and it hurt like hell. So I ended up feeding him soy milk from a bottle."

• Rebecca, a retired actress who ran a repertory theater, refused to mother her infant, saying she could not bear the smell of diapers or the messiness of feeding her son. The odor of feces made her nauseous. The way he played with his food and mashed it in his hair made her want to throttle him. She said she had little to do with him "until he could carry on an intelligent conversation." Fortunately, Rebecca could afford to hire surrogates. She saw her role as that of administrator—she told the nannies what to do and what not to do, decided when and where he was to go to school, what lessons he would take, where he would go to summer camp. In this way Rebecca exerted her influence over her child, staying connected with him but at a distance.

Child rearing during the first three years of a baby's life often demands that we give without getting anything in return. Some infants are more difficult than others—colicky, for instance, or extremely hard to feed and comfort. Some babies are by nature sensitive and high-strung. One mother described the agony of having a daughter who never stopped crying:

• Margaret's baby was too fussy to breast-feed and screamed with colic for six months. Four months before the delivery of her daughter, Margaret and her husband had left family and friends in Tulsa, where they'd lived all their lives. Her husband had been transferred to the San Francisco Bay area where they knew no one. "I was so lonely to begin with, and then this baby just wouldn't stop crying. I mean that kid screamed day and night for months. Imagine never, never being able to comfort your own baby. It nearly drove me nuts. You get mad, you know, when you try everything and nothing works. At times I just wanted to kill her. There were nights I almost choked her, anything to stop that awful wailing sound she makes. I remember one morning at five, when I thought I couldn't stand another minute, running out to the garden and ripping out all the baby tears we'd planted around the pond.

The effect of a baby's prolonged crying and whining on some mothers is excruciating. One mother said her pediatrician actually prescribed phenobarbitol to give her sick baby who had been screaming for days. "If she didn't stop crying, I don't know what I would have done." Another mother told me a story handed down to her of her grandmother's household in southern Russia:

• While preparing the evening meal, the servants would fill socks with cloth and small amounts of opium and give them to the crying infants to suck as the large, heavy cook and bone-thin serving girls rushed around the kitchen. As they passed the infant, they would kick the cradle so it would rock back and forth while they worked.

The continuous offering of physical care, protection, and empathy can cause care-givers to feel not simply fatigue but acute emotional deprivation. In this country, many mothers feel such extreme impoverishment they become vulnerable to disturbing forces both within and without: depression, rage, guilt (for who can feel anger toward a defenseless beloved infant who needs you?), and feelings of worthlessness which come from our culture's devaluation of the intensive labor of child rearing.

The Fusional Experience

Without consciously knowing it, most mothers try to protect their babies, not only from physical harm but emotional trauma as well, working to intuit their infant's unique characteristics and sensitivities so they can prevent intrusions that would be disruptive to that particular child. In the attempt to know what a baby feels, care-givers must sometimes dissolve into the infant's wordless world in which sensation, not reason, directs perceptions. Expanding on the ideas of Winnicott, psychoanalyst Thomas Ogden in his book *The Matrix of the Mind* describes the mother's function during the first months as:

> *delaying the infant's awareness of separateness . . . Meeting the infant's need before need becomes desire . . . For a brief time the mother creates the illusion that need does not exist.*

The mother tries to become one with her infant to support its fragile sense of being, at least until the infant becomes resilient enough to accept the disturbing fact that it is small and relatively weak, separate yet entirely dependent.

What is the effect of this kind of giving on a mother? In her short story "Tell Me a Riddle" Tillie Olsen describes maternal love as something so intense and blinding that it can temporarily wipe out a person's identity or sense of self:

> the passion of tending . . . [rising] with the need like a torrent; and like a torrent drowned and immolated all else . . . And they put a baby in her lap. Immediacy to embrace . . . warm flesh like this that had claims and nuzzled away all else and with living mouths devoured; hot—living like an animal—intensely and now . . . the long drunkenness; the drowning into needing and being needed.

When we become immersed in caring for children, they often lead us *away* from the self as well as toward life. In this story, a dying grandmother refuses to even touch her grandchild because in dying —in her withdrawal from all she loves—she is also making a "journey to her self," postponed until now by a lifetime of giving, tending, needing, and being needed. Selflessly caring for an infant makes us, for a time, self-*less*, and every mother who does not have help is often threatened with temporary feelings of obliteration.

In a poem entitled "Morning Song" Sylvia Plath describes the experience of selflessness involved in the bearing and nursing of an infant as something animalistic, impersonal, like the sea—so overpowering that it makes the mother-narrator jump the second she hears one cry from her baby:

> One cry, and I stumble from bed, cow-heavy and floral
> In my Victorian nightgown.
> Your mouth opens clean as a cat's . . .

Yet the infant in the poem is like a mirror that reflects the mother's sense that she is somehow disappearing:

I'm no more your mother
Than the cloud that distills a mirror to reflect its own slow
Effacement at the wind's hand . . .

As words like "drowning," "drunkenness," "immolation," and "effacement" suggest, all care-givers of infants lose the sharp edges of the boundary between self and other for a time, to intuit what the child needs. Some women love this stage; others enjoy it, but only if they can do it part-time. Some like parts of it but cannot immerse themselves in it for long stretches without feeling their identities are being wiped out. (One mother said she kept having dreams of being swept away in a flood while trying to hold her baby's head above the water.) One thing is certain: the early bonding stage of infancy requires more giving on the part of the care-giver than most women can imagine before having a child.

The Symbolic Significance of the Baby

What is an infant to its mother? First, it is a part of her body that mysteriously, inexplicably detaches as it enters the world, a part of her own self that she must nurture and then send out beyond her realm, beyond her control. To some mothers, the child is a possession; to others, a passionate lover. An infant can provide tremendous solace, become a buffer, shielding the mother from unpleasant circumstances. An infant can be all these things to the same woman in rapid succession.

Some psychologists believe the infant is at first a narcissistic extension—something that cannot, for a time, be considered separate. Psychoanalyst Elizabeth Loewald thinks that an infant temporarily becomes, for some mothers, a kind of transitional object—something both herself and not herself, beloved but not yet distinct from her fantasies and wishes. According to British psychoanalyst Enid Balint:

> *Maternal love is intended—according to its instinctual sources— only for the very young child, the infant depending upon the mother's body . . . Thus just as the mother is to the child, so is the child to the mother—an object of gratification . . .*

The constant caring for children pulls us back upon our deepest memories. In her book *Parenthood as a Developmental Phase* psychoanalyst Therese Benedek claims that children pull us inward because of memory traces conjured up by the smells, touch, sounds of the infant, baby, toddler, child—its hunger and helplessness, incessant movement, fears, delight, play, the joy and terror of its struggles for autonomy remind us of our own. This makes it difficult at times to distinguish our needs and early experiences from our children's.

Psychiatrist Peter Blos says that there is a temporary regression— normal and essential—with the birth of each child. Blos says the mother's

> *greater access to childhood memories, unconscious wishes, conflicts, and fixations, and loosening of defenses outlasts the physical and endocrinological changes of biological pregnancy and the postpartum period. This psychic openness is sustained for many months and begins to attenuate only during the middle of the young toddler's second year . . . this period of psychic flexibility is brought to a close by the toddler's increasing awareness of his or her own psychological separateness and the mother's recognition that this has occurred . . .*

Care giving during the first months can be so exhausting, it may be important for a mother to experience her baby as a partial extension of her psyche. Yet a time comes when this initial blurring of self and other must end. At this crucial time the mother must learn who her child is, quite apart from her wishes and fantasies.

Weaning and the Return of Rationality

One of the first crucial breaks in the fusional relationship between mother and infant is labeled "weaning" and is associated with the actual weaning from bottle or breast. Weaning, which brings on the full realization that mother and child are *not* one, is always something of a jolt, especially if the care-giver has recaptured with her infant the intimacy and sense of completeness of her early relationship with her own mother. Often the ability of the mother to think rationally again is ushered in with differentiation, and her reexperiencing of what it is like to be separate, alone, and to have wants and needs of her own.

Unlike the small separations that occur each day and are softened by the infant's dependency and the hard work involved in child care, weaning from the breast or bottle is the beginning of the end of something. Weaning is a state of mind as well as a response to changes in the infant's development. It is an event symbolic of a shift in the relationship between the mother and the infant, who can no longer be seen as a passive, helpless recipient of the mother's ministrations.

For some mothers, weaning is like the end of a honeymoon or the infatuation stage of a love affair: if the relationship is going to last or grow, the real work must now begin. For other mothers, weaning is a welcome relief, the end of an intense, cloying intimacy with a creature too helpless and too dependent. After weaning mothers often feel, "My baby's a real person now, a unique individual." An infant's strong, fierce personality emerges sooner or later. Every mother fantasizes about her baby long before it even comes into the world.

What it is or becomes is always a surprise—at best, a welcome surprise; at worst, a personality denied.

Whether weaning is rushed or prolonged, painful or experienced as liberation, it is always a rite of passage for both mother and child. It is highly idiosyncratic, executed differently by each individual mother. Some women have a low tolerance for dependency, encouraging their children to be autonomous at an early age:

> • Twenty-five-year-old Roberta, a housewife from Houston who'd been transplanted in the Bay area, told me over coffee how she couldn't stand to see her son sucking on his bottle after he was a year old. "I kept feeling it was making a sissy of him," she said, "watching him sucking on that nipple all day." When her son was eleven months old, Roberta gathered all of his bottles and threw them away. Her son screamed and cried for a week, refusing to eat the gourmet meals she prepared and ground up for him in a baby food grinder, using the freshest vegetables and the highest-quality meats. When he finally stopped sobbing and ate his gourmet baby food, Roberta felt she had finally begun to make a man of him.

The time a mother decides to wean her baby is dependent on both internal and external factors. Some husbands cannot tolerate competing with a baby for their wife's attentions. Women sometimes hurry the weaning process no matter how much they've enjoyed it for fear of alienating their husbands or endangering their marriages:

> • Francis said her first marriage crumbled after the birth of her son. "I was so young at twenty-one, and after the baby came, I just couldn't do two things at once—be a wife and be a mother." When, at thirty, she married for the second time, Francis was determined not to let mothering come between herself and her husband. For this reason, she weaned her daughter at three months and left her infant with a nanny for a week while she and

her husband flew to the Bahamas to try to reestablish their relationship. Unfortunately her breasts bulged and ached with milk the whole week, and every night she wept for her infant as she lay in their expensive condominium. "My baby didn't recognize me when I came home. But then when she heard my voice, she sobbed for hours."

The loss of the intimate nursing relationship can become symbolic of other painful losses and cause temporary feelings of depression:

• Elena, who had so enjoyed nursing her two babies, became despondent when her youngest child was a year old and refused to breast-feed anymore. "I knew we weren't going to have any more children. So this was it." Elena said she became overwhelmed with irrational feelings, as though she'd been rejected by her baby. "It seemed like she just lost interest in me and I couldn't stand it." Elena then began hating herself for feeling so selfish and possessive. "I got unbelievably morbid and began missing my dead mother. At one point I wanted to fling myself on her grave I missed her so much."

Alarmed by the rapid downward spiral of her emotions, she went to see her obstetrician. Part of this depression, her obstetrician told her, was hormonal, due to the changes the body goes through when lactation stops. But part of the depression had to do with feelings of loss—the loss of the closeness of the nursing relationship.

Some mothers find breast-feeding so gratifying they disregard their children's needs for autonomy, retarding their children's attempts to become independent:

• An ardent member of the La Leche League, Ruth spent five years counseling mothers who had problems nursing their babies. When her youngest child was two years old, he looked up at her after breast-feeding, milk dripping from his chin, and said, "Mama, can I drink from a bottle now?"

In retrospect, Ruth said that she'd been insensitive to earlier signs of her son's desire for liberation from breast-feeding. But she had so enjoyed the nursing experience, she had not wanted to wean her son. "Sometimes they have to persuade you to let them grow up!" she said.

In her book, *Of Woman Born*, poet Adrienne Rich says that many mothers, throughout their children's infancy and childhood, must work to wean themselves from their children and the passionate intensity that accompanies the different phases of mothering. Rich is one of the first women to openly acknowledge how difficult this separation process is for the *mother*. Some women compare it to withdrawal; however, it is good for neither mother nor child to do it "cold turkey."

Separation/Individuation from the Mother's Perspective

Allowing a very young child gradual autonomy, individuation, and a truly separate self is one of the most complicated tasks for parents. Letting our children go takes a great deal of strength and maturity, especially if the love and attachment we feel toward them is intense.

We can only speculate about an infant's subjective experience—it will always be something of a mystery. As most mothers will attest, around the second year of life an enormous change occurs, both within the infant and in the relationship between the care-giver and infant. Many people label this phenomenon "the terrible twos." Psychoanalysts now feel it is a crucial and extraordinarily complex stage of development that has a profound impact on the rest of the child's life. Margaret Mahler has done the research on this phase of development in children and her theories are based on extensive observations of children and mothers.

The technical term in psychoanalytic theory—"separation/individuation"—was coined by Mahler and is a kind of shorthand for what unfolds in a child's emotional life roughly between the ages of eighteen to twenty-four months. With the exception of Louise Kaplan in her book *Oneness and Separateness,* Nancy Chodorow in *The Reproduction of Mothering,* and a small but growing number of articles and case histories, few people have attempted to examine this experience from the mother's perspective—what goes on inside her when her children begin the struggle to become more autonomous. It is easy to understand, however, why we find it difficult to talk about the emotions this developmental stage stirs up in women. Conflicting passions—loss, longing, disgust; the experience of being a rival, being taken advantage of, used; disappointment, even hatred —all these emotions flare up from time to time in every parent once the toddler begins to differentiate herself. Such negative feelings are taboo for a mother to have, yet they are inevitable, universal during the separation/individuation stage and thereafter.

Child care during this phase can drive some women to distraction. In one of her last poems, "Lesbos," Sylvia Plath vividly describes her young daughter having a temper tantrum while her baby son—she calls him a "fat snail"—leaves a trail of slime on the floor. The scene is familiar to mothers, at least in our culture—one of those fleeting nightmare moments we try to forget—when a mother picks up her daughter from "face down on the floor . . . kicking to disappear," and puts her in her room until she cools off or calls a baby-sitter for relief. But Plath does more than describe what is common fare for anyone who must deal with toddlers. Instead of chalking it all up to the "terrible twos," Plath *recreates* through poetry how it feels to take care of two demanding little ones, to feel as full of rage and out of control as a screaming toddler and then to blame yourself for everything that has gone wrong.

The articulation of such disturbing feelings is new in both life and literature. We have enormous resistance to acknowledging the emotions that boil up, simmer, grow cold as we care for children of that age. Unfortunately our culture bombards mothers with images of saintliness on the one hand and harsh judgments on the other. The message is that feelings like possessiveness, envy, and grief (when the child is not dead) are so unacceptable they should not be felt, much less acknowledged.

Separation for mothers is a complex phenomenon. A mother must endure the child's separation from her at the same time that she experiences her own separation from the child—the two events occurring simultaneously. Also, child rearing evokes her own experiences as a baby. As her two-year-old rages against its powerlessness, its smallness, and begins to desire autonomy, *the mother may feel all these things herself* as well as feeling the loss of an infant whose devotion shortly before was untainted by such painful ambivalence.

If all has gone well, her child will become closely attached to others now, lessening the exclusivity of the mother-child relationship. As the toddler begins to show strong affection for others, some mothers are ashamed to admit the jealousy this can evoke.

Separation/Individuation from the Toddler's Perspective

The child's first introduction to the world beyond her mother and herself is associated with curiosity and excitement. Even under the best of circumstances, the first tastes of autonomy create in both children and mothers feelings of exhilaration and rage, joy and betrayal, loss as well as delight.

In her book *The Psychological Birth of the Human Infant,* Margaret Mahler explores in depth the toddler's anger, ambivalence, and pulling away from the mother during the "terrible twos." At this time, the care-giver must allow herself to be used in a way she did not when the child was younger and totally dependent. This time requires the most altruism, giving, and disinterested concern. For now the mother must learn to tolerate being ignored one minute and clung to the next, having to *be there* when the child wants her yet be disregarded when he wishes to be left alone.

Toddlers, after tasting the first delicious fruits of autonomy, still need "refueling"—in other words, they need their care-givers to be there to run back to after they have explored the world. As babies learn to creep, crawl, walk, and run from the mother, they feel elation that comes from the glorious, simultaneous experiences of movement, exploration, and mastery. In an article exploring the separation/individuation process in baby girls, Anni Bergman, who worked closely with Margaret Mahler, described the illusion of being one with the mother and the "sense of safety and protection this entails."

> *Mother is still at the center of her world, and the baby needs to take her for granted and to return to her periodically for "emotional refueling" . . . Emotional refueling is an important phenomenon of that subphase. It describes the way in which a tired baby receives sustenance from brief physical contact with mother and has renewed energy to go forth and explore the world again with zest and pleasure, to begin the unending explorations anew.*

However, this glorious state is doomed to rupture as the child develops. As children grow, they discover they're small, clumsy, and vulnerable. Inevitably they fall down, hurt themselves, learn they can't do all the things they want. Slowly they realize that their mothers are quite separate beings and that they are alone. By two years of age, Bergman says, the "illusion of unity, oneness, can no longer be maintained." This produces behavior which Mahler labeled "ambitendency":

*alternately a wish to be on one's own and to have mother present to
provide solutions, only to reject them as soon as they are forthcoming . . .*

How aggravating from the mother's point of view to be constantly
needed and rejected, expected to be there—feeding and protecting
—yet not interfering except when they need you. No wonder mothers feel used and taken advantage of at this time. A toddler's bursts
of rage are common as the child finds that her mother is not an
extension of herself, nor a servant at her beck and call. Yet no matter
how toddlers behave—no matter how outrageous their demands—
mothers must watch them incessantly.

The Emotional Impact of Setting Limits

In an attempt to learn the extent of its powers, a child constantly
tests the limits of his/her world. In our strangely permissive society,
the need to discipline a child, to limit, to say "No, you can't do
that!" begins in earnest at this time. Some parents do not feel good
enough about themselves to set limits for their children. Some believe that if they restrict their child, he or she will stop loving them.
One father of a boy of two said, "I'm afraid he hates me now. What
can I do to make him stop hating me?" When a toddler hits, bites,
spits, flashes a hateful, spiteful look, it seems like adult hatred, as if
toddlers are capable of the same feelings of revenge that we as adults
feel. Of course this is not true. One of the most startling things
about two-year-olds is that they do not hold a grudge, at least not for
long.

According to child psychiatrist Dr. Henry Massie, a child's need
to know what his parents are *really* like—what kind of behavior they
can tolerate, what they cannot stand, and the limits of his own power
in relation to them—is as great as his need for air, food, and water:

Far too many of the parents I work with are so guilt-ridden over any notion of saying no to their children and meaning it, they can't set limits with their kids. This is especially true of working mothers who are often badly troubled by leaving their children every day. But kids desperately need to know who their parents are. They also need someone to help them control their impulses when they can't quite manage on their own. A lot of child patients I see in my practice are terrified of their impulses because no one has set limits —helped them restrain themselves. One kid is so wild he wreaks havoc in my office, then pretends he's a policeman and puts himself in jail.

Loving parents may have trouble understanding that their flashes of rage are a normal response to children's constant and highly provocative testing of limits. Many educated parents are shocked when they find themselves shouting at their children as they would an adult. Some parents fear that if they tried to curtail obnoxious behavior they might seriously hurt their children. Many who staunchly oppose physical punishment are appalled when they find themselves spanking their child. Children frequently put our most strongly held beliefs and values to the test:

• When Dan's seventeen-month-old daughter reached for the light socket for the seventh time, he finally gave her a swat on the backside. A professor of philosophy at a major university, Dan shares the care of his daughter and three-and-a-half-year-old son with his wife, a full-time working mother. Apologetically Dan admitted, "I never thought I'd ever hit a child. But now it's no longer whether to spank or not to spank but how many times am I going to spank my child today?"

Before his daughter reached for the light socket, we joked about what Kant and Hegel would have been like as care-givers and how it might have changed their thinking. Smiling guiltily,

Dan said, "How was I to know what my kids would drive me to? It's made me look at philosophical systems in a whole new light."

Fearing she would become abusive to her child, one mother began isolating her daughter in her room until she could get a handle on her emotions:

• Jeanette was laid off work for a month during a nurse's strike when her daughter was two and a half. Delighted to finally be able to spend whole days with her child, something she had never been able to do except during two vacations, she temporarily took her daughter out of day care. "Little did I know how difficult she'd become. On the third day she started hitting me every time I told her she couldn't do something. I got so mad at that kid. It took everything in my power not to hit her back. One day I must have put her in her room at least ten times. Outside of the fact she was acting obnoxious, I was afraid I'd really hurt her if I didn't."

Another mother expressed disappointment and disgust at her son's behavior:

• When Elena was pregnant with her second child, she became short-tempered with her son's constant tantrums and contrary behavior. "Whenever I said, 'Let's go inside,' he'd want to stay outside. If I said, 'Okay then, let's stay out!' he'd say, 'No!' Whatever I wanted him to do, he did the opposite. Sometimes I'd find myself hating him—or hating the way the kid was treating me. Who else on earth would you let spit at you? I went through about a month or two when I wished I'd gone back to work and never become pregnant again."

During this time, some mothers fall back on how they were handled by their parents; others deliberately try different methods, sometimes resorting to the opposite of their parents' treatment:

• The day before I talked to Lorraine, she said she had washed her four-year-old's mouth out with soap. "I really hate it when I have to do things like that, but I swore to myself I'd try never to hit my kids—which was what was done to me." Though Lorraine spoke respectfully of her parents, she said physical punishment had been the norm when she and her seven brothers and sisters were young. "Both Mom and Dad used the strap on us. I remember being so scared of that thing. I can't say I haven't spanked my kids. Some days I wouldn't get through as a sane human being if I didn't spank at least one of them. It's the worst thing about being a mom, keeping them in line. But you just have to. They'd kill themselves or each other if you didn't."

The phrase "testing of limits" does little to convey the child's behavior or the care-giver's response. When my oldest daughter was two, I remember feeling shock and confusion at those first signs of unmistakable hostility, an anger I had never seen before. One of the most vivid recollections of my first years as a mother was an afternoon I spent with several other women, strangers for the most part, all with children my daughter's age. We had recently banded together to form a "play group":

• I am on a sunny, flower-filled terrace. Toddlers weave and totter around a stone bench, in and out of shrubs and pots of geraniums, exploring stones, leaves, petals, snails, drops of water.

I watch my daughter, who is unself-consciously exploring the world. She is delighted to be among so many young bodies her own size. Obviously this is what she needs right now—to be with other children, but with me around so that she can explore the world freely yet know that safety is not far away. Out she ventures bravely. The stiff, guarded mothers remind me how lonely I've been since the birth of this precious daughter, for her birth has drawn me away from work, colleagues, and shared interests into a strange, foreign world of "mothers with children."

One mother carries a Bible around with her. She has had the most trouble with her baby, who was born with a congenital heart defect. This woman seems kinder, more human than the others, though we have little in common.

Suddenly I see her little daughter, smaller than the others, pick up a stone and throw it at her mother. It hits the woman's face below the eye. "You hit me!" the mother flares. The daughter comes closer and whacks her mother as hard as she can. Embarrassed, everyone pretends not to notice.

But it reminds me of the flashes of rage that I, too, have begun to get from my daughter and how upsetting they are. My daughter's devotion to me keeps slipping into what seems like deliberate malice, then back to the love and hugs and cuddles which are sometimes what sustains me. This has driven me to a good friend who, with her thorough knowledge of children, informs me of what is going on: "They're discovering they're not God and it pisses them off," she says. "You're not the appendage they thought you were. They're little runts in a world of giants. They'll start loving you and hating you at the same time now—they have to, it's the only way they can begin to separate. It means they feel sure enough of your love. But don't let her hit you. It makes them feel awful if they see they've really hurt you."

The Bible mother winces again and again as her daughter literally thrashes her. Someone says, "My daughter has started doing the same thing now—she bites, kicks, even spits at me!" Another mother says, "I've had to start locking my son in his room—that's how obnoxious he gets." For a time, relief spreads, defenses drop, and every mother has a similar story:

"Mine bit my knee so bad it bled."

"Bobby kicked me in the shins."

"Suzy pulled out a clump of my hair."

Slaps, pinches, hate, anger, rage. And it's all directed at us. It is like a dog biting the hand that feeds it; like Eve and Adam biting the apple in Paradise, after God created such a nurturing place just for them. Betrayal: they betray us by hating us and wanting to be free after we have given them so much. We betray them by holding on, or else by leaving them first, before they are ready to have us leave them, because we can't stand their offensive behavior.

Parental Guilt, Rage, and Self-Discovery

Some mothers try desperately not to hurt their children the same way they feel *they* were hurt as children. Yet this impulse can cause unforeseen dilemmas. Recently Carol, an old friend, called me from the Midwest, in tears. That day a kindergarten teacher had said that her daughter was demonstrating wild, uncontrollable behavior in the classroom, acting emotionally disturbed, and needed psychotherapy. Carol and I had grown up together in the same neighborhood. The child of divorced parents, she had always spent as much time as she could with my family. I remember Carol's mother as an unpleasant, vindictive woman who traveled a lot and eventually had a bad second marriage which left a trail of misery. Carol's surrogate care-givers were chosen haphazardly and were frequently fired and replaced. Carol was now sacrificing her career as a public defender to raise her daughter in the way she felt best, not leaving her child except for brief intervals when it couldn't be helped.

Carol seldom set limits with her daughter. When she visited me the year before, she told me that limit-setting was confused in her mind with the strict, sometimes abusive forms of discipline she had experienced with her own mother. Carol felt her mother's way of keeping her in line had seriously hampered her as an adult. She was afraid that if she drew the line with her daughter, she might thwart the child's creativity or harm her in the same way she had been harmed. In tears she said to me:

• How can any mother be sure of anything? I hate mothers who are cocksure of themselves! I've done everything I could to give Jenny a happier childhood than I had. My mother used to scare the hell out of me when she was home. I swore to God never to do that to Jenny. And some of those people she hired to take care of me I still have nightmares about. I've devoted my whole life trying to be a better mother than mine was, so that Jenny won't have to endure what I went through . . . But now I'm told I may have done something just as bad if not worse to my own kid.

Guilt. Uncertainty. Trying to do it better this time around. Trying to give more. Trying to be a better mother than Mother was. In spite of such feelings or because of them, the guilt that many mothers feel is endless and tyrannical. Guilt for providing too much attention or not enough, for giving the child too much freedom or not enough, for spanking or not spanking—these feelings are common yet often hidden. The guilt of the working mother, the guilt of the mother who does not have to work, the guilt of the mother who tries to do both—work part-time and mother part-time—and feels both jobs suffer because of it; the guilt of the mother who just wants to get away from her children, but doesn't feel she has the right; the guilt of the mother who bolts, abandons her child; the guilt of the mother whose child is showing signs of disturbance, unhappiness, physical illness; the certainty you've somehow damaged your child permanently, no matter what you've done or failed to do.

Where does this horrid, oppressive guilt come from, and why does it fall so heavily on the mother's shoulders? How much of it is real, important to feel, to spur us on to look at ourselves, to be better parents? If we felt no guilt, we might never be moved to correct and learn from our mistakes. But the maternal *mea culpa, mea culpa, mea maxima culpa* is surely excessive; mothers tend to blame themselves for everything.

Most of this guilt is socially induced, cruel and destructive to mothers, heaped upon them so that others do not have to bear responsibility for the well-being of the next generation. Part of the guilt stems from the rage we feel as our children begin to expose the naked anger they feel toward us, asserting themselves in shockingly obnoxious ways, doing things we would allow no other human to do to us without swift retaliation. We are enraged when we realize that our children are furious at us (even temporarily)—after all, we have worked so hard to take care of them. Yet wrath felt toward small, defenseless children whom we adore seems *so* wrong.

Parents often feel they have erred in one direction or the other, either by being too lenient or too strict. A strong set of religious beliefs used to help parents with the problem of discipline. Unshakeable convictions made parents confident that *whatever* they were doing was right, even if it was child abuse. In contrast, the absence of certainty in our secular age has made us all question values that were once taken as absolute truth. Feelings of helplessness and bewilderment lead to the overly permissive attitudes so prevalent now. When we are confused or self-absorbed, we often cannot find the inner conviction to say "No."

Not only do we tend to behave the way our parents behaved, we often feel toward our children whatever our parents felt toward us at this stage. Whatever was painful in our relationship with our own mother returns when we care for a child. The emotional tasks of child rearing involve caring for a precious, vulnerable new life while reliving early ties and conflicts. It is not surprising that people grasp at new theories on how to "parent" in order to ward off the feelings children stir up in them. Few parents, however, can sustain the use of these trendy techniques with a deep sense of conviction. One of the most challenging yet threatening aspects of child rearing is finding out, for the first time, who we really are and how we respond to such conflicting emotional experiences.

During the first three years of a child's life, a primary care-giver must perform extraordinarily complex tasks: she must create a bond with a tiny new being whose helpless dependence requires that someone be constantly available; she must also work to order the child's world and support its fragile budding self. As soon as the care-giver masters these intuitive skills, she must learn a whole new set of cues, tasks, and behaviors: how to make demands on the toddler; how to curb and mold his actions; how to tolerate and accept the child's rage and devotion, adoration and rebellion—the whole spectrum of negative and positive feelings. While this crucial early relationship is being established, a mother must simultaneously re-experience and rework previous tensions and conflicts—longings for her own mother and the longing for freedom, the need for someone to help master and control unruly impulses and the pain of that process.

Chapter Three

THE LONGING FOR CHILDREN AND LONGING FOR THE MOTHER

Giving birth . . . may be for the mother a kind of fulfillment of the . . . double wish to be a baby and have a baby . . . Her own symbiosis with mother may be experienced . . . and thus the loss at the growing separation would be a double one—the loss of [a child] and the loss of the mother.

—Anni Bergman
Early Female Development

The wish for a child is probably what is least human in man.
—Janine Chassequet-Smirgel,
"The Femininity of the Analyst"

Notes from Interviews

• *If you've ever suffered from a sense of insignificance, having a baby takes that feeling away completely. Totally. I've never felt so powerful as when I pushed that baby out and the midwife put this bloody little living, breathing thing on my breast! Like I'd created something real! This real, live baby! It was too much. I've never experienced anything like it, ever, and I don't expect to unless I have another one. And I'll tell you something, there's a part of me that would like to just keep on having children, year after year. (Maxine, twenty-four, mother of one)*

• *When you're pregnant, you just feel like somebody! You are somebody! While you got that baby inside of you, ain't nobody can take that feeling away! (Serena, forty-three, mother of seven)*

• *Some of these pregnant teenagers are so damn needy and lonely. It's frightening, the hunger I see in these teenage mothers. The younger the girl is, the greater the hunger, the more restless . . . The kid I talked with today was so sad . . . I think she got pregnant because she thought the baby would be like one of her dolls. The problem is, babies are so damn much work. And here's this kid, sitting there in that dirty kitchen, listening to rock and roll, dying to go out roller skating with her friends and she's stuck with a tiny, helpless thing, holding this baby like he was a ragdoll. Acting "as if" she were a grownup. Of course she had access to birth control . . . What on earth pushes a child to ruin her life like this? Two lives ruined really, not just one. (Social worker)*

―――――

Whether it is a biological imperative, a psychological need, or a cultural force, the human wish for offspring is strong and sometimes quite independent of the resources available to nurture children after birth. For some women, the yearning to be pregnant and give birth is entirely separate from the capacity or even the desire to care for a new, young life. Stronger than intellect, remote from common sense, the longing to have children seems to have its roots in the irrational, in our biology, or in the dark recesses of the unconscious.

The birth of an infant is awe-inspiring and brings with it not only the sense of power and mystery but also the feeling of a new beginning. Under favorable circumstances, the decision to have a child usually indicates hope, faith in oneself and the world, and a belief that the creative forces of life will ultimately defeat the forces of destruction. Hope, faith, and belief are words associated with religious yearnings, with the spiritual aspects of human life. It is not surprising that the central symbols of both ancient and modern religions are gods who create, the birth of a savior, and goddesses of fertility.

The longing for children seems so natural, it is seldom questioned. To look closely into this mystery seems impious, almost a sacrilege against human nature. The impulse of some religions to forbid birth control may originate, in part, from a reverence for life and our miraculous ability to recreate ourselves. However, this veneration of uncontrolled fertility makes sense only when there are ample resources—emotional as well as material—to give children the nurturance they need.

The Longing for Children

Ideally the conception and birth of a child is a concrete expression of the love between two people: the embodiment of their desire to share in the creation and nurture of a new being who will be both unique and a part of themselves. The birth of a child may also be the open manifestation of a more private wish of two people to "mix blood"—to symbolically mingle and unite in the body of another.

People reproduce for other reasons, less mystical and esoteric. Some people have children because they are lonely, others because of social pressure; still others have baser motives that have much more to do with feelings of competition and self-aggrandizement than the desire to nurture a child.

Now that most people have a choice about conception, why do they want to have children? When I interviewed college-educated, middle-class whites, some of the conscious motivations they gave for wanting children sounded strangely prosaic. One man said he wanted a son to "follow in his footsteps." When I asked him what that meant, he said he wanted someone to take over the family business when he retired. Two older women spoke of being strongly influenced by social and parental pressures:

• During my childbearing years (the 1940s), having children was expected of women. I would have been pitied or ridiculed if I did not have children. I don't even know if I wanted children, but women didn't ask themselves those questions then. I don't think I had the strength to be "different."

• My parents wanted grandchildren. They were after me about it all the time. I felt I would be letting them down if I didn't have kids.

One woman said she had children because she was "curious":

• I wanted to experience everything. I was afraid I'd be missing out on something if I didn't have at least one child.

Another mother admitted feeling envious of a younger sister's fertility. The sight of her adorable nieces and nephews made her feel so jealous, she finally "gave in" and had two children of her own, despite the fact that her stressful career as a trial lawyer made it impossible to spend much time with them.

One woman claimed that childbirth was an adventure and child rearing was so much fun she felt sorry for people who deprived themselves of such joy. Another said:

> • I can't imagine not having children. I have so many happy memories as a child. I've always wanted to have children just so I could give them all the things my parents gave me when I was a kid. My mother was so wonderful. Dad too. We were a very close family. It never occurred to me there was a choice involved. It's hard to imagine anyone not wanting children.

There were other reasons to have offspring: the fear that the experience of old age without offspring would be unbearably empty; a desire for immortality; a quest for meaning; the desire to recapture, albeit vicariously, the innocence of youth. People verbalized these motivations for wanting children in the following ways:

> • I never wanted children until I was in my thirties. Then everything I was doing got to seem meaningless without children. Maybe it was something biological—the "biological clock" as they call it—but I don't think so. It was more like an emotional or spiritual clock. I wanted to have children because nothing else seemed important.

> • My poems, novels—they'll be nothing but dusty artifacts, read once or not at all. But my children are alive, real, and their children and their children's children will bounce and vibrate throughout eternity.

> • The thought of growing old without children is awful. I'm afraid of waking up one morning and feeling barren and empty

and totally alone. Maybe that's a selfish reason to have kids, but it's one of my greatest fears.

• Here I was, thirty-four years old, cynical about everything, wrinkles all over my face, my flabby body gone to seed. I wanted to create something young, innocent. It was the innocence I wanted. There is nothing so precious and beautiful as the innocence of children.

Some couples, it seemed, had children for the wrong reasons—to avoid an impoverished relationship or as glue to salvage a failing marriage:

• My wife and I never could stand sitting across the table from one another, just the two of us. Maybe that's why we had so many kids. We just didn't have much to say to one another and with so many kids we never had to.

• My ex-husband and I were having awful problems getting along. I think we were hoping a baby would save the marriage. Somehow we thought a kid would do the trick, bring us closer together, but the opposite happened. It made us fight more and grow even further apart.

Others spoke of intense feelings of loneliness and the desire for a kind of intimacy they felt they could get from no other relationship:

• After my divorce I felt like no one loved me. I was incredibly lonely. I remember saying to a friend, "I wish I had a baby. Then I would have someone who really loved me." After my second marriage, I got pregnant immediately, and I think in part it was so I would never experience that kind of loneliness again.

· A friend kept telling me about the intimacy and closeness she had with her baby and how much better and more intense it was than with her husband.

Several parents spoke of their need to master a traumatic childhood by giving a "normal" one to the next generation. As one father said:

· Childhood for my brothers and me was a nightmare. I guess I wanted to do it right this time around, give my kids the best of everything. My dad was such a mean son of a bitch. I don't think you'd believe some of the stories if I told you. I've always wanted to have kids, though, even when I was a kid. Then give them the good life I never had.

Some people expressed both the longing to be loved and cared for and the desire to love and nurture. One woman described feelings of intense longing for her mother and the hope that becoming a mother herself might ease such yearnings:

· I missed my mother. We moved clear across the country and I got so lonesome. I figured the next best thing to having my family with me was making a new one. Fortunately, my mother came out when the baby was born, but she didn't stay long enough. I can't tell you how hard I cried when she left.

The deep gratifications of child rearing are often intense and exquisite precisely because they conjure up the times we were nurtured. Through caring for children, the wish for a loving care-giver is reversed, made active, into a kind of "making over to others the right of having one's own wishes fulfilled" (which is Anna Freud's definition of altruism).

Longing for the Mother

The desire to be loved and taken care of is perhaps the most denied yet influential of human feelings, affecting thought and behavior on all levels. How the need for care is met by mother/caregiver/society establishes patterns of longing and gratification, thinking and feeling, which ultimately affect how we treat the earth itself.

Soon after we are born, the need for food, warmth, and protection is transformed into longing for the person who provides it. Contentment, satiation, the fulfillment of our most basic primitive needs becomes, eventually, the feeling of being loved. As need becomes attachment and attachment becomes love, boundaries between infant and mother are blurred, so that the one who tends and mirrors back the child's gestures becomes, for a short time, the infant self. Though longing for the mother is soon repressed in the child and denied by adults, you can get some idea of its strength by watching a nine-month-old baby screaming when its mother is out of sight. By this age, if a normal bond has been established, the mother has become essential to the child's feeling of well-being. Forces within the baby soon thrust its attentions out onto the world. Mobility and language must be mastered, the immediate world explored. Eventually the child learns to tolerate longings, especially as physical and mental maturation push the child toward independence and a desire for more and more autonomy.

Though longing for the mother is rigidly kept from awareness in most adults, it persists in the unconscious, surfacing in disguised form during times of heightened experience, such as before and after the birth of a child or in periods of distress. (For example, a commercial airline pilot said on the flight recorder just before his plane crashed near San Diego, *"Mother, I love you."*)

Children provide us with an opportunity to satisfy, on a vicarious level, our own wishes to be loved. One of the strongest motivating factors for having children may be the longing to repeat or re-create the experience of being cared for, by caring for others. Many are driven to have children by the desire to reexperience their own early care-giver's treatment (or, if it was painful or traumatic, to experience the opposite of their care-giver's treatment—in an attempt to master or right the wrongs). Our deepest yearnings for a loving mother are thus transformed into the longing for children.

There is a difference between the idealized mothers we yearn for and our real mothers. Because of our need to imagine the perfect love of an all-giving mother, we frequently distort whatever happened during childhood. In other words, longing for the mother is often independent of what our real mothers were like.

After the exhaustion of labor and childbirth, one of the first emotional realities a mother must face is the infant's urgent need for continuous care. Ideally, during the first year of a baby's life, the mother will have practical help, emotional support, and protection from disturbing external influences. Without loving figures around, mothers are frequently overwhelmed by the complex and arduous tasks of nurturing a new life. But even under the best circumstances, women feel strong irrational yearnings for their own mothers during this vulnerable time.

One woman I interviewed, whose relationship with her mother had always been a troubled one, said she longed for her mother after the birth of her daughter. Twenty-seven-year-old Patricia told me she begged her mother to fly out to Sacramento from Connecticut. Shortly after her mother arrived, however, reality clashed harshly with the comforting fantasy that her mother would now care for her lovingly as she learned how to nurture her baby:

• How could I have forgotten what my mother was like? But right after the birth, I wanted her so bad I completely forgot how critical she's always been with me yet needy at the same time. It was awful . . . like having two babies in the house—only my mother was more demanding than the baby. I was so relieved when she left. But then I got horribly depressed. Here I was, twenty-seven years old, wanting a "Good Mother" to come and take care of me so I could take care of my baby!

Another new mother said she was so overwhelmed with confusion and exhaustion after her son was born that she spent a good part of her savings to pay for her mother's airfare from Baltimore to the San Francisco Bay area. She completely forgot how controlling and competitive her mother was. The day after her arrival, Judy said that her mother began acting as though the baby belonged to her:

· I desperately needed my mother to help me out after the baby was born. The midwife had told me during my pregnancy how important it was to just enjoy my baby, but how could I with all the laundry and cleaning and grocery shopping? I was hoping my mother would help me with that so I could learn how to *cope* with this new baby. It's such an unbelievably big adjustment and I felt I couldn't do it alone. After a day or two, I got the creepiest feeling—like my mother was going to take over, steal my baby away from me. I felt so inadequate—like she could take better care of him than I could. She kept making me feel like I was doing everything wrong. It was a nightmare until she finally left. By then I was more exhausted than when she came.

Though postpartum depressions are due in part to the profound hormonal changes that occur after the birth, they also stem from the intensity of the longing for the mother and the now certain knowledge that such primitive yearnings can never really be fulfilled.

Shortly after the birth of her second son, twenty-nine-year-old Ella suffered a postpartum depression so severe that she had to be hospitalized for several weeks. Ella said that during the first week of her son's life she called her mother several times a day, weeping over the phone and begging her to come help her. Her husband left on a business trip when her son was ten days old, and Ella became frightened by horrifying fantasies that the baby would die. When she began thinking seriously of suicide, Ella called her doctor, who recommended immediate hospitalization.

Ella's mother flew out immediately from Minneapolis to take care of both boys. Though Ella was appreciative of this, she confessed that she felt unbearable longings for her mother:

• I felt so ashamed, I wanted to die. The awful thing was that I wanted my mother to take care of me. I wanted to be held and fed just like my baby. I'm still ashamed of this feeling. But the thought that I now had two babies to take care of was absolutely overwhelming—like it was impossible because I felt I couldn't even take care of myself. I wanted to trade places with my baby just so my mother would be that loving with me. When the fact that this could never ever be finally sunk in, I must have cried for days.

Giving birth forces a woman to revise her relationship with her own mother. For a mother to respond to her infant's complete dependence on her, she must reexperience and work through the longings she once had toward her own mother. By giving love and care to an infant, we can make reparation with our own mothers—for whatever they did or didn't give us. A mother can feel vicariously nurtured by caring for her child. When all goes well, active caring for the baby replaces longing for the mother and becomes gratifying in its own right.

Longing and the Origin of Intolerance

Perhaps longing for the mother is best understood by what it is not: contentment, fulfillment, a feeling of safety, autonomy, independence. This suggests the frustrating nature of longing, and it is this aspect that exerts its influence on our thinking and behavior. Mothers have to frustrate their children to a certain extent to encourage them to grow up. Even under the best circumstances, when this is a gradual process, some rage toward the mother is inevitable. But under trying circumstances, the child's anger toward the one she loves most in the world can be overwhelming, especially if it is felt too intensely, at too young an age, and is not mitigated by consistent, loving care. Rage toward those we love, love toward those we hate, whose power we envy; longing for the one who frustrates us: ambivalence is so painful that children put off feeling it for as long as they can, splitting maternal images into the "Good Mother" and "Bad Witch" of fairy tales.

Some psychologists say the realization that we hate the one person we love most in the world is the most painful feeling of childhood. For a child, simply to love is the greatest happiness; not to be able to love is psychic devastation—suffering so great it is difficult to consciously imagine. The need to believe in a Good Mother is a psychological necessity—even if it means the total distortion of reality. Because children cannot bear to hate their mothers, they divert their anger and disappointment onto someone or something else. If it persists into adulthood, this diversion of hatred can become dangerous. If intense feelings of love, hate, and longing for the same person cannot be integrated and resolved during the course of childhood, they can create in adults a propensity for intolerance and prejudice— in some cases, a life-long need to hate. To protect the idealized image of a loving mother, one must deflect and vent one's rage on someone or something else. In other words, the pain of ambivalence can become so excruciating in adults that it can lead to acts of irresponsibility and violence.

Another way to ward off this extreme suffering is to confuse this painful kind of longing for the mother with the desire to have a child. Pregnancy and childbirth can become defensive maneuvers, acted out for the purpose of staving off the unbearable feeling of disappointment and the mental pain of recognizing that we hate and need and long for the same person. To become a mother is a way of disclaiming the intense desire for the all-giving, all-loving mother of fantasy. Some women have children only to express how desperately they want to be loved as only babies are loved, and to try to wrest from the experience of giving birth the nurturance they never received from their own mothers.

Compulsive Pregnancies

One of the greatest human tragedies is the birth of a child who is not loved or wanted and who cannot be provided for. Perhaps only the horrors of the twentieth century and the possibility of global annihilation could motivate us to question the very premise of procreation and to examine when and why the longing for children is not matched with the resources or even the desire to care for those children.

The fragility of a newborn infant can evoke in mothers an animal ferocity at the thought of harm coming to the child. Strong protective feelings toward offspring seem so normal, many believe they are genetically passed down from generation to generation. Thus, when we see the drive to reproduce coupled with neglect, abuse, or inadequate child care, we are mystified. With the advent of birth control and widespread sex education, people can now match the desire for offspring with circumstances that are most conducive to creating healthy, happy children. Yet, as so many unwanted and neglected children indicate, the reasons some people procreate remain obscure.

On a subliminal level, pregnant women often feel like their own mothers, who nurtured them symbiotically for nine months. Under favorable circumstances the feeling of unity with the nurturing mother is transformed into a feeling of unity with the infant after it is born. The infant can seem for a time like a tiny version of oneself that was once cherished and now will be cared for again.

If the longing to be loved and cherished is too intense, some women will try to get nurturance from their babies instead of giving it. Under such circumstances, love is replaced with resentment, emotional hunger, and a grasping need to try to take from their children what they never got from their own mother. When they discover how arduous infant care is, other mothers lose interest in their babies and have as little to do with them as possible.

According to clinical psychologist Dr. Christina Wendel, some mothers cannot allow their daughters to develop as individuals. A needy mother may actually feel a daughter's growing autonomy as threatening, a kind of abandonment. This can put pressure on the daughter to become a mother rather than betray her own mother and experience herself as separate. As Dr. Wendel explains:

> Sometimes a daughter will become too much a part of the mother's life which she cannot relinquish. Because the mother is lonely and unfulfilled, she clings to the daughter as though she were a part of herself. To ward off feelings of emptiness, she won't let the daughter go. Unconsciously, the daughter feels the mother's panic at being left. Leaving the mother, growing up, equals betrayal and abandonment of the mother. Though the young girl's body is pushing her out into the world and into relationships with others, guilt keeps her tied to her mother. Despite information, every kind of birth control device available to her, she gets pregnant so that she will not have to feel she has deserted her mother or experience herself as separate.

Dr. Wendel says the young girl may become pregnant to give the baby what she herself never got. Yet in reality, caring for the infant makes the young mother feel despondent with deprivation:

> After the baby's born, the teenager realizes she doesn't want to

take care of it because what she wants is to be taken care of her-self—loved exclusively—the way infants should be loved but she probably wasn't. Since she's too old for this, she keeps on having babies, trying to get it through them. Then, like her own mother, she tries to get her children to take care of her . . . And then her daughters, when they are teenagers, get pregnant—it becomes a vicious circle.

The failure to provide loving care results in feelings of scarcity. Emotional impoverishment in early childhood sets the stage for insatiable yearnings for a loving mother. The longing for nurturance can easily become disguised or confused with a longing for children. In some women, the desire to maintain the fantasy of an idealized Good Mother, by *becoming* a mother, leads to compulsive pregnancies, but without the desire or ability to mother each child after it is born.

Good Mothers and Real Mothers

In developed nations, the trend in the twentieth century is for people to have fewer children (or to decide not to have children, an option that has become culturally acceptable). Such decisions can evoke in women both primitive longings for motherhood *and* the urge to develop other kinds of creativity. Children may exhaust us and consume our energies, but they also protect us from feelings of emptiness, loneliness, even the fear of death. Thus the experience of childlessness or our children's separation from us as they grow up often requires courage, further development, and individuation in most parents.

In the 1920s, Virginia Woolf—a writer who chose *not* to have children—wrote a novel that gives poignant expression both to the nature of our longing for the mother and the longing for children.

At the same time it subtly hints at the growing desire in some women to be exempt from the stresses of child rearing. In *To the Lighthouse*, Woolf also laments the loss of a mother-figure whose sole task in life is to comfort, protect, and nurture her children and those around her. In the character of Mrs. Ramsey, devoted mother of eight children, Woolf creates someone who exudes all those qualities we associate with the word "maternal." This mother wants only what is best for all her children, which she intuits effortlessly. She gives freely to them without asking anything in return. She wants only to love and work to provide what will make others happy. She is the mother we secretly long for and the mother we would like to be for our own children, but somehow never quite can.

The power of the novel comes from Woolf's ability to show us Mrs. Ramsey, the "Good Mother" in whom we long to believe, and Mrs. Ramsey, the *real* mother who gives and gives until she is exhausted, yet is still driven to try to fulfill everyone's deepest wishes to be cared for. Virginia Woolf subtly hints that because this loving mother has devoted her life to taking care of others, she is devoured by everyone's insatiable desires and, perhaps, by her own need to be needed.

The novel is so rich in the subtle connections between longing for the mother and the longing for children, the feminine, maternal world of fusion with another, that feeling of symbiotic unity which makes giving to another seem like giving to oneself—*only not quite*. The longing in Mrs. Ramsey for children—and her power to create eight—blots out in her all feelings of aloneness and inadequacy. Through her role as mother and giver, she is defined and thrives, and is ultimately consumed.

Though Mrs. Ramsey is described as a "rain of energy," a "delicious fecundity," the "fountain and spray of life," her constant giving is doomed. For one thing, no one nurtures her, no one gives back to Mrs. Ramsey. There is no reciprocity in her relationships, not even with her husband. Woolf foreshadows this mother's inevitable collapse, describing moments when ". . . the whole fabric fell in exhaustion upon itself, so that she had only strength enough to move her finger."

Virginia Woolf suggests that when women's responsibilities as emotional care-givers become so overburdened and compensatory, the masculine intellectual traditions become one-sided and consequently grow nerveless, watery, and stale. Because her husband has Mrs. Ramsey act out the role of his mother as well as his wife, Mr. Ramsey remains limited, and his significant intellectual powers are reduced to game playing and showmanship. Because he never has to face himself or his longings, he grows cowardly, childish, and demanding. Insatiable in his desire for sympathy and attention, Mr. Ramsey must be constantly reassured and protected from the truth. Oddly, even as a recipient of such loving ministrations, Mr. Ramsey exaggerates his wife's ignorance by thinking her "not clever, not book-learned at all. He wondered if she understood what she was reading. Probably not, he thought."

When the image or role of the "Good Mother" is inextricably confused with mindlessness and ignorance—even by those who reap the benefits—something in the world has gone terribly wrong. Woolf leaves little doubt as to how humanity has belittled and distorted both the longing for the mother and the object of that longing.

Most readers love Mrs. Ramsey. Indeed, she may be one of the last "Good Mothers" in literary history. Yet Virginia Woolf also makes her a real person, intimating that when mothers are devalued, undernourished, and emotionally deprived, they often have only the dependency of others with which to satisfy their needs. The idealized mother, created in fantasy out of our repressed longing for her, can become in reality blind and oppressive. Woolf shows Mrs. Ramsey as nurturing yet controlling, sometimes treating adults as though they were children. This loving mother's overly intuitive intelligence blurs boundaries and distinctions. Because she is unable to wean herself from the mothering role, even in relationships where it is inappropriate, Mrs. Ramsey is unable to distinguish her own needs from the needs of those who remain dependent on her, never quite seeing them clearly enough to recognize how different they are from herself.

Because of the severe stresses of nurturing, many overburdened mothers tie others to them, suffering a kind of spiritual "failure to thrive." (This term has been used to describe children who mysteriously stop growing despite the fact that food is plentiful and there is nothing physiologically wrong with them. I use it in this book to describe mothers who stop growing emotionally, in mind as well as spirit, though materially they seem to have "everything.") In a world where mothers are devalued and overburdened, where fathers are as hungry for love as their children are and either compete for the wife-mother's attention or withdraw, care-givers cannot, without heroic effort, create conditions favorable for nurturing children. Severe emotional deprivation can become the societal "norm." Woolf subtly suggests in *To the Lighthouse* that women who need others to be dependent on them are not only devalued by those they care for, but can also become instruments of their own oppression. Because of their emotional hunger, they can fulfill neither their own nor their children's needs. Despite exhaustion, they may continue to have children in order to ward off feelings of impoverishment, the knowledge of how much they are used and surreptitiously resented, and the pain of their ultimate aloneness.

Are we creating a society in which severe emotional deprivations perpetuate failures to nurture our children and ourselves? In the creation of our advanced technology, are we diminishing our capacity to love and care for our children?

The birth of a child not only engenders feelings of joy and possibility, it also creates opportunities for us to love in new, life-affirming ways. Never before have we had such opportunities to "do things right this time." In addition to our material well-being, we are gradually gaining knowledge of what would benefit both care-giver and child so that conditions for optimum child care can be realistically examined and created. By looking at how much we devalue the mother and the nurturing role, we begin to understand that it is a part of ourselves and our children we are devaluing.

Paradoxically, it is through insight into the deep connection between our longing for the mother and our longing for children, our profound identification with both mother and child, that we can finally face painful feelings of deprivation and work toward repairing and transforming scarcity into fullness, want into love.

Part Two

THE

RELUCTANCE

TO KNOW,

THE

RELUCTANCE

TO CARE

THE FEAR

OF KNOWING

. . . the first notion of identity in the infant, what is most his own, comes from the outside . . . through the mother's gaze, the infant (receives) precise instructions as to "who he is" and "how he must be" in order to be loved and recognized . . .

—Raquel Zak de Goldstein,
"The Dark Continent and Its Enigmas"

. . . the behavior of the environment is part of the individual's own personal development.

—D. W. Winnicott,
Playing and Reality

Notes from Interviews with Mothers, 1983–84

• *Going back to work when my daughter was a year old nearly killed me. I kept imagining her crying for me hour after hour. I would think about her all day, feeling I was missing the best part of mothering and ruining her somehow, like I was damaging her development. I had to leave my son even earlier—at six months. I envy mothers who can stay home with their children. They don't know how lucky they are.*

   (Sheila, thirty, mother of two)

• *Why do we keep it a secret? Pretend it's not work? Act like staying home with our kids is easy, self-indulgent, the glorious reward of the affluent life? I envy mothers who have to work. Yet I feel so guilty about this I can't bring myself to tell my husband when he comes home from the office that taking care of our two-year-old son is the most exhausting, difficult thing I have ever done. Instead, I listen to him complain how exhausted he is.*

   (Gloria, twenty-eight, mother of one)

• *The most difficult time of the day for me is 5 P.M. when I come home from work and have to deal with my two boys (two and four) who are usually crazy—I mean off the wall—by this time. They're so hyperactive from being in that day-care center all day I can't think straight. I find myself wanting desperately to go back to work where it is quiet and peaceful—where I can get some self-respect, order.*

   (Lenore, thirty-four, mother of two)

Because child rearing is not based on instinct, but rather on learning and ultimately on choice, our treatment of our children is a kind of theater of the soul, revealing our deepest hopes, longings, destructive urges, and capacities for love. It is not surprising that we have resisted knowing many things about ourselves as care-givers. We do not choose our feelings. They arise spontaneously whether we want them to or not. For this reason, the emotions and conflicts evoked in us by our children are sensitive areas of inquiry, places where we are most fragile, for they expose much of what we try to keep hidden from ourselves and others.

Reasons for the Silence

There are historical reasons why we have not, until recently, uncovered the deeper conflicts that child care stirs up in us. Centuries of high infant and child mortality rates made it difficult to look closely at our feelings toward our children. Loss cancels out curiosity; fear of loss obliterates thought. In addition to profound love and concern, parental feelings include envy, resentment, narcissistic involvement, and possessiveness. If the chances of children surviving to adulthood are low, admission of negative feelings arouses too much guilt and anxiety. Also, our feelings toward our offspring are as intense as our feelings toward our parents; consequently they are subject to repression or amnesia.

For centuries a succession of pregnancies kept most mothers mute about their experiences. Pregnancy, childbirth, and child rearing leave little energy or inclination for introspection. The modern luxury of having fewer children has given people the opportunity to feel and observe their children's gradual individuation and growing autonomy. When a woman has more time to watch and experience a child's various developmental needs and changes, her emotional responses to her offspring become more accessible.

In the past those who have been the most educated and articulate either did not have children or, if they did, were not involved in the selfless demands of child care. Only recently have the majority of women had the same educational opportunities as men and consequently acquired similar aspirations and ambitions. Never before have so many educated women had so few children—and the time to experience all the feelings and conflicts that arise when they tend a child.

Freedom from financial pressures has allowed some women to look closely at the emotional aspects of child rearing rather than focus on external factors such as survival and economic oppression. This subject is an extremely touchy one. We can understand a mother leaving her children each day in order to make a living. When a woman is poor, oppressed, and observably desperate, we can even comprehend her cruelty or neglect of her child. But when a woman has no financial worries and leaves, neglects, or abuses her children, she is now instantly judged as a "bad mother." We need enormous courage to look beneath this epithet at the underlying emotional experiences that cause such behavior.

Certain beliefs obscure our culture's lack of curiosity about the realities of child rearing for both mother and child: the belief that women leave their children only because of financial necessity; the opposite belief that fulfillment in our society comes only through work outside the home that is highly paid and highly esteemed. There is the myth that it is effortless to be a working mother and that this is the best thing for both mother and child; and the belief that when a mother leaves her infant during the first years of its life she does the child irreparable damage. Most pernicious is the myth that mothers are instinctively more loving and maternal, meaning that by nature they do not want for themselves—only for others. Slowly the pressures of urban technological societies have begun to erode the myth that the needs of the mother and the needs of her children are the same, exposing the disturbing fact that in a growing number of cases, the needs of mother and child actually oppose each other.

Two Kinds of Powerlessness

Mothers in this country experience one of two kinds of powerlessness: (1) the loss of power to influence and direct a child's life in an intimate, immediate, daily, hourly way which subtly shapes the young child's mind and soul; and (2) powerlessness in the outside world where ambitions can be played out instead of lived vicariously —where action and excitement, power and money seem more within reach, where muscle can be developed to pull one's own weight and to influence decisions that affect both family and world. When a mother chooses to stay home and care for her child, she must to a certain extent withdraw from the outside world. Because of the incessant care infants and toddlers need to survive and the arduous tasks involved in care giving, these mothers must render themselves more or less powerless in our man-centered culture.

If a mother chooses to work outside the home, she assumes more power and control in the marketplace, the law courts, schools, universities, big business, the political arena—places where decisions are made that affect all our lives. She must find others to tend and rear her child a good part of the day. A mother who chooses or must work outside the home to survive financially, lessens her daily, hourly contact with her children, diminishes intimate time spent with them, and her influence over them as primary care-giver. Part-time mothers become absolutely dependent upon others, often strangers, to provide the emotional and physical care their children need. If they are lucky, they have loving husbands or relatives to take over the tasks of child care, but care giving usually falls upon day-care centers or baby-sitters. Few women in this country can afford highly trained and qualified nannies, nurses, or tutors—people we expect to know a lot about the care of children.

To understand the conflicts of the working mother, we must be capable of imagining the anxiety of leaving a beloved child each day, sometimes with an "unknown" or in a place we feel is not the best for our child. It is unsettling to imagine doubt, guilt, loss of control and intimacy—loss of that sensual gratification and delight which can come only from contact with young bodies, what Dorothy Dinnerstein so aptly describes in *The Mermaid and the Minotaur* as "the flesh of babies . . . uncontaminated with self-rejection."

At the same time we have great resistance to imagining how awful it feels to be trapped at home with demanding children, powerless in the world at large, a loser in the great American game of winning at all costs (even if it is only winning the right to change jobs if you feel like it). Mothers find it hard to talk openly about these feelings of powerlessness because few people in our society are willing to listen; the care-giver's experience is seldom mirrored back with genuine empathy and understanding.

Many mothers now must learn to live in a world that may provide jobs, even material support but gives them no help with the conflicting dilemmas of child care. Again and again during interviews, I heard mothers who were torn and conflicted. What disturbed them was either the lack of esteem for the complex tasks mothers must perform each day if they choose to care for their children, or the pain of having to leave a child too soon, before they were ready to hand that child over to another person, often a stranger. For some mothers, it was the isolation and loneliness of urban living that makes conflict inevitable when one's social life centers around work rather than neighborhood.

Two Points of View

There seemed to be two separate camps: mothers who worked outside the home and those who remained home to take care of their children. Neither had much knowledge or sympathy with the other's concerns, which seemed so unlike their own. For example, immediately after the birth of her daughter, twenty-eight-year-old Patricia said she became totally disoriented. Only by returning to her work as a lobbyist in Sacramento when her daughter was three months old could Patricia regain her former sense of identity. When she described the turbulence of her first months as a mother, it was difficult for me to imagine that this meticulous, well-groomed woman could have been bewildered by anything. Yet she said it had been the most difficult time of her life:

· After I came home from the hospital with the baby, I became totally disorganized. I had no idea how to take care of a baby and felt more alone than I'd ever been before. All I wanted was to go back to work just so I wouldn't feel so weird. My I.Q. must have dropped at least twenty points. I felt like I'd lost my whole personality—I mean the part of me that really functions. I'd never felt so disorganized. I don't know how mothers who stay home with their kids can stand it without going crazy.

Betty Sue's response to the birth of her children was the opposite of Patricia's. Though she and her husband are desperate for the money, they decided to "do without a lot of things" so that he could continue in graduate school while she took care of their two children. They were living on his small stipend and some meager savings. Betty Sue said she couldn't understand how any mother could leave her children during the early years, no matter what the circumstances. While we talked in the kitchen of her tiny apartment in Berkeley, Betty Sue nursed her four-month-old son while her daughter, two and a half, played quietly on the floor at her feet. Raised on a farm in the San Joaquin Valley, Betty Sue said that the most important thing to her was being a "good mother" to her babies:

· I'm not a great believer in welfare, but I honestly think I'd accept foodstamps rather than leave my kids with someone else. I guess I just believe children need their mothers. And the stories I've heard about day-care centers—even here in Berkeley, even the places that are supposed to be the best—it gives me the chills. I know a lot of mothers don't have a choice. They have to work or their kids would starve. But a lot of mothers I know do have a choice, it seems to me. They don't really have to work and yet they do, even when their kids are babies, because they want a slightly higher standard of living. It's these mothers I'll never understand.

Jeanine's experiences as a mother seemed remote from both Betty Sue's and Patricia's. A marine biologist doing research for the U.S. Geological Survey, Jeanine said she had to return to work full time when her daughter was only two weeks old:

• My husband and I separated when I was six months pregnant and he'd left town. In order to complete my research I had to leave Laura with the day-care mother from 7 A.M. to 6 P.M. Monday through Saturday. I think the day-care mother has done a great job. (She's in the middle of toilet training right now, though this is hard to believe because my daughter wets the bed every night.) Some days, Laura acts like she doesn't recognize me. There have been times when she acts like I'm a stranger. I guess I've always felt guilty even though she seems like a real happy kid. She seems real independent even at two and a half. I love buying her things. That's probably my favorite "mommy" thing to do. Her room is filled with every toy on the market. Sometimes it's real hard but we make out all right.

Thirty-six-year-old Florrie also leaves her children every morning at seven, not returning until evening. Florrie said her biggest conflict as a mother is the jealousy she feels toward the nanny whom she hired when she weaned her first child at two months. Because of her demanding work as an anesthesiologist, Florrie has had to forfeit her role as mother except on the weekends. Yet she finds her feelings toward the nanny, whom she appreciates and respects, somewhat troubling:

· I feel so lucky to have found Helen (the nanny). She's absolutely great with the kids and I can leave each morning assured that they're in really good hands. I just never expected I'd feel so jealous when I see them prefer her to me. It's Helen my son cries for, even when I'm home. Helen's the only one who can comfort the baby. I know their closer attachment to her is normal—a blessing considering my schedule. It's just that it's real painful for me sometimes, because it really seems they love her more than they do me, like I'm a stranger, an outsider. They're my children, but sometimes it's like they're really more hers than mine.

Like Betty Sue, Carla, who recently moved to the San Francisco Bay area from Scarsdale, has purposely chosen to stay home and raise her three children herself. Yet to her, mothering is often an exhausting, thankless job which everyone seems to take for granted. Carla admitted that she frequently found herself feeling resentful and unappreciated:

· How many times a day do I wipe noses, change diapers, keep the middle one from hurting the baby, the oldest busy with some activity to keep her out of trouble or to try to improve her self-esteem? Of course, my husband thinks I have it real easy because I don't have to go out and work! And whenever we go to cocktail parties and people ask me what I do and I say, "I'm a mother," eyes glaze over and they lose interest in me completely.

What's so hard about taking care of kids is keeping it up day after day, week after week, especially when a lot of people around you don't value what you're doing or even consider it work. There have been times when I've come close to hiring someone and going back to teaching. Yet I keep putting it off. I want to wait until Tommy's at least in kindergarten. But taking care of these kids has got to be the hardest thing I've ever done—both physically and emotionally—no matter how much I love them.

Women like Carla and Betty Sue, who stay home full-time to care for their children, are becoming rare in our society and often feel devalued. Though many women must work outside the home to survive financially, the reasons why many mothers leave home and children to enter the work force are more complex than we like to assume.

Socioeconomic Realities of Child Rearing

The trend in this country is for women to want more highly paid jobs—so that they may achieve the same status as men, both socially and economically. In the United States, child rearing is not work that is highly rewarded financially. Mothers who choose to stay home to care for their children are increasingly looked down upon for not joining the work force. The enormous amount of work a mother does each day taking care of children is often not considered work. Men tend to look upon taking care of children on a day-to-day basis as beneath them unless they have the status of teacher, child psychologist, etc., and are paid for it. We live in a society in which the lowest form of work, both in terms of status and financially, is day-to-day child care. Domestic work is more highly paid; baby-sitters do not receive even minimum wage. Garbage collectors make more money than our teachers. Day-care workers are grossly underpaid. Those who work with children in just about any capacity (except physicians and psychotherapists) make very little money, especially compared to those who go into other professions.

The trend in the twentieth century has been a gradual weakening of the family structure. The nuclear family has replaced the extended family; single-parent families, usually involving only the mother and her children, now equal the number of two-parent families. The once deeply revered family ties have dwindled in importance compared with commercial ties. In *The Reproduction of Mothering*, sociologist Nancy Chodorow attributes the weakening of family relationships to the grim fact that ". . . ties based on kinship no longer function as important links among people in the productive world, which becomes organized more and more in non-kinship market and class relations."

We tend to define society in terms of social and economic power and our interest is often focused on those who hold and wield the most power. In our culture, it is men who make most of the legal, social, and economic decisions which influence the family. Though women have started to take on powerful roles in the world, those who do succeed usually have to adopt aggressive, competitive behavior, and ethical systems that do not value or respect nurturing. Consequently, on a legal and political level, those who wield power continue to ignore the needs, experiences, and work of the care-giver.

Alexander Mitscherlich, in his book *Society Without the Father* also explains the weakening of family ties in economic terms:

> in predominantly peasant cultures children represent capital, a natural source of cheap additional labor, security for the parents' old age. In modern industrial society, prolongation of the period of education represents a using up of capital, and the task of providing for old age has to a large extent been shifted to institutions; each generation has to fend for itself . . .

Children are no longer considered the hope of the future in the most primitive sense; as Mitscherlich points out: "Less material advantage is nowadays to be gained from one's children, for parents and children each go their own way."

In his book, *Cultural Materialism*, anthropologist Marvin Harris carries this idea even further, suggesting that what we feel toward our children is in direct relation to what we get back from them. Because we now have little use for our children, who have become too expensive for any cost benefits, we do not have as many. In the past, children provided cheap labor, soldiers to fight wars, reliable care when old age enfeebles us. Now he says:

> . . . the population growth rate in the developed countries is moving steadily downward as the cost to parents for rearing children to adulthood rises beyond $100,000.00 per child, and the expected long-term economic benefits fall to zero (Minge-Kalman, 1978). In the United States, this is happening at the same time that resources are being depleted and domestic capital is flowing overseas at an increasing rate in search of cheap labor, leading to inflation and the necessity for having two wage earners per middle-class family . . .

This kind of thinking in regard to children seems cold and extreme, except when analyzed in the light of an economy that is depriving the next generations of financial security as well as natural resources.

Giving Without Getting

In our society we are taught to expect rewards for everything we do. Giving without getting anything in return (at the very least a tax exemption) is considered unintelligent in our culture. Yet the mother-child relationship is not a reciprocal one. Except for the transitory pleasures—the smiles and hugs and devotion of children (which are enough for some women)—there is little mutuality between the child and its care-giver. For a long time, one gives, the other takes. This can deplete and consume a mother's strength.

The relentless giving that children demand can stir up unacceptable hungers, guilt over disappointments, and feelings of ambivalence. Many mothers I interviewed, whether they worked outside the home or not, found it painful to acknowledge how little emotional support they had actually received from anyone. Unless they paid for it, the majority of mothers received no practical help whatsoever. One woman said she was shocked to find that even those closest to her had very little to give, even in the way of understanding or empathy. Another woman said the only way she could survive when her children were small was to make herself numb by keeping busy: "I just wore myself out so I wouldn't have to feel the hurt."

What is most denied about child rearing is the altruism required and how draining it can be to constantly give care, protection, and empathy. We seem to be most reluctant to examine the spectrum of emotions evoked when we give time, attention, understanding, and compassion to someone who cannot really return these gifts, at least not for a long time. It is hard for us to acknowledge how easily care-givers of children can be ground down in our culture, depleted by the enormous energy the work requires, labor that is devalued and unappreciated.

What is the effect of giving to someone who gives little or nothing in return? When I tried to talk to mothers about feelings other than love and devotion, I felt like a foreigner walking into a strange village. Doors slammed shut, locks clicked, shutters and windows banged to a close. It is not surprising that many women remain shy and mute when asked to speak honestly and openly about the experience of mothering. The acknowledgment of intensely ambivalent feelings toward their children is often equated with being a bad mother. To be found wanting as a mother is the worst crime most women feel they can commit.

Other mothers I interviewed became competitive, aggressively asserting how happy, smart, healthy, successful, talented, agile, athletic their children were, what a close relationship they had with them, or how well they had everything under control. The underlying meaning of this competitive spirit seemed to be the need to reassure themselves and others that they were not bad mothers; that they had done a good job raising their children. What bothers parents more than anything else is the possibility that they may have hurt or failed their children. Few can admit how impossible it is *not* to demand something back from our children in return for all we have given them.

Most parents encourage behavior from their children that they feel will reflect well on themselves. We want our children to look and act a certain way and to perform well so they will make us feel proud (at the very least, not embarrass us). Nothing makes modern parents feel more ashamed than the awareness that what they have encouraged their children to do and be has nothing to do with the *child's* best interests but has been motivated by their own selfish behavior. The impression we want our children to make on others, the achievements we want them to accomplish, may often have more to do with our own best interests than with the child's. It is extremely difficult for us to acknowledge how easy it is to use a child, unwittingly, to gratify personal needs or act out our own unfulfilled ambitions. Using a child comes so naturally, so easily, we must reassess our ability to sustain the disinterested love and concern children need for any length of time.

How can we distinguish between using a child for our own narcissistic purposes and giving the child crucial opportunities to learn and develop important skills? As the mother of a gifted nine-year-old said to me before her daughter's concert, "I don't know who's more nervous, her or me. When she's out there playing the piano, I feel like she's fulfilling all my dreams."

While we raise our children, we are also trying to take care of ourselves and fulfill our own ambitions. Whatever it was we wanted, perhaps the opportunities we still want, we try to give to our children. What may be much worse for a child is indifference, neglect— the extreme opposite of narcissistic investment in their lives.

We seldom examine how difficult (and wondrous) it is to be able to distinguish our own needs and best interests from those of another. When you consider human nature and the competitive, materialistic society we live in, for anyone to constantly (or ever) put the best interests of a child before his or her own is miraculous. (One mother said she thought it was "unnatural.") Nonetheless, the rigorous, exacting demands of child rearing call for a kind of giving that is unrewarded. One Jungian analyst I interviewed considers the work involved in nurturing children "heroic." Heroism, to that analyst, is whatever takes the most courage to endure. In this culture at this time, giving to a child what is truly best for that child is just such a heroic task.

The Resistance to Knowing About Mothering

When women writers begin shattering sentimental idealizations of the mother, they explore the more painful aspects of child rearing. The pendulum has now swung away from the loving Madonna and Child image (which represents our longing for a mother who will love, comfort, and protect us), to themes and images that express the darker, more complex aspects of maternal experience.

In an article entitled "The Fantasy of the Perfect Mother," Nancy Chodorow and Susan Contratto find recent literature on the experience of the mother dominated by "primary process thinking" (i.e. thinking dominated by irrational, unconscious feelings). They feel such writing suggests: ". . . having a child is enough to kill a woman or make a woman into a murderer . . . having a child destroys the mother or the child . . ." Chodorow and Contratto see some of the literature by Adrienne Rich, Jane Lazarre, Dorothy Dinnerstein, and others as works in which "maternal violence is described but not opposed" and speculate that "if antifeminists have tended more than feminists to blame the mother, feminists tend to blame the child or the having of children."

Because of our identification with the vulnerability of children, we have a tendency to see everything that is not loving or bland in the mother-child relationship as irrational and frightening. We are not used to examining the mother unmerged with her child and when we do so, it is disconcerting. Sometimes what is good for the child *is* harmful to the mother and vice versa. When mothers speak honestly, this unfortunate (sometimes tragic) fact becomes apparent. The airless detachment of many scientific articles falsifies and distorts the intensity of the mother's experiences, which include rage, frustration, and anguish as well as joy and gratification.

Why is there so much resistance in our society to knowing what mothers feel? According to psychoanalyst Thomas Ogden, the empathy that leads to understanding demands that we "try on for size one identification and then another (i.e. to play with the feeling of being the other in different ways)." In his book *The Matrix of the Mind* Ogden explains that this kind of "play" is possible only when we feel there is no danger of being "trapped in the other and ultimately losing oneself in the other." Without the capacity for empathy, the capacity to "play with the feeling of being the other," we back off from understanding the deeper meanings of a mother's behavior.

We may fear that empathizing with the mother will make us lose our identity or feelings of separateness. The fear and devotion we felt as infants toward our own mothers distort our perceptions of all mother-child relationships, making us prone to both emotionalism and scientific detachment. If we were to truly understand what a mother feels on a deep level, we might feel engulfed in her pain, trapped in her frustrations, overwhelmed by the anguish of her guilt and ambivalences. Getting involved in the mother's emotional experiences may evoke the helplessness we once felt as small children. We idealize or blame the mother to maintain distance from the person who was once so close to us she seemed to be too much a part of ourselves.

Whether we become shrill in our judgments or cold and unfeeling, all of us (men as well as women, feminists as well as antifeminists) resist knowing about our unwillingness to nurture and care for children. By refusing to examine the experiences of mothers and the real needs of children (as opposed to the many impossible demands all normal children make), we block our own reactions to those needs and do not learn the extent to which *we* can and cannot give.

The Fear of Ambivalence

We think of maternal love as something unsullied by mixed feelings. A good mother doesn't feel rage, envy, indifference, or boredom when she is with her children. On the contrary, we associate a mother's love with pleasure, joy in nurturing, the *desire* to spend time caring for young lives. During the past three decades, however, studies in child development have given us a glimpse of the ferocious ambivalences every child feels toward its parents. Though we tend to look away from our children's rage toward us, even a small amount of observation shows us the intense ambivalence that is often concentrated on the mother. Unless we are saints, ambivalence usually begets ambivalence.

In developed countries, many mothers who stay home to take care of their children live isolated lives, penned in with their children. Working mothers come home exhausted and often have little energy or patience to deal with their children's needs, demands, *and* mixed feelings toward them. Because few people in our society become involved in the care of children unless they are paid for it, many mothers cannot afford to escape their children even briefly to vent their frustrations or replenish their energies.

Nevertheless, recognition that we have complex, contradictory feelings toward our children deeply troubles us. Conscious awareness of our ambivalence toward children arouses deep subliminal fears: of our unwillingness to love and care for others, of our indifference to the well-being of our children because of more immediate, short-term gains; there is also the fear that our own needs for love or power make us resent whoever receives care but cannot give it back in return. Yet we all harbor mixed feelings toward our children, just as we harbor mixed feelings toward our parents.

Underlying all our fears of knowing is the shadowy figure of the primary care-giver who once awakened us to the world, who reemerges when we care for our own children, and whose influence will be a part of us forever. Early child care rekindles primitive, unconscious emotions: irrational yearnings for the sensuous body of the mother as well as fears of being overwhelmed and controlled by her, longings for intimacy and fantasies of engulfment. Beneath the tendency to blame or idealize the mother lie the feelings we have retained for that primary care-giver who set limits on our impulses, who witnessed how small and weak we were, how dependent on her ministrations. Residues of this infantile rage toward the one who made us aware of our powerlessness and "rubbed it in," so to speak, may remain in the unconscious forever, emerging later as a devaluation of all women, mothers in particular. Without realizing it, some women incorporate this ambivalence toward mothers, devaluing the importance of the nurturing role and even of themselves as nurturers.

Our earliest memories of the mother have to do with whatever she mirrored back to us during our infancy. It was the mother who instructed us in who we were to become, intimately intermingling herself with our own sense of being. Perhaps on some level we never learn to distinguish ourselves from that first primary care-giver. In our unconscious, she remains forever, a kind of "ghost limb" torn from us when she ceased reflecting whatever it was she saw and wanted us to be.

As parents, we too instruct our infants, toddlers, and children, never knowing fully the depth and extent of the unspoken messages we are delivering. Unable to avoid mirroring back yearnings and images of what we want and need our children to be, parents cannot avoid limiting their children's potential to a certain extent. Care giving constantly teaches us crucial lessons in humility and the importance of forgiveness. Perhaps we can never know for sure all the things we are communicating to our children, whether we are expanding or retarding their capacities, how we are molding their gifts. Perhaps it is only after *we* become the "ghost limb" of our children's unconscious that we can acquire the potential for mercy toward ourselves and our mothers.

When we care for our own children, we cannot help but find ourselves limiting them while we love and protect, thwarting as we nurture, saying "no" because we must. Parenting forces us to acknowledge the ways we sometimes *cannot* meet our children's legitimate needs, frequently requiring that we face and accept our limitations. Perhaps we fear knowing what care-givers experience during the daily, mundane tasks of child care because such knowledge makes it impossible to blame or idealize anyone.

Our fear of knowing about mothering is derived from deep feelings of ambivalence toward both our parents and our children, and from the ways in which this ambivalence is transferred from one generation to the next. It also stems from an unwillingness or refusal of many to involve themselves in the exacting, selfless demands of child rearing; this has contributed to our resistance to knowing about the nurturing capacities of men. We avoid understanding empathically the kinds of powerlessness care-givers experience in this culture because of an irrational fear that we might lose ourselves or become trapped in their overwhelming frustrations. Perhaps most painful to all parents is the knowledge that we sometimes fail our children and cannot always fulfill their legitimate needs.

ON FATHERS AND MALE MOTHERS: THE MYTH OF THE BAD FATHER

The young male is, in the beginning, plunged into the mother's "femaleness." This primary symbiosis must be undone in order that masculine identity can be developed by separating off from the maternal identity . . . Identification with the father . . . enables the child to cut his tie to his mother and to turn toward reality . . .

—Janine Chassequet-Smirgel,
"The Femininity of the Analyst"

The father . . . is never as close and constant in bodily relationship with the young infant as the mother . . . must be. Nature has seen to that.

—Phyllis Greenacre,
Emotional Growth

Although the mother's body may have been the original prenatal metronome, these infants (nurtured by fathers) seem to have increased their repertoire to include a rhythmic synchrony, or cadence, with the father's body as well. Does this suggest that there is an innate potential in all human beings regardless of gender identity to establish such intimate reciprocity in and through the nurturing of one's own infant?

—Kyle D. Pruett, "Infants of Primary Nurturing Fathers," from *Psychoanalytic Study of the Child*

Notes from Interviews

· *What I see more and more frequently in my practice are marriages breaking up because of the stresses of child rearing. One woman I'm seeing is divorcing her husband because he refuses to help her take care of their child. This couldn't be happening at a worse time for the child, who is four and adores her father! Another patient got a separation because she was unable to say to her husband, "I can't do it alone. You've got to help me. I can't raise these children by myself." She said she felt less alone as a single parent because of all the support groups for single mothers, but I also think she wanted to get back at her husband, punish him. The myth that best describes this feature of our society is the myth of Jason and Medea—children destroyed by the parents for purposes of revenge. (Jungian Analyst)*

· *Men have always wanted to be where the action is—racing around the colosseum in their chariots. The trouble is, now women want to do it too, so there's no one to do the drudge work of taking care of the kids. The collusion between Freud and Helene Deutsch in not discussing her difficulties as a mother probably had to do with the fact that neither one of them wanted to know how much fun it is not to be home taking care of some snot-nosed brat. Maybe that's what men (and now women) don't want to face—how easy it*

is to leave the whole mess of raising them with someone else . . .
(Clinical Psychologist)

When I was a child, fathers were not expected to be nurturing. In the 1940s, men were supposed to protect and provide for their families—to shelter their wives as they bore and raised the children but not participate in the intimate tasks of care giving. Whenever my own father was nurturing to me, it was like a rare gift—treasured and remembered to this day. But this happened seldom because it was considered much more important that he generously provide for us financially. Good fathers made sure their children *had* things—opportunities as well as freedom from "want." The Depression left a scar on my parents' generation. "Want" was physical hunger and a kind of poverty difficult for us to imagine now. In my neighborhood, the notion that someone could hunger for anything more than financial security and socioeconomic elevation was viewed as alien, silly, or suspect, most certainly emotionally self-indulgent.

Of course this idea of the Good Father has changed drastically, especially now that over fifty percent of all mothers work outside the home. At the present time we expect more nurturing behavior from men. Images of the Good Father now projected by the media show males lovingly involved in all facets of care giving, even changing the baby's diapers. It is unclear how much this change in image accurately reflects men's actual behavior with their children. Most mothers I interviewed complained that their husbands avoided child care whenever possible or else did as little as they could get away with. As working women request their husbands to participate more in rearing their children, they often find men strangely reluctant.

The Myth of the Bad Father

What often seems easy for women—sensitivity to the needs and feelings of others —appears to be very difficult for men, especially in regard to their children. Though some women are unable to establish close ties to their children, in our culture it is men, generally speaking, who have more difficulty with intimate, nurturing behavior. The inability of some men to empathize with others, even their own children, often goes unnoticed. This failure in relatedness can seem quite "normal" by our cultural standards because it is obscured by material success or "macho" values. Yet the incapacity to feel compassion can result in a kind of inner, spiritual death leading to a lack of concern for anyone or anything beyond the self.

If there is a corresponding myth of the Bad Father to match the myth of the Bad Mother, it is the belief that men are not only more remote and unfeeling than women, but also more destructive and inhuman. Just as we hold mothers responsible for damaging the lives of their children, we blame fathers for the larger disasters, tragedies which occur on a grander scale. A woman's power to destroy stops with her children. Men's power to destroy seems limitless: presidents and generals playing golf while they decide on bacteriological warfare or which nuclear warheads they'll launch; the Nazi who played Mozart while sending Jews to the ovens. Though a mother may be cruel to her children, it's hard to imagine her tinkering with global destruction, coolly ordering masses to be slaughtered, or devising machines of unprecedented destruction. The images that epitomize the Bad Father and the Bad Mother are those in the films *Dr. Strangelove* and *Mommie Dearest.*

What are the emotional realities underlying these two mythic counterparts? With so many mothers away from the home most of the day, children urgently require their fathers to be more intimately involved in their upbringing than ever before. Men's reluctance to participate in the daily care of their children now appears to be worse than indifference. Considering the desperate need so many children have for loving care-givers, a father's resistance to nurturing his off-spring seems irresponsible. Yet many fathers act as though the incessant tasks involved in child rearing are really none of their business. Even when men have a keen awareness of what their children need, they have on the whole more difficulty following through and responding with the kind of time, attention, and concern children need. *We must consider why fathers remain so detached from their children or resist participating in care giving, even when they have the opportunity, for these questions yield clues as to what it is about child rearing that makes it so difficult for anyone.*

Some people feel that mothers remain more responsive to their children throughout their development because of innate biological, hormonal mechanisms. Others believe that because a woman carries an infant inside her for nine months, she feels her children to be a part of herself and thus maintains a more vested interest in their well-being than men do.

In her book *The Reproduction of Mothering,* sociologist Nancy Chodorow suggests that mothers form closer, less clearly differentiated bonds with their daughters than with their sons. According to Chodorow, mothers see boy infants as distinctly different from themselves and treat them early on as if they were more independent. Mothers experience their girl infants, on the other hand, as though they were more of an extension of themselves rather than as someone quite separate and distinct. Consequently mothers tend to treat their daughters with more warmth and intimacy, and to blur boundaries and downplay differences. For this reason Chodorow believes that the girl-child is predisposed to a greater sense of connectedness to others, as well as a desire to reproduce the closeness she experienced with her own mother by becoming a mother herself and nurturing her children.

Despite the mother's predisposition for closeness, however, glaring failures in nurturing occur in women as well as men. Many interviews revealed that some men enjoy infants and care giving as much if not more than their wives do. In fact, recent studies prove that the ability to provide intimate love and care for our children is as genderless as talent, genius, ambition, and the desire for control. Research during the past twenty years indicates not only how crucial a father's participation is in his child's development, but also how good men are at nurturing.

The Importance of the Father During Early Childhood

Studies carried out by Mischel in 1958 and Siegman in 1966 found that the absence of the father before the child's fourth year causes antisocial behavior and difficulties in the ability to delay gratification. The Glazer and Moynihan Report in 1963 discovered the average I.Q. of children whose fathers were absent was at least six points below that of the control group, regardless of economic and educational level. Other studies done by Kotelchuck (1976), Parke and Sawin (1977), and Pedersen et al. (1980) revealed that when babies from the ages of five to twenty-four months were bathed, fed, changed, dressed, and played with by their fathers, they were more socially responsive, could withstand stress better, and had higher cognitive and motor skills. In a study done in 1976, Ernst Abelin found that early attachment to the father was not easy to differentiate from attachment to the mother. The relationship of the infant to both parents had symbiotic qualities. Abelin noted that toddlers "refueled with both parents, seeking comfort and nurturance from whichever parent had been absent the longer time: the longer the absence, the greater the need for refueling."

Though pregnancy and lactation give women a physiological head start in mastering the tasks of care giving, recent studies indicate that personality, style, and the desire to nurture override biology, refuting the idea of the father as a remote, unattached bystander. In 1978, when researchers Frodi and Lamb measured the psychophysiological responses of mothers and fathers while they watched a tape of their smiling and crying infants, it was found that "patterns of autonomic arousal and reported irritation to crying or unpleasant emotions . . . were indistinguishable for male and female parent."

Though men seem less willing than women to involve themselves in the selfless demands of child rearing, the research of child psychiatrist Kyle D. Pruett (1983 and 1986) indicates that when fathers become the primary nurturers of their infants, these children thrive better physically, emotionally, and intellectually than those cared for by mothers. Pruett and his researchers speculate that father-nurtured infants thrive better because the baby has two parents in such cases. Though the mother may work full-time, she usually remains intensely involved with the infant, much more so than a father would, so that instead of "one-and-one-fourth parents" (due to quarter time or less involvement on the father's part when less care is demanded of him), the child has the benefit of two active care-givers. Pruett concludes: "Children raised primarily by men can be vigorous, competent, and thriving infants who may be especially comfortable with and interested in stimulation from the external environment . . . These men are capable of forming the intense reciprocal nurturing attachments so critical in the early life of the thriving human organism . . ." Pruett's work also suggests that sons can and do establish intimate attachments and identifications with their mothers, nonthreatening to their masculinity, which they, like daughters, wish to reproduce by becoming primary care-givers.

Despite the fact that children respond with equal affection to fathers and profit so much from paternal love and care during infancy and early childhood, most men in our society have little to do with their children except at a distance. Given that children benefit from the care of both parents, we must examine why it is so hard for men and women to share the responsibility for their children with genuine mutuality.

Forms of Paternal Caring

Recently men have developed more consciousness about their role as parents, examining their deepest feelings toward their children and the intrapsychic conflicts child rearing provokes in them. Many fathers I interviewed were open and articulate about the pressures within and around them that decrease their ability to sustain nurturing attitudes toward their children, despite the deep love they felt toward them. The men also spoke of how arduous it was to develop the capacity for constant physical care that young children must have.

More men than I expected had experienced full-time care giving. Most were forced into it. Once they got over the initial shock, some fathers had no desire to lessen the intense involvement in their children's lives that primary care giving had fostered. The experience left a vivid and lasting impression on all who took on full-time care of their children.

One father stressed how difficult care giving was, both physically and emotionally. When I spoke at length with David, a thirty-seven-year-old chemical engineer from Tucson, he said that until his wife became seriously ill, his household had been run in the traditional manner: he was the breadwinner and his wife raised his three children. Though he loved his children dearly, he had never been able to spend much time with them except on weekends. Even then, David said, he spent the afternoons playing tennis or golf.

- It's not like my kids and I were strangers. I just never spent that much time with them until my wife's illness. But then there was a period of several months when she was in the hospital. It was a nightmare. Until I found a housekeeper I had to do everything—cook, clean, get them to school. I've never felt so lost—like I'd been dropped in a jungle without a map or supplies! Maybe boot camp is a better way to describe it. You never have a minute when you're not running around. It was exhausting. And then the youngest got real sick (fever 104, ice baths, the works). I had to spend three days at home with my six-year-old son, watching him suffer, afraid he was dying, and it nearly killed me. What was so terrible was sitting there and not being able to do anything to make him feel better except just wait it out. I wanted to change places with him. I'd never appreciated my wife before that time and I've never been so relieved to have her home.

David claimed that this experience of intensive care giving "changed his life." Never again, he said, would he be able to take his wife for granted or underestimate work involved in child rearing.

Another father vividly described the intensity of the ambivalence his children evoked in him. After working for eight years as a middle manager in an aerospace company, Joe had been laid off his job, and his wife had gone back to full-time teaching in an elementary school. When I went to meet Joe at a local playground, he was comforting his three-year-old son, who was in tears from a fall off a jungle gym. Joe's two other children, five and seven, were in school. When his son stopped crying, Joe humorously described the joys and frustrations of full-time care giving:

• I don't know how my wife did it. I don't know how my mother did it. My hat goes off to all mothers who stay home and take care of their kids because they have the hardest job in the world. Children are greed machines; they're inhuman, amoral; they're monsters. Children don't give back—that's what blows my mind. You give and give all day long, and they take and take, and maybe once in a blue moon some goddamn teacher will say, "Great kid—you must be a wonderful father." (That happened the other day.) I mean, I know in the great scheme of things you reap what you sow and all that bullshit, but to take care of children who either need or want something every minute of the day, who interrupt your thinking, your conversations, your work, your life . . .

Then sometimes I ask myself, what else is there?—and I'll tell you something. Now that my wife works, she's grown insensitive to them. She comes home and growls at them, like I used to. She used to get on me about it, but now I tell her to lay off. I can't stand it. I tell her to get away from them until she cools off . . . You can't love children in the abstract, not if you take care of them every day. There's absolutely nothing abstract about kids. You have to get into self-sacrifice or you'll end up abusing them.

But it's been the best thing that's ever happened to me. I know my kids now. You can't love anyone you don't know. I may feel like killing them ten times a day, but I love them. And they love me. I'm no stranger who comes home with the paycheck and tells them to get lost. I'm their flesh-and-blood dad, and they adore me no matter how much I spank them or yell at them.

Fathers who took on the full burden of responsibility for child care spoke of the deep attachments they had formed with their children, the development of strong protective feelings, and the gradual enjoyment of the intense physicality involved in their care. There was no doubt that twenty-nine-year-old Larry, a single father of two, felt profound devotion toward his children. The produce manager of a grocery store, Larry had been raising his children alone since his wife "ran out" when the youngest was twenty months old, four years ago. Though he hears from his ex-wife every few months, Larry said that she still has a serious drug problem and is unfit to be a mother. Meeting me on one of his coffee breaks, Larry confided that he has resisted remarrying—for fear his children would once again be burned by someone who didn't care about them:

• I consider myself mother and father. Twice I almost got married again, but if you want to know the truth, I chickened out at the last minute because I got scared that the woman wouldn't be a good mother to my kids. I've gotten real picky about the women I go out with. I'd always wonder how they'd treat the kids. Their own mother hurt them so much, I could never stand for a stepmother to do the same thing.

I'll be honest with you. It's not easy. I have to work eight to nine hours a day to pay bills. I put them in day care during the day and it's not what would be best for them. Sometimes I'd cry when I picked them up. You can always tell how miserable they've been. I've never found a day-care person worth her salt. When I'm with them, I do everything, of course. I've taught them how to use the potty, clean themselves, tie their shoes, get dressed by themselves. The hardest thing is not spanking them every time you feel like it, and I'll be honest—if you raise your own children, you just naturally want to spank them a lot because kids can drive you nuts.

But I'll tell you what happens—you start loving them so much —loving their hugs and holding them in your arms. Children are physical . . . and they make you physical—they make you love hugging them as much as they love hugging you. No woman could ever make me feel so loved as my kids make me feel . . .

Like Larry, other men who took on the role of primary nurturer spoke not only of the stresses of child care but also of the gratifications of being passionately loved by their children—a kind of affection they got from no other relationship.

Exclusion of the Father

Some interviews indicated that mothers tend to exclude their husbands from child care, unwittingly making them feel left out and inadequate. Many women I spoke with felt that they are the only ones who can really take care of children or do it well. Because society reinforces these attitudes, we must question how true they are.

Several women swore that their young children are not physically safe with their husbands. Because some fathers are neglectful, self-absorbed, or incompetent, the mothers literally fear for the child's well-being whenever they are forced to leave their children with their husbands. Without a trace of resentment, Martha, a Los Angeles housewife who is married to a research scientist, explained:

· I've always taken care of our three children and I've loved it. I have no qualms. My husband is very absentminded. He has neither the time nor the inclination to take care of the kids. He always says I am the "empath," and basically that's what you do when you take care of children. We each do what we do best. I think he is helping humanity more by the research he's doing. Some men should never be given responsibility for child care. Otherwise people get hurt. My husband is often distracted when he's with the children. It doesn't matter really who he's with. When my oldest son was two years old, I asked my husband to watch him for half an hour while I went to the store. When I came back, my son was toddling along the edge of a twelve-foot ledge. Another minute and he could have fallen down and cracked his skull. This absentmindedness has always made it dangerous for me to leave the children with my husband. Now whenever I have to go anywhere, I hire a sitter to watch the little ones.

These mothers indicated they would not even bother to confront their husbands or demand that they be more responsible and help out with the tasks of child care, because it would be of no use.

Because a man's involvement with his children is in no way biologically motivated by a nine-month pregnancy or the capacity to breast-feed, he might need more encouragement to involve himself in child rearing. It is important to explore how much and in what ways women collude in keeping men distant and consequently insensitive and unconnected to their children. One child psychiatrist speculated that some mothers feel so unimportant in the culture at large, they unknowingly keep their husbands from participating in child rearing. Experiences described from the father's perspective suggest an unconscious collusion on the part of both men and women as well as rigid male/female roles and behavior patterns handed down from previous generations.

When forty-two-year-old Frank married for the first time at age twenty, he had not finished college. After quitting his studies at a university in Seattle and working for a year in a brokerage firm, Frank moved with his wife to the country where he tried making a living as a free-lance writer. Everything was fine until his wife gave birth, after which the marriage began to disintegrate:

• My first wife didn't let me near the kid when he was a baby. I thought that was normal, the way things were done. My own father never had much to do with my brother and I. I just figured it was OK not to have that much to do with him. Right after he was born, I remember feeling like an outsider. My wife was always holding him, feeding him, changing his diapers, giving him baths. We were living in the country at the time, pretty isolated. I remember at one point feeling incredibly lonely, and she'd become a real bitch.

I'm sure it was the birth of my son that made us break up. We drifted further and further apart after he was born. She had no interest in my work. I don't know if things would have been different if I'd done Lamaze (like I did with my second wife), helped with the birth, held the baby right after he was born— done all the bonding stuff. Maybe. Of course, men didn't do that then. That was in the late fifties. I was only twenty-one. I've never had much to do with my first son. I still feel a lot of resentment toward my ex-wife because she always seemed to encourage the distance. She'd make me feel I was too clumsy, like I'd drop him. She told me I played too rough with the baby and scared him.

My part in it? That's hard to know. It was a long time ago. Maybe I didn't make enough of an effort but neither did she. I don't think I really cared that much about the kid, about kids in general. Maybe I was too hurt by my wife ignoring me. But I was pretty self-centered then—if I couldn't be the center of my wife's attention, I wanted out. Maybe I wanted out anyway.

When Frank became a father for the second time, his experiences with both wife and baby daughter were the exact opposite. Frank attributed this to two factors. First, times had drastically changed, and men (at least where they lived in northern California) were expected to participate in both the birthing and rearing of their children. Second, Frank said that at thirty-eight he had begun to long for a child and wanted nothing more than to immerse himself in caring for his daughter.

In families where both parents are involved in child care, mothers and fathers frequently find themselves competing over their children's affections. A child's devotion can be extremely gratifying; and to lose it—or seem to lose it—can feel temporarily devastating. It takes a great deal of maturity to allow a child to love someone else with all the passionate intensity of early childhood. Some mothers feel possessive of their children, especially if they are not used to sharing their children's attention with their husbands during infancy. Many women admitted feeling especially jealous of their daughters when their affection for their fathers eventually grew into adoration.

Though the father is always an important person in a child's life, he definitely becomes the preferred parent at certain stages. Some of the mothers I interviewed remarked that this was a hard blow. When I asked an old friend about her feelings toward her daughter when this happened, she said:

• I'd gotten so used to her crawling into bed next to me every morning and giving me a big hug. Then, around age three and a half, she started crawling in between my husband and me. It seemed she was trying to pry us apart like a crowbar. Then it was him she started hugging in the morning. I felt spurned! Here I'd given that kid three and a half good years of my life, and what does she do? Turns away from me and hangs around him.

Anne Sexton has a poem about the more complex aspects of maternal possessiveness. In "Pain for a Daughter" Sexton describes a situation in which a daughter, wounded by a horse that has crushed her foot, is helped by the father instead of the mother.

> . . . her father, hydrogen peroxide in hand,
> performing the rites of cleansing . . .

It is not the mother whom the child runs to or prays for, or who ends up nursing the wound. "Blind with fear" and "arched against . . . pain," the daughter cries:

> . . . Oh my God, help me!
> Where a child would have cried Mama!
> Where a child would have believed Mama!
> She bit the towel and called on God
> and I saw her life stretched out . . .
> I saw her torn in childbirth,
> and I saw her, that moment
> in her own death . . .

Some mothers commonly equate a child's separateness with death. Such feelings of separateness can evoke in mothers irrational feelings of panic, grief, and aloneness. Consciousness of a daughter's distinct identity is one of the most difficult aspects of mothering for many women. Allowing a child to have a special and exclusive relationship to another, even with someone as important as the father, can make a mother temporarily feel like she is losing a part of herself. Sometimes it takes tremendous strength to allow a child to form intimate attachments to others, even when we know how crucial this is for their well-being.

Aversion to Children

Now that more and more women have entered the work force, men are expected to take an interest in their children and are encouraged, if not pressured, to spend more time with them. Yet many mothers felt that though it has become more fashionable for men to spend time with their children, their involvement in child care is only slightly greater than in previous years. The consensus was that men's concern for the emotional well-being of their offspring (revealed by actions, not words) does not come close to matching that of mothers.

According to a public relations specialist, society's attitudes toward the father are definitely changing:

> • The first thing you do to restore someone's public image is get photographs of him playing with his kids. It works every time. And it doesn't matter if it's George Bush or somebody radical— you convey to the public how much this man loves his children or his grandchildren. This hasn't always been the case. It wouldn't have worked with Nixon or even Reagan. But it's true now. That's how fast times are changing.

When I asked this same man about his own experience as a father, he said he sees his sons, two and four, on Saturday mornings. Sitting in the elegant offices of his public relations firm, Steve explained that his business demands that he reserve Saturday afternoons and Sundays for work and the kind of socializing he must do to establish good relationships with his clients. Steve and his wife, a real estate developer, have a full-time nanny and take their vacations together without the children. On weekdays Steve leaves early in the morning and does not return from work until after the children are in bed. When I asked Steve if he was satisfied with seeing so little of his sons, he said he thought his relationship with them was a good one and that this was the "normal" arrangement for most of the fathers he knows.

In fact, Steve's arrangement was normal for many fathers I interviewed. These men did not have or want much contact with their children. The responsibility they felt was primarily financial. Some said that as the family breadwinners, they did not have the time or leisure to spend time with their children. When I interviewed George, a senior partner in his law firm, he said:

· I work a twelve-hour day, at the very least. That takes time away from my wife and kids. But the benefits are—my kids get a good education. They go to the best schools, they get the best academic training. They'll get into the best colleges and they'll do well. Already they're both top in their class. They get to travel. They ski in the winter. They get flute lessons and piano lessons and tennis lessons and riding lessons. Without my paycheck, they wouldn't be able to learn how to do all these things. I think everybody benefits from the work I do. Though I may not spend as much time with them as I'd like, I'm providing them with as good a life as I can.

Ernie also sees his role as a father to be that of a provider. The owner of a large trucking firm, Ernie is proud of how he has pulled himself up by his bootstraps:

· I started my business eight years ago. If you were to ask me any second during the day where my trucks are, I could tell you within a hundred yards where each one is pounding the pavement. My wife's a great mother. I suppose I'm not the kind of father that hangs around with his kids. The way I was brought up, kids took care of themselves. I never even saw my father. By the time I was in high school, I was holding down three jobs at a time. My wife's wonderful with kids. That's her domain.

In most families the stereotypical division of labor went unquestioned: the women took care of the children, whether they worked full-time or not. Children seemed to make some men feel anxious, bored, or inadequate. Some fathers sounded as though they had an aversion to child care and were more comfortable relegating the care of their children to someone else. A year and a half after the birth of his first child, twenty-seven-year-old Tom, a computer programmer, said:

· Babies just don't come naturally to me. Every time I have anything to do with her, she's always screamed bloody murder, right from the very beginning. Of course I'd rather my wife take care of the baby. What man wouldn't? My computer doesn't whine. Computers don't have temper tantrums, smelly diapers, and you don't have to feed them. You turn on the juice and they do what you tell them to do. My wife has the baby, I have my computer— so we're even. Seriously, though, I spend my time writing code and designing programs. This is what I do and it brings in a bigger paycheck than what my wife makes as a substitute teacher. Also, it comes naturally. Child care doesn't.

Why is it so easy for men *not* to be involved in caring for their own "flesh and blood," even in their spare time? It is easier to understand men staying away from their children because they are frightened by sexual or violent impulses that child rearing can sometimes bring forth. Some men fear they will actually hurt their children and for that reason spend as little time with them as possible. They stay away from their children to protect them from violent outbursts which they fear they cannot contain. Peter, for example, learned to leave the house when he felt one of his "rages" coming on. When his children were small, Peter had trouble controlling his temper:

• I've always had a tendency to fly off the handle. My wife had to clue me in. She said, "You don't hit kids like that. You'll hurt them." I was just doing what I thought all fathers did. When I was a kid growing up in Nebraska, we all got whipped. It was just no big deal. And kids can kind of egg you on, you know. So I had to learn to split when I felt the urge. My wife told me to get away when I felt like hitting them so that's what I did—and still do.

Patrick, a veteran of the Vietnam War, is a more extreme and tragic example of someone who lives in fear of violent fantasies and impulses. When Patrick returned from Vietnam, he said he tried hard to fit into "ordinary life," which to him was marriage and children. But after his son was born, things fell apart:

• My ex-wife started back to work about four months after the baby came. I was taking courses at the university then and would give him his bottle and change his diapers when she left for work in the afternoons. I love my son, but eventually I couldn't continue to live with him or my wife. I blame this on the three years in Nam. It got so that every time I was with my son, I saw Viet Cong children being blown to bits. Pretty soon it was whenever I shut my eyes I'd see mutilated children—exploding right in front of my eyes—like a four-year-old or a two-year-old. I ended up on a psychiatric ward at the V.A. for about six months. My wife filed for divorce. I haven't seen her or my son in a year.

Patrick's tragic experiences with his son may have been caused by the trauma of war. But others, women as well as men, who have not been soldiers or victims of war, are tormented by similar fantasies; this causes them to have an aversion to being with their children.

Particularly horrifying to men are sexual feelings and fantasies evoked when they are with their children. As one father said:

> • I'll tell you something, but I would never want my name mentioned. I'm telling you this because if it's happened to other fathers, maybe they won't feel bad. I used to get erections whenever I held my baby daughter. I couldn't help it—it just happened. It was different after my son was born, it didn't happen. But I've always felt a little uncomfortable around my daughter . . .

Women, because of their ability to breast-feed, can enjoy deep, sensual feelings toward their babies which are literally life-sustaining. If a mother does have disturbing sexual feelings, there is never a danger of anything so physically overt as an erection to confuse her in her role as care-giver. Because infants and babies stir up all kinds of sensuality, a man might have more to repress when caring for them.

Sexual and sadistic impulses can make the attachment to a child threatening, in some cases overwhelming, to both men and women. Given such frightening feelings, some people seek safety in any work outside the home that keeps them away from the painful emotions evoked by their children.

Child Care and Regression

In attempting to understand why so many men do not participate in the care of young children in our culture, other cultures, and in the past, psychoanalyst Grete Bibring writes:

> *In addition to the custom in our culture that fathers do not take over the regular care of little babies, a man is inclined to ward off his own childhood impulses that are aroused by the infant's helpless*

dependence, nursing, weaning, teething, and soiling, by avoiding tending to the baby . . .

According to Bibring, when we are able to avoid close, intimate attachments to children, we do not have to experience the many infantile feelings evoked by our children's needs and instinctual urges. Though some fathers feel comfortable with the closeness and intimacy that relationships with young children can generate, others have trouble with this aspect of care giving.

Men in our culture are expected to be independent. Many fathers treat their children the way *they* were treated and expect them to behave the way *they* were rigidly conditioned to behave. These men find it extremely difficult to accept their young children's neediness and dependence: the younger their children, the more difficulty these men have in caring for them and responding to their dependency needs.

Though some people feel it is economic pressures and realities that keep men away from their children, others think it is social conditioning. Child rearing is considered women's work and makes men feel effeminate if they participate in it too much. Because men do not have the power to create life inside their bodies, they tend to enjoy machinelike extensions of themselves (cars, guns, motorcycles, computers) or athletics—activities involving strategy, power, and physical prowess. Yet none of these theories explains the care and devotion parents feel toward adopted children. And many women enjoy achievement, agility, power, and making money much more than mothering children, especially now when it is not just acceptable but expected of women to define themselves outside their role as mothers.

Because of the regressions child rearing stirs up, it may take more ego strength, courage, and commitment for a man to involve himself with his children. Child care pulls everyone back into the "world of the mother" (unless one was raised by both parents); a man who felt uncertain of his masculinity might be threatened by having to perform what our rigid cultural stereotypes label "maternal behavior." The care of infants demands that we empathically respond to the infant's need to be passively held, loved, nurtured; this can easily stir up our own passive longings. According to clinical psychotherapist Jack Erwin:

> *Women can slip in and out of feeling what a baby feels in order to determine what the baby needs and wants. To take good care of an infant, you've got to know what it's like to "want your mommy." A man who "wants his mommy" is considered a wimp in this society. Men have to work harder than women to repress longings for their mothers. Of course, if a man has been nurtured by both father and mother, then he is not going to fear losing his masculinity when he takes care of a baby.*
>
> *I've had several male patients who literally "mothered" their children after they were first born. The wives worked full-time. The men were excellent nurturers. One man told me he began to sit down while urinating. I don't know whether this threatened his masculinity. He said it became necessary because he was carrying his baby in his arms. But this could make some men frightened of turning into women, losing their manhood, that sort of thing.*

For men, care giving is often a voluntary act—and inherently threatening. This makes it easier to avoid and, at the same time, more demanding of courage and inner conviction when a man decides to care for his children.

Effects of Paternal Distance

In traditional psychoanalytic thinking, the father's role includes: providing support for the adult ego of the mother, helping to limit and control the child's fantasies of omnipotence and destructive wishes, and encouraging mastery and achievement through sustained effort. This rather bloodless view reflects the culture's attitudes toward fathering: men are not expected to become a crucial source of love for the child, but rather to enhance separation and independence from the mother.

In 1955 Margaret Mahler intimated that the relationship with the father may be important much earlier in a child's life:

> . . . the stable image of a father or of another substitute for the mother, beyond the eighteen-month mark and even earlier, is . . . perhaps a necessary prerequisite to neutralize and to counteract the ego-characteristic oversensibility of the toddler to the threat of reengulfment by the mother . . .

Reengulfment here means the intense longing of the toddler for the mother and the fear of this very longing because it undermines the toddler's proud strivings for autonomy. If reality reinforces inner fears and the father doesn't mitigate the tie to the mother, this primary relationship can become contaminated with ambivalence that is too intense. Mixed feelings—dependency and anger, rage and longing—bind rather than loosen. Like the daughter in Ingmar Bergman's film *Autumn Sonata*, some people feel so much ambivalence toward their mothers that they cling to them throughout their lives, and are unable to establish satisfying relationships with anyone else.

Unfortunately, the love of a child for its father is often stronger than the love of the father for the child. Many interviews with mothers suggest that when the father was emotionally unavailable, which was frequently the case, the mother took on the responsibility for *all* of these emotive tasks *herself*, including encouraging her children to separate from her. In fact, many mothers went to great lengths to help their children achieve autonomy, finding or creating experiences that promoted individuation, encouraging relationships that helped each child feel strong and independent. These mothers were often overburdened with the *total* responsibility for their children's well-being, whether they were single mothers or had husbands, worked outside the home or devoted their days to child care. In other words, many fathers had little to do with their children— even when they had many opportunities to participate in child rearing, even when both wife and children were obviously suffering from his avoidance and neglect.

The effects of a father's emotional distance, death, absence, or of his inability to respond with love and care can be devastating to a child. Without an uncle, grandfather, or other man who is willing to take on such an important relationship, a child can become attached to an absence, a shadow, which she must try again and again to fill or make real. Industrial and postindustrial societies have increasingly drawn the father away from the home most of the time; many children have been deprived of that crucial intense relationship, which can develop only with a father's physical presence and through close day-to-day interactions with him.

Under ideal circumstances, the child identifies with the father as well as the mother, competes with both, and eventually tries to outdo them. The ancient Buddhist proverb "Honor your master by surpassing him" suggests that identification and successful competition with the parent can be wisely seen as a gift to the parent.

Unfortunately, in urban technological societies, the father has become a shadowy figure—gone most of the day, often with little to give to his child when he does come home. Though this is changing, the change is slow in coming.

So much energy must be expended to conjure up a loving father image when one does not have the real thing available. Men who had little contact (or had painful experiences) with their own fathers often must struggle to conjure up some loving model to help them care for their own children. Ironically, through nurturing, men can create their own model of a loving father. In his studies on fathers who became primary nurturers, psychoanalyst Kyle Pruett suggests that "identification with the infant . . . may ease or aid in the resolution of the father's disappointment and grief over his own father's nonnurturance."

Sylvia Plath's Father Poems

In two of her most widely read poems, "The Colossus" and "Daddy," Sylvia Plath describes extreme emotional reactions to the absent father. The earlier poem, "The Colossus," expresses both the profound need all children have for a loving, protective, flesh-and-blood father and how, if he is not around, the child will create and re-create him in fantasy until his image takes on mythic proportions. Yet in this poem, the dead father has become so vague and ambiguous in her memory, the narrator feels:

> *I shall never get you put together entirely,*
> *Pieced, glued, and properly jointed.*

> *. . . I crawl like an ant in mourning*
> *Over the weedy acres of your brow*
> *To mend the immense skull plates, and clear*
> *The bald, white tumuli of your eyes . . .*

The narrator tells us she has spent thirty years trying to discover who her father really was, what his real message to her was, but the most benevolent image that she can come up with is an ancient colossal statue ruined by time and anarchy. It does not seem to matter that his protection is as impersonal as stone:

> *. . . Nights, I squat on the cornucopia*
> *Of your left ear, out of the wind . . .*

The need for a loving father of abundance, who protects us from the harshness of the world, is so important that the narrator has forfeited much of her life to sustain even this vague figure:

> . . . *My hours are married to shadow* . . .

Many of Sylvia Plath's poems suggest that neither the reality nor the fantasy of a loving father could help her separate from her over-burdened relationship with her mother, or aid her in sustaining nurturing ties to others. When the image of the father turns up in "Daddy," one of her last poems written before her suicide, it is saturated with rage and paranoia. The father in "Daddy" is described as "Not God but a swastika . . . A man in black with a Meinkampf look." The father is no longer distant but close and viciously persecutory. It is significant that "Daddy," a poem in which the father is indistinguishable from a Nazi, has become one of her most widely read works. "Daddy" seems to express our massive, underground rage toward all the fathers who were responsible for the Third Reich, the atom bomb, Hiroshima and Nagasaki, the napalming of Vietnam, the growing stockpiles of nuclear weapons—the list could go on and on. The remote, distant father who turns into the sadistic SS man reflects our deepest nightmarish fears. We suspect it is men—fathers—who are running the world, and very badly. In positions of power, where broad policy decisions are made and executed, it is our *fathers*—the city-fathers, the fathers of our countries, our flesh-and-blood fathers—who are creating conditions in which war, destruction, violence, and needless suffering persists.

Sophie's Choice: The Metaphor of Sacrifice

Is there any truth to the conviction that men are ultimately more ruthless and sadistic than women? Are *fathers* responsible for the atrocities of this century and the impending threat of global annihilation?

In the novel *Sophie's Choice*, William Styron created a scene that epitomizes the limitlessness of human cruelty. Sophie, a Polish mother who has been imprisoned in a concentration camp with her two children, is told that one of her children must die. One will be saved from death, but *she* must choose which child is to be sacrificed.

Preceding this horrifying scene, Styron shows us the SS men, their wives and children, inside their homes where Sophie has been given a menial job. Their children are brash, self-centered, cruel, but not *that* bad, not *that* different from ordinary children. Their wives work hard to run their households. The SS officers suffer from headaches, stress; they worry about their jobs, want to "get ahead," please their bosses. Styron portrays the SS men the same way concentration camp survivor Primo Levi describes them:

> *They were made of the same cloth as we, they were average human beings, averagely intelligent, averagely wicked: save the exceptions, they were not monsters, they had our faces . . .*

Styron focuses on the SS man responsible for choosing who is to die. He is suffering from depression because of the strain of so much ghastly decision making. To get temporary relief, he makes Sophie suffer the burden of choice instead of himself. On the spur of the moment, when he comes to where Sophie and her children are standing in line, he makes *her* decide which one of her children must die. Sophie sacrifices her daughter to the SS men.

This grotesque scene is a metaphor: as men put into action their brutal machinery for destruction, deciding who is to live and who is to die, they feel guilt, horror, self-loathing. To get some relief, perhaps to avoid examining what it is they are really doing, they make women, *mothers*, choose who of their loved ones will be destroyed.

But the key point is this: it is *men* who are behind this unnecessary misery.

So the myth of the Bad Father continues: because of their positions of power, it seems as though men *could,* if they wished, transform horrible destructive acts into creative ones, artificial scarcities into more wisely distributed abundance, war into peace. Of course men do not have a monopoly on acts of viciousness. Because men *seem* to have more trouble than women empathizing with and responding to others, it becomes easy to blame them for economic and political decisions that are life-threatening. This blaming ignores the complex issues of complicity and collusion.

As a society we are all choosing who must be sacrificed; it seems someone or some group must always lose, suffer, not thrive—whether the choice is between black and white, men and women, husband and wife, mother and child, son and daughter, older child and younger. The choice may be to send some individual or group to a spiritual or emotional death rather than a physical one (though in our inner cities, it is often both).

We are all involved in decisions about who will thrive and who will not. Our affluence doesn't make a difference. There just doesn't seem to be enough to go around. There is so much deprivation—both emotional and economic—that anyone capable of escaping or getting relief grabs the chance and forgets those left behind. Our tragedy is the creation of a culture in which profit for one group necessitates loss and suffering for another.

Children and Moral Visibility

Does participation in child rearing make us all better people? Obviously not, in many cases. Nonetheless we do not know how much of our humanity is sacrificed, kept undeveloped or simply atrophied by avoiding children. The refusal of men to involve themselves in their children's lives at an early age seems to harm not only the child but to dehumanize the father as well, if only by blinding him further to what he is and to the consequences of his acts. Every act we do with a child has visible consequences which we either register or ignore. Child rearing seems to make us either better or worse than we are, more or less sensitive, empathic, humane. At the very least, child care offers us the opportunity to see, understand, and develop parts of ourselves that would otherwise lie dormant or hidden.

The discipline and strength required to care for a child—the ability to discern the best interests of another and to give without getting anything immediately in return—can cultivate and deepen a kind of consciousness that involves empathy and compassion. Caring for children can crack open—as nothing else can—the shell of our narcissism, humanizing us as it teaches us both about our children and our deepest selves. This kind of consciousness is not limited to mothers or to women. When applied to the world, it can make us want to solve the problems of hunger, injustice, war, poverty and racial prejudice.

Though the roles of father and mother are changing, the tasks of care giving remain the same: forming the close initial attachment that draws the infant out of its sleepy, womb-tinged world; the intense nurturing and protection required for many years; toilet training and the setting of limits and boundaries; the long, slow separation/individuation process that involves the gradual introduction of the child to the real world and the affirmation of its individuation and autonomy. Whoever takes care of a child during its first years, man or woman, does all these things. Many find it difficult, painful, or tedious. Some would rather involve themselves in more immediately gratifying occupations. But the stresses of nurturing in our society cannot be resolved without fathers taking a much more active role in the rearing of their children.

With mothers and fathers both working outside the home, we have opportunities for genuine mutuality in raising our children. For the first time in history, fathers and mothers can share in the tasks of child rearing, and men can have equal responsibility and determination of the outcome of their offspring.

Bonding with a child right after birth and close involvement during infancy and early childhood, when the child needs and demands more time, love, empathy, and understanding, has a profound intrapsychic impact on the father, promoting a deeper bond with his child. The acts of nurturing children transform how we see and treat the world. As men establish an intimate and loving connection with their children, they will care more about the earth and the future.

Part Three

LOVE AND

RELINQUISHMENT

Chapter Six

THE WORK OF

SEPARATION

When the child must be weaned, the mother blackens her breast, it would indeed be a shame that the breast should look delicious when the child must not have it.

—Søren Kierkegaard,
Fear and Trembling

. . . [most people] even when capable of an adult altruistic form of love which acknowledges the interests of the partner—retain toward their own mothers this naive, egoistic attitude . . . that the interests of the mother and child are identical . . . the measure of goodness or badness of the mother is how far she really feels the identity of interests . . . the mother must not want anything contrary to the wishes of the child.

—Enid Balint,
"Love for the Mother"

It is almost too long ago to remember—
when I was a woman without children . . . / that/
instant when I gave my life to them
the way someone will suddenly give her life over to God . . .

—Sharon Olds,
"That Moment"

Notes from Interviews

• *I really don't understand all this family album stuff. I just keep a few pictures of them, that's it. It's gotten so that I can't stand to see photographs of my kids when they were babies. I mean what good are memories? It's a time that doesn't exist anymore—it's gone, finished, and I just can't bear it. It makes my heart ache. Look how cute she was. She couldn't go anywhere without that filthy "blanky." And look at him standing there with his teddy bear. Whenever I see how adorable they were, I want to weep. How can anyone get any comfort or joy from remembering something that's over and done with? It's just too painful. Not that they aren't cute now. But they seem so grown-up. They're different now. All they want me to do for them is have dinner ready or drive them over to their friends' houses. It's like I'm not really a mother anymore. I've become a cook and a chauffeur. (Antoinette, thirty-five, mother of two)*

• *Now that they're both in school all day, I've finally had time to organize this album. I've been meaning to do this for about six or seven years and haven't had a minute. I've put all these photographs in chronological order, starting with their birth. We have so many wonderful memories of when they were small. Look at this one. Doesn't he look adorable? He was such a good baby. She was*

a hellion but so darn cute, you wouldn't believe it. We had such
happy times when they were babies. Now I'll always be able to
recapture those precious moments. (Nora, forty-one, mother of two)

———

During the first years of an infant's life, we form a bond so intense
we cannot break or even loosen it without enormous effort. In per-
forming the tasks of nurturing, we mirror, contain, and often share
our child's intense passions and sensations. Just as we have gotten
used to the sensations of physical closeness and the daily assaults on
our defenses, our children's wild and naked emotions begin to go
underground, from highly visible to more or less invisible.

After the first five or six years of children's lives, their unbounded
energy gradually becomes contained by the acquisition of new skills
and repeated attempts at mastery and self-restraint. If we have
grown used to their physical affection, their dependent kind of love,
we will have some kind of reaction to their new strivings toward self-
reliance and control. At this time, our caring changes from a sensual
experiencing of them to a more vicarious enjoyment of their newly
won mental and athletic skills. If we have come to love the intimacy they teach us during the early years, we must learn now to
relinquish it.

One of the most intricate tasks of child rearing is the gradual
letting go of our children, which inevitably demands of the mother
further growth, development, and individuation. To allow our children to grow up, we must develop the capacity to appreciate, encourage, and from time to time grieve the various stages of their
detachment from us.

Historically few mothers have been able to establish an identity
beyond the role of care-giver. For centuries most women were dis-
couraged from achieving any kind of individuation. Though they
encouraged autonomy in their sons, mothers were reluctant to foster
independence in their daughters. On the whole, women were raised

to take care of others. Intellectual and emotional development was such a lonely, painful process for mothers that only the most gifted, rebellious, or unhappy women attempted it.

Because of different socioeconomic pressures and greater opportunities, more and more women have begun to develop and achieve in realms outside the role of care-giver. At the same time, immersion in the intense experience of child rearing influences the way one develops as a separate being. The gradual relinquishing of the early tie between the mother and the child is still complex and problematic.

Just as our children will always be a part of us, so too will our mothers. In the symbolic realm there may be no such thing as separation from the mother. Our initial connection with the primary care-giver is a fusional one, an intermingling of our own being with that of another. We may keep the mother or parts of her with us always, in the pleasures we allow ourselves, the pain we create and endure, the work or play we choose, the relationships we form. In the unconscious, the place of dreams, separation from the mother may be experienced as a kind of psychic death, severing us from all of humanity. Because we reexperience this close tie to our mothers when we give birth and nurture our children, caring for the next generation can ward off feelings of unbearable aloneness as well as provide our lives with meaning.

In the cold light of day, however, there is no such thing as fusion with another. What our culture prizes most is independence and distinct individualism. During our waking hours, we do not like to think of ourselves as dependent or confused with someone else, least of all our mothers and our children. We feel most separate and are happy to be so. When we have children, our society expects us to encourage them to be autonomous. When the time comes, a good or "good enough" parent is expected to let his or her children go.

What is the emotional impact of this transition—from the intimate, "hands-on" care demanded in early childhood to the more distant relationship necessary when a child becomes school-age? We have, in fact, few in-depth studies or extensive firsthand accounts about the process of separation from the *care-giver's* perspective. Except in the realm of fiction and poetry, we do not really have much information about the deeper feelings and issues evoked in mothers by the experience of relinquishment. Psychotherapy usually focuses on a patient's childhood, not his or her experience of parenthood. Many contemporary case studies analyze the quality of the adult's separation *from the mother,* not the quality of the parent's separation from his or her own children. Empathic understanding of what goes on inside care-givers during this phase is usually not taken into consideration or felt to be important.

Devotion at a Distance

The physical and emotional withdrawal of a child, which begins in earnest at this stage of development, has a profound effect on many parents. There are obvious benefits: less attention to the incessant baby-proofing, the constant modifications in surveillance required during those early years to keep children safe from danger. More and more time is spent away from the child, which often releases feelings of liberation in the mother. The withdrawal, however, produces more complex responses than is usually expected. It is a time of loss as well as of gain and, ideally, an era of profound transformation.

By the time children are old enough to go to school, they have become more manageable, adoring and adorable, and also distant. Temper tantrums and frequent outbursts of tears are contained more and more in games, sports, and imaginative play. It is a time of moderated fantasies; increasing interest in rules, measurements, standard views on what is right and wrong; and strenuous efforts, sometimes unsuccessful, to behave and to mimic and comply with the adult world. Psychoanalysts call this stage of development—from around five or six until whenever puberty begins—*latency* (presumably because sexual urges seem to be dormant at this time).

For some parents, the desirability of children is enhanced by this new, distanced relationship. The child's growing competence and agility lessens the need for the constant provision of external controls. In both parent and child amnesia sets in, though for different reasons. Children need to forget how dependent they once were and still are to a certain extent. Parents need to forget the times that were so exhausting or emotionally troubling. Yet part of the tendency to sentimentalize the gratifying moments of intimacy has to do with very real and painful feelings of loss.

Working mothers who must leave their children many hours a day, long before they are school-age, are not immune to feelings of loss at this time. For what changes drastically is the *quality* of the child's attachment and the lessening of the parent's influence and control. As one eight-year-old daughter said to her mother, "I still love you, Mommy, but I don't want you."

After making herself a vehicle for the fulfillment of others, the mother of school-age children must recede into the background while the children try to overcome and forget about their previous dependence on her ministrations. Forty-one-year-old Marsha, a computer graphics designer, experienced excruciating feelings of loss at this time:

> • I've always worked at least part time, often full time. I didn't pay much attention when the older two kids started school. It was a relief not having to worry about them part of the day. But now that the youngest is in school, it just kills me. She doesn't even want me to kiss her good-bye anymore. She won't let me walk her into her classroom. She doesn't even want me to read her stories anymore. The other night she said to me, "You don't have to sing me any songs." That's when I'd get to cuddle with her, just before bedtime. Sometimes I think this is the most painful thing I've ever been through.

For some mothers nothing is more gratifying than raising their children. When the intimate part of it is over, some mothers feel intense grief. When I spoke with forty-six-year-old Carrie, a mother of four, she said that for her nothing could ever match the experience of caring for her children:

· When my youngest started school, I almost died. He loved it— couldn't wait to get out of the house every morning. I remember crying so hard I practically went into convulsions. Here I had four kids leaving me every day, even the baby. Eventually I went back to the university and became a school psychologist. I love working with kids. But nothing could ever take the place of caring for my own kids when they were young. I still dream of being pregnant again.

Sharon Olds's poem, "Looking at Them Asleep," expresses the devotion she feels toward her school-age son and daughter, describing them in minute detail while she watches them sleeping. Her close observance of them at this age must be done in secret, lest they notice how passionate her love for them really is and feel guilt for their growing emancipation from her. The narrator lists the strange, quirky things they do when they are asleep, their differences and peculiarities. It is a poem about the details of loving, about intimate knowledge of the things that make each child so unique. This love must now be hidden, kept under wraps so that it will not interfere with the child's flourishing sense of independence. Keeping this affection clandestine seems to increase its depth, scope, and intensity:

> . . . *oh Lord how I*
> *know these two. When love comes to me and says*
> *What do you know, I say This girl, this boy.*

At this time of more and more distance, how do we stay connected with our children? It becomes difficult at this stage—especially if a mother works outside the home—to stay in close touch with children whose overt message often is: "I still love you, Mommy, but I don't want you. I'm independent now and don't need you anymore!" They do still need us, of course, but more and more on the periphery, except when they're sick, injured, troubled, or in danger.

In other poems, Olds speaks of the agony parents feel with every high fever, cracked skull, broken bone—the times when all you can do is watch, hope, or pray. Every sore throat, bout of stomach flu, earache hurts not just the child but the mother as well (or whoever has made a deep connection with the child). This close identification is one of the most painful experiences that comes from loving children. Olds harkens back to the time when her children were sealed within her womb or small enough to be held and protected by her physical presence. To a baby, one can feel Godlike. It can be tremendously comforting to hold and rock an infant who is ill. To care for a sick school-age child, who is working hard to ward off passive longings for his mother and the regressive pleasures of being babied, it is much more difficult.

During this time of longer separations, many mothers feel elated by the new sense of freedom. After years of self-denial, they now have more time to do what they enjoy. For example, thirty-four-year-old Lara, after ten years of intensive mothering, claimed she felt both liberated and guilty when her third son, the youngest child, started first grade. "I felt so deliciously free . . . but it seemed wicked—to be so happy *not* having to take care of my own child." When I asked her what she did, now that all three boys were in school, she said,

• Sometimes I feel like I've been let out of prison. I keep thinking I'm doing something wrong, like I'm neglecting them, but then I think—how can I be neglecting when they're in school! As soon as I get off work at noon, I play tennis instead of rushing to the day-care center. Sometimes I swim laps. Sometimes I just do nothing for the first time in years.

Parents feel a sense of achievement when a child becomes old enough to go to school. We cannot help but feel pride and relief when children show signs of self-reliance and become more capable of taking care of themselves. The responsibility of child-rearing is officially shared with others. The discipline of mothering becomes more of a noninterventionist endeavor and, in many ways, much less exacting. As one mother said, "Once they learned how to swim and cross the street without getting run over, my whole life changed. Now it's the teachers who have to deal with them most of the day."

Parents are not completely emancipated, however. In our society, children from six years to whenever puberty begins are still considered children. From this time on, the care they require is quite different from before. Their problems are more likely to show up in school rather than at home. Parents are more likely to be gauging how much distance or "space" a child needs, rather than how much closeness and protection. Parents are often judged by how well their children perform and are blamed if a child is doing poorly. In other words, child rearing becomes more public. How well the child is doing academically, athletically, socially provides standards of parental excellence or failure. As one father of two exuberant school-age boys put it, "The way the teachers talk to me about my sons— sometimes they make me feel like I'm on parole."

In this country, even in areas of affluence, the outside world into which we send our children is a perilous one. Many mothers complain bitterly of the poor quality of the schools they must send their children off to each day. What was hardest for one mother during this time were the insensitive, impatient teachers she had to turn her dyslexic, hyperactive son over to, and how it took several years to find the right program that would help him. Another mother said her daughter's second-grade teacher was so cruel, her child would come home crying every day. Others speak of bullies, drugs, violence—

what is now the child's "holding environment" for most of the day. This pushes some parents to be active and work, in the schools or in politics, to make things better for their children. Others do not have the time, inclination, or energy to try to change the educational system. Some feel too hopeless to attempt such a task.

Emotional Realities of Caring for School-Age Children

For some mothers this is a time of confusion and discovery, resentment and reevaluation. The experience of thirty-six-year-old Rose Ann illustrates the fate of some mothers who find themselves altering career choices because of their children. Tall and lithesome, Rose Ann talked of the six years she worked as a dancer in New York and how hard it was to give it up:

· Before I had children, I was a professional dancer—it was my whole life. But then after the first cesarean, I couldn't dance for a long time. By the time my body was getting back into some kind of shape, my husband and I decided we wanted another child. So my whole life changed. When my second was three or four, I went through a period of time when I began to resent them. Like I realized it was too late and I blamed them—they'd taken away what I loved to do most in the world, made it impossible. I'd had real high hopes as a dancer. Instead, I got into teaching dance. Of course, that's what every dancer does, eventually. I just did it sooner than I would have wished . . . I don't think a mother can talk about children and not talk about self-sacrifice, at least to a certain extent. But then I weigh the sacrifices with these two kids and how much I love them. I keep having to ask myself what's really important?

Jeanette's story is another example of the reevaluation that is sometimes required when children get older. When her daughter, an only child, started school, Jeanette found her work as a pediatric nurse strangely depressing. For financial reasons Jeanette and her husband had decided not to have another child, despite the fact that she longed for one. It wasn't until Jeanette decided to switch to a different specialty, psychiatric nursing, that she realized working with young children had become too painful. Her own daughter, a fifth-grader, was spending more and more time away from home. All the babies Jeanette saw as a pediatric nurse reminded her of how desperately she missed the closeness she had once had with her daughter and how much she wanted another child.

At this stage, parents must deal with the more frequent partings and longer stretches of time when the child is away from them. Some of Sharon Olds's poems describe how a mother's affection is often felt most poignantly at bus stations and airports, before an impending separation. In her poem "The Signs," parents anxiously wait around a camp bus that is about to leave. To keep the ache of loss at bay, they peer into the dark-tinted windows for one last look at their children. The narrator marvels how each parent can pick out his or her child by just a tuft of hair, the curve of a chin, the wave of a "thin, finny hand / rotating like a windshield wiper." The children abandon their parents in a "Stygian stink of exhaust," leaving them in a "cloud of fear and longing / [that] hangs above the long drawn-out departure."

Unable to bear the loneliness of these more frequent separations, some women long to become pregnant again. Elena, who loved mothering during infancy, found the growing distance between herself and her children extremely disturbing at this time. For a period of time she desperately longed to have another baby. Though she loved her work as a marriage and family counselor, her urge to become pregnant after her youngest child was in school all day was quelled only by the fear that another child might be disastrous for the marriage:

· Though we could have afforded a third child financially, my husband and I couldn't have afforded it emotionally. I remembered how hard it had been on him those early years when I was completely wrapped up in the babies. The older the kids got, the more I could give our relationship. As much as I wanted another child, I decided it was too risky. Also, I'd just seen a good friend's marriage go on the rocks after a third child.

Unlike Elena, some mothers do have another child when their youngest goes off to school. According to clinical psychologist Dr. Bruce Bess:

It's normal for parents to get dependent on their children. Child rearing during those early years fills you up in a way few other things do. It's hard to be left by children you've given so much to. If a mother works outside the home, this may help her separate from her kids to a certain extent. But I've seen working mothers feel profound grief when their kids start school. Some full-time working mothers in my practice have gotten pregnant again when the youngest starts school because they realize how quickly its over and how much they've missed. When their kids were babies, they were working outside the home and didn't get to enjoy any of the intimate care giving.

Though many mothers breathe easier when their youngest is in school, others find it a time of turmoil. According to marriage and family counselor Barbara Kinsey, marriage problems inevitably surface at this time because there are now fewer distractions:

Kids are real hard on marriages. I've had to deal with so many divorce cases in my practice because of neglect of the marriage when the kids were young. Usually they bring the youngest kid into the child guidance clinic—around first grade—but often the kid's not the problem. What's happened is the parents have become strangers. All the energy has gone into child rearing and there's been nothing left over for the marriage. Then suddenly there's time. Only you've got years of resentment built up that no one could deal with when the kids were babies.

Some working mothers who temporarily put themselves on hold in terms of their careers have trouble determining how much their children really need from them at this stage and how much they can now devote themselves to their work. Though somewhat less dependent, children still need care giving at this time, someone available for emergencies or refueling—just in case. Unlike adolescents, whose physical maturity makes it clear they are becoming adults, latency-age children have an obvious need for guidance and protection in our society. Sometimes it's hard to know what kind and how much. Many mothers are anxious to throw their energies back into their work; to use their skills and abilities in the marketplace and make up for lost time. After working three years at a forward-looking Silicon Valley firm, thirty-four-year-old Sarah took time off to have a child:

· I purposely didn't work full-time again until I felt my son was ready for me to leave him. When he was four, I became project manager for a really innovative new program. Though I worked longer hours, I was still able to spend a lot of time with my son. When I went back to work full-time, they eventually asked me to be vice president in charge of finance. By that time my son was in first grade and I thought for sure I'd be able to immerse myself in my work without any problem. But the job demands such long hours. I drop Randy off at school early in the morning and sometimes don't get home until seven or eight. People tell me that he'll adjust, that it's better for him for me to be successful in my work, but there are times when I just don't buy this. Yet what's good for me and my career doesn't seem to be all that great for him. Since I've gone back to working full-time, he doesn't seem all that happy. A lot of times when I come home from work, he's either sick or frayed around the edges.

How much should school-age children influence a working mother's life? Whose needs are ultimately more important at this time? While on the job, if working parents are dominated by concerns about their children, they are not able to perform well. Yet most working parents *are* deeply involved with discerning and trying to achieve what is best for their children, though they might not know what this is. What disturbs parents most is when the needs of their children seriously conflict with—or oppose—their own needs.

One reaction of some mothers to their children's growing detachment is either physical or emotional abandonment: when the child begins to separate, the mother leaves first, to ward off intolerable feelings of loss. Another reaction is symbiotic clinging and constant undermining of the child's attempts to separate. Janice, a fourth-grade teacher in the San Francisco public school system, told me she sees both reactions:

• There's a mother who brings her nine-year-old a hot lunch every day. She literally walks into the classroom and brings him a fully prepared meal right in front of all the other kids. Another woman walks her son to and from school every single day despite all the teasing the kid gets. These mothers just can't let go. But then the other problem is worse. There's a kid in my class who comes to school filthy, spaced-out. Another kid never has a lunch and looks emaciated. You get the feeling that somewhere along the line the parents just lost interest.

How much does a child actually need from his parents at this stage? As Janice suggests, overinvolvement and underinvolvement are key issues that mothers of school-age children must grapple with.

Maternal Clinging and Compulsive Flight

There are dangers that arise at this time, pitfalls that make separation for the mother a more complex process than is usually assumed. Individuation can be tortuous for women, creating in some a tendency to hold on to their children. Other mothers find parental bonds either too painful or too stifling, and feel a compulsion to flee.

In her short story "To Room Nineteen," Doris Lessing examines the psyche of a woman suffering excessively from what many mothers experience to a much lesser extent when the tyranny *and* the gratification of their children's needs begin to wane. Lessing's heroine, Susan Rawlings, is unable to wean herself from a kind of voluntary bondage to her children. In this story, Lessing shows her heroine compulsively giving to her children, letting them constantly interrupt and consume her with their demands, even after she hires a mother surrogate to take over. Lessing gives us an excruciating picture of the driven need in some mothers to give without asking or receiving anything in return, and how this can retard the crucial tasks of individuation—even now, when further development is expected of women. This compulsion is what Dorothy Dinnerstein calls, in *The Mermaid and the Minotaur*, "an overdeveloped talent for unreciprocated empathy." (An example of the advertising industry exploiting this tendency in mothers is the Kraft cheese television commercial that has a male voiceover saying: "You've got to give one hundred percent—isn't that what a mother is for? . . . for mothers who give one hundred percent.")

In *The Awakening*, published in 1899, Kate Chopin deals with the opposite (or perhaps underside) of voluntary bondage to one's children: a mother's *refusal* to be dominated or possessed by her children's needs. Chopin's enigmatic heroine, Edna Pontellier, reflects the current woman's struggle not to be held down or back by the burdens and responsibilities of child rearing. Like most educated women now, Edna struggles to live and develop in ways once considered the birthright of men only: the enjoyment of both sexual freedom and intellectual enlightenment. The idea that it is her *children* that make Edna feel "overcome," "possessed," "overpowered"— more so than her husband or the conventions of provincial society— is prophetic of one of the meanings of women's liberation today: emancipation from the daily, hourly care of one's children.

Lessing and Chopin subtly prod the reader to consider: How important should our children be to us? When should we allow them to dominate our consciousness? When can (or should) we forget about them?

Like most women in our society now, the mother-heroines in these stories grope toward something more than motherhood to give their lives meaning. Both try to make that necessary journey back to a part of themselves that has been put "on hold" during the early years of child rearing. When the early years of care giving are over, both heroines find the "self" they return to undernourished, undeveloped, and unbearably alone. Even though they are intelligent, creative, and resourceful women, they cannot make it through their children's latency years. At a time when they should feel liberated to become themselves again and do what they want, both mothers suffer from "failure-to-thrive."

Kate Chopin, who was the mother of six as well as a successful and prolific writer, gives her heroine perhaps the most sought-after yet subtly problematic situation she could think of: choice, leisure, and liberation from the constant demands of child rearing with the freedom to enjoy her children whenever she wishes. In addition to those things, Doris Lessing gives her main character a successful career that she could resume when her children reach school age. Chopin and Lessing then use the mysterious suicides of their heroines to suggest the extraordinary complexity of the separation/individuation process in mothers.

The Refusal to Be Dominated by Children

Because of the fusional aspects of the maternal role, some women fear that they will not be able to separate themselves from the needs and personalities of their children. A mother can feel as though she is the property of her children, just as she once felt herself to be the property of her own mother. The compulsive flight from the emotional demands and responsibilities of child rearing can be motivated not so much by indifference or negligence (as is often thought to be the case), but by a fear of dissolution and a desire to preserve a separate sense of self. Such mothers feel that if they do not flee, they will lose their identity.

Written at the turn of the century, *The Awakening* is most modern in its subtle insistence that the heroine's conflicts have as much to do with her role as mother and her feelings toward her children as with a failed romance. Edna Pontellier's attitude toward her children is much like that of the contemporary working mother's.

By today's standards, Edna is an ideal mother until the end of the novel. She feels toward her two sons what any good career woman might. If she lived now and were a professional—doctor, lawyer, teacher, artist—her feelings toward her children would be considered normal. Edna loves her two children but, like many late twentieth-century mothers, provides them with loving surrogates so that she is a part-time parent.

Chopin goes to great lengths to describe Edna as both a loving mother *and* as someone struggling for and achieving an identity separate from her role as care-giver. We are given carefully wrought glimpses of the love and intimacy that exist between Edna and her two healthy, happy sons. Because their mother does not hover around them like the other mothers in the novel, Edna's sons are described as much tougher and more independent than the other children.

The plot of *The Awakening* is tinged with romantic overtones. Superficially Edna is similar to preceding literary heroines—Anna Karenina, Emma Bovary—who commit suicide because of failed love affairs. Edna Pontellier falls in love outside her marriage and has a sweet, short-lived summer romance. While Edna's husband is away during the fall and winter, Edna has both a sexual and an intellectual awakening. At the end of the novel, Edna's young lover returns, declaring his love for her but, presumably because he is too conventional, cowardly, or not willing to bring about her social ruin, he ends the affair. Edna goes to the resort where they spent the summer together, swims out to sea, and drowns herself.

For the modern reader, Edna's last perplexing thoughts uncover one of the most profound dilemmas a mother can have. Edna does not think about her lover but about her two sons. Chopin reveals Edna's last thoughts before her death:

> *The children appeared before her like antagonists who had overcome her; who had overpowered her and sought to drag her into the soul's slavery for the rest of her days. But she knew a way to elude them . . . They were a part of her. But they need not have thought they could possess her body and soul . . . she would give up the unessential, but she would never sacrifice herself for her children.*

The implication here is that children can make a mother feel owned and controlled, body and soul. Yet this is what *children* unconsciously feel: despite the fact that they are in school, away from their mother's physical presence, they secretly harbor fantasies that they belong to her. In dreams, fantasies, and imaginative play, children during latency give many indications that on a subliminal level, they feel their bodies (and souls) are still essentially the mother's property. (It is not until adolescence that children claim exclusive rights to their own bodies.) What Chopin suggests in *The Awakening* is that

this feeling is reciprocal in some cases. A mother can feel as dominated and controlled by her children as they can by her. Just as the
child must gradually extricate herself emotionally from the mother,
so the mother must from the child.

The separation/individuation process in mothers is a precarious
task. Sometimes it mirrors in adulthood what children go through
during the first three to four years of life. Newly felt autonomy can
be as pleasurable and exciting for mothers as it is for toddlers. Chopin describes the elation of Edna's unfolding into an independent
being in toddler imagery:

> *that night she was like the tottering, stumbling, clutching child,*
> *who all of a sudden realizes its powers, and walks for the first time*
> *alone, boldly and with over-confidence . . . A feeling of exulta-*
> *tion over-took her, as if some power of significant import had been*
> *given her soul. She grew reckless and daring . . .*

Chopin also describes the panic and aloneness women feel when
they reexperience this complex process in adulthood. Like a toddler
venturing too far from mother, Edna's elation is short-lived—she hits
the fear and vulnerability children often feel when they realize how
small and powerless they are in comparison to the vastness of the
world and how much they are still dependent on others.

> *As she swam, she seemed to be reaching out for the unlimited, to*
> *lose herself . . . She had not gone any great distance . . . but to*
> *her unaccustomed vision the stretch of water behind her assumed*
> *the aspect of a barrier which her unaided strength would never be*
> *able to overcome.*

Metaphorically Edna swims too far away from the support she
needs to explore her real self and the world. To encourage our children to separate and experience themselves as autonomous (without
pushing them to do it or abandoning them to experience it alone)

demands, ultimately, that we do the same thing in our adult lives, except that, as adults, we separate without a loving mother disinterestedly encouraging us along the way, allowing us to run back to her to refuel, then run off again to the freedom and excitement of the outside world. Though Chopin hints in this novel at how instrumental adult sexual and romantic relationships might be in helping women to separate from their children, husband, or lover, romantic fantasies do not, ultimately, help Edna in her attempts to stop being an appendage to her children and husband.

Women's recent recognition that they need each other for refueling (in order to separate/individuate from patriarchal society and from their own oppressed mothers, thereby understanding them) has been a breakthrough. No one can struggle for autonomy alone. Everyone needs tremendous support and encouragement to break out of the symbiotic unity—the "fusional universe" into which we are all born and which women reexperience when they become mothers themselves. The terror of further individuation in adulthood, for both men and women, is the terror of having no one there to return to and, in the case of women like Edna, the fear (or reality) that if you become yourself and not an appendage, you will be rejected or abandoned.

Voluntary Bondage

Like *The Awakening*, "To Room Nineteen" also hints at the tremendous support women need to achieve further individuation and a separate sense of self. Devoid of any romantic illusions, "To Room Nineteen" describes a woman who, after devoting ten years of her life to her four children, cannot find a way back to herself—her "True Self." The fruits of Susan Rawlings's labor have gone to others, her children. When this mother's youngest child is finally in school all day, she feels restlessness, "tension, like a panic . . .

Emptiness." It is only then that Lessing's heroine begins to feel that her large lovely house and family are a prison and that she is in bondage—bondage more deadly because it is voluntary. Intellectually she grasps why she feels so empty and useless: "Children can't be a center of life and a reason for being. They can be a thousand things that are delightful, interesting, satisfying; but they can't be a wellspring to live from." But emotionally Susan cannot understand or justify her feelings.

When a child has serious problems—becomes diabetic, for instance, or is handicapped—voluntary bondage may be necessary. It could be an important way for a mother to stay deeply connected to a child who will need very special attention for several years, maybe forever. One mother told me her son had a severe learning disability and became seriously hyperactive at around seven years of age. This required her to spend enormous amounts of time helping him, to literally bind herself to his pressing needs; otherwise she could not have stood the amount of self-sacrifice demanded by his situation.

But under normal circumstances, it is difficult to know whether some mothers simply need to be needed in order to feel important and worthwhile, or whether they become slaves to their children to ward off feelings of loneliness or emptiness. One mother, who had devoted herself completely to her three children until they went to school all day, had a particularly difficult time when her children were this age. Hattie, a housewife from Cleveland, admitted that for a time she literally *created* needs in her children so that she could fulfill them:

· I tried to make them need me. I couldn't bear the fact that they were getting so independent, despite the fact there was a part of me that resented the hell out of them. Here I was waiting on them hand and foot, taking them breakfast in bed, feeding them special things any time they wanted, and they acted like spoiled brats! They began to expect such treatment—as though they deserved it! When they got older, they became completely dependent on me to help them with their homework. Every night, we all did their homework together. My oldest daughter told me she couldn't do her math without me. I'd always help them with their science projects (several I even thought up myself). It wasn't until their last years in high school that they got more independent—but that's when I started getting more independent . . .

Like Lessing's heroine, Hattie was not pressed to go back to work, though she had had a career as a remedial reading teacher before she had children. Fortunately, by the time her children reached adolescence, Hattie rediscovered horticulture—something she had loved to do before she had children. By involving herself in this old hobby and eventually establishing a business, Hattie gradually weaned herself from needing to be needed.

The ending of Doris Lessing's story is excessively bleak. Eventually her heroine rents a room where she sits undisturbed for hours, first three times a week, then five, trying to get back to "the essential Susan" which, since the birth of her children, has been "in abeyance, as if she were in cold storage." "Why?" she asks herself. Again she answers intelligently—but this does nothing to assuage her feelings of emptiness: "Not for one moment in twelve years have I been alone, had time to myself. So now I have to learn to be myself. That's all." This kind of selflessness—which we define as mothering, and more or less take for granted—has disastrous effects.

Sitting in a room alone, with no children to distract her, Lessing's heroine experiences the limits of her emotional hunger and inner impoverishment. Voluntary bondage to the care of children has warded off for ten years something that seems much worse—total aloneness and stark confrontations with frightening parts of the self. Because of the distractions of child rearing, painful facets of Susan's inner life were inaccessible until now. Her feelings of inner impoverishment eventually become unbearable.

Lessing's story deals with the fact that the intimate mother-child relationship is a terminal one; it must end. This is not to say that mothers and daughters cannot maintain a loving attachment to each other throughout life. But the *mother/child* relationship must end. If all goes well and the connection was a close, gratifying one, the termination may be rapid. If mother and child are not very well connected, both may have trouble letting each other go. (When children get the love and caring they need, they are more able to walk away from their relationship with their mothers without excessive guilt. When a mother-child relationship is disturbed, it tends to make children cling to the loved-and-hated object, to try to get what was lacking or to make sure they have not hurt the mother with the anger they feel toward her.)

What Lessing stresses are the totally irrational elements stirred up during this time. Finding nothing inside or outside to sustain her through this difficult weaning, Susan Rawlings ends her own life. Though the story exaggerates the "empty nest" syndrome, Lessing suggests something more ominous: that attachment to and caring for children can lend itself both to a kind of inner oppression as well as oppression by others. "To Room Nineteen" shows how the intense connection between a mother and her children can reinforce an emotional dependency that can lead to a stifling servitude. Stripping her heroine of any romantic or sexual involvements, Lessing lays bare the bone-chilling state of deprivation, the downward spiral of emotional impoverishment that, on the surface, mothers *seem* to bring on themselves.

During latency, children still need a loving figure around. This increases the difficulty for some women: to give up the intensely-loved-and-needed phase for the only-sometimes-needed-and-don't-intrude-if-I-don't-need-you phase, only to become the recipient of constant interruptions. Other mothers thrive during this interlude by participating at a distance (as a Girl Scout troop leader or 4-H teacher, for example). Fathers get interested in Little League or soccer. But within the mother's psyche, it can be a jolt when children are suddenly in school all day, keeping their mothers more and more at arm's length, developing close relationships with others, becoming separate people so that sometimes they seem like strangers. Why is this so easy for some, felt as relief, but so difficult for others?

Maternal weaning from the gratification of being so intensely loved and needed by young bodies and of giving so much of oneself to another can obliterate a part of the personality that a mother must develop all over again. Without tremendous support for inner development, Lessing's story suggests, the separation/individuation process can be more difficult for mothers than it is for their children. After the self-sacrifice and self-denial imposed by the rigors of early child care, some mothers find it hard to learn or relearn how to gratify and fulfill themselves. Lessing's story explores how that very intensity of being needed and of giving so much to others can actually destroy an important part of the self. To survive, some women have to start from scratch, developing a new identity—transformed by the discipline of mothering—bringing it forth painfully after it has been discarded by children who once profoundly needed the care-giver but now only need refueling and respect for their growing independence and individuality. The problem is that children (and husbands—or anyone who enjoys the benefits of being waited on and tended to) get used to having someone serve them. In the short run, it is not to their advantage to have this person stop serving them. To acknowledge the mother's self-sacrifice—and its emotional cost— would arouse too much guilt.

What is startlingly new in Lessing's story is her intuitive grasp of the dilemma all women must face if they have participated in raising their children: the painful letting go, the maternal weaning from the gratification of being so intensely loved and needed by young bodies. For some women it is a narcissistic blow to suddenly become "irrelevant." And it hurts; it is a kind of abandonment. It is painful to be left by creatures to whom you have given so much—who needed you and suddenly (especially if you have been good at it) do not really need you except on the periphery.

Maternal Individuation

Lessing hints at the loss and grief so difficult for women to face and to feel, when they realize that the last child no longer needs them in that intense, gratifying way, that this part of mothering is over forever. Young children can come to seem like beloved companions, possessing a quality of adoration, malleability, and gratitude impossible to find in adult relationships and, once experienced, difficult to do without.

Sometimes further individuation in a mother does not occur to a radical extent until her youngest child goes off to school and begins to develop interests and relationships that begin to equal the mother's in importance. If she has been intensely involved in caring for her children, the mother has been indelibly altered by this experience. Something so permanent and deeply felt has taken place that no one can remain the same.

The dilemma of individuation in mothers can be put into a larger, more universal, genderless framework. As Jungian analyst, Dr. Arthur Colman, explains:

Jung felt that one of the tasks of the second half of life for everyone, not just mothers, is to confront those parts of themselves they had rarely consciously dealt with before—skills and talents too mediocre to be used well in the outside world as well as parts of the psyche that seem too negative to be faced. Though it seems as if the development of these parts of the psyche could only lead to danger, pain and humiliation, Jung believed that it is just those elements that contain hidden creativities and, when integrated, lead towards a sense of wholeness and meaning. Women who keep having children can put this task off for a longer time; but it is the same with workaholics, childless women, men who have never explored the

*nurturing parts of themselves that could be well used by their chil-
dren. The real danger is to leave the dark and inadequate side of us
undeveloped—we must face all the different parts of ourselves or
suffer the consequences of a half-lived life.*

This can be a difficult time for a mother. If she cannot make the
journey back to herself, she is in danger of using her children to
obtain gratification—either by making them live out the dreams she
cannot make come true for herself—or by keeping her children tied
to her, refusing to allow them to separate. Or what occurs more
frequently now, running away from the pain of loss, a mother runs
away from her children before they can run away from her.

Child rearing demands from us the ability to fuse with our children, to know what they feel and need so that we can properly care
for them. Child rearing also demands the ability to let children go, to
separate from them to set them free. Separation requires further
development on many levels as well as integration of the profound
psychic restructuring that occurs when we nurture a child through
the various stages of their passage to adulthood.

Most parents delight in their children at this time and enjoy their
greater freedom. Yet complicated feelings of deprivation, loss,and
confusion are stirred up as well. Sometimes these feelings are dis-
avowed or misunderstood. No matter how successful we are at letting
our children grow up and away from us, we always on some level
yearn for reunion.

ADOLESCENCE
AND THE END
OF CHILDHOOD

I have used the phrase "adolescent doldrums" to describe the few years in which each individual has no way out except to wait and to do this without awareness of what is going on . . . There is no established identity, and no certain way of life that shapes the future . . . We expect defiant independence to alternate with regression to dependence, and we hold on, playing for time instead of offering distractions and cures . . . There is only one cure for adolescence, and this is the passage of time . . .

—D. W. Winnicott
The Maturational Processes and the Facilitating Environment

Even when growth at the period of puberty goes ahead without major crises, one may need to deal with acute problems of management because growing up means taking the parent's place. *It really does.* In the unconscious fantasy, growing up is inherently an aggressive act. And the child is now no longer child-size.

—D. W. Winnicott
Playing and Reality

Notes from Interviews

· *When my daughter was a teenager, I bleached my hair, had my face lifted, and went out on the town. I don't know who had more dates—her or me. (Mitzi, forty-eight, mother of three)*

· *If you've got a teenager in the house, take it from me, you just better learn to get your strokes from somewhere else because they'll just trash you. I'm serious. They'll treat you like garbage. And you can't tell them anything. They know it all. Believe me, they're not going to listen to a thing you say. And if they do, they'll just do the opposite. (Hazel, forty-one, mother of one)*

· *I never had any trouble with my oldest son until he got to be a football star. Well, in the fall it was football, in the winter it was basketball, in the spring, baseball. The kid's an athlete. But not a day went by when he didn't challenge me about every damn thing you could imagine. I got so sick of him and all those pissing contests. Pretty soon, he wouldn't do a thing I said without a big blow up so I finally gave up or gave in. What's the use? It's his world now anyway. My time in the sun's just about over. (Dick, fifty-six, father of four)*

In a culture that is both repressive and titillating, permissive yet filled with sexual peril, puberty is an outrageous event. Even under the best circumstances, adolescence is an extreme and unsettling form of consciousness. Radical hormonal changes create sensitivities that are pure and untranslatable. The sensory experiences of adolescents have an acuity that is different from that of adults, an extreme physicality that we have lost. It is hard for us to recapture the time when our child body first began wildly transforming itself into an adult body—the size and strength of our parents. Try to recall those first overwhelming sensations of sexual arousal—leading ultimately to a temporary loss of self—and all happening in a family (and a society) in which one's status is still that of a child.

Something about the volatility of adolescent sexual feeling puts us all at risk. Taboo desires, both voluptuous and violent, make greater distance and separateness from the parents a necessity. Incest, matricide, patricide have now entered the realm of physical possibility. Shifts and cracks are likely to appear in the power structure of the most solid families. To withstand the emotional storms of adolescence, parents have greater need of patience and maturity than ever before. As our children create more distance between themselves and the seductions of childhood, they cease their endearing attempts to mold their behavior to please us. At this juncture the older generation must educate their offspring in earnest while making room for them to follow in their footsteps.

Unintended Feelings

Adolescence is a time of tremendous energy, when the body acquires amazing prowess and asserts its new powers. Not only must we prepare adolescents for taking our place, training them to channel their energies so they will be able to survive and surpass us, we must watch them grow stronger and more nubile than ourselves. Often this happens just as our own powers are beginning to decline.

Usually parents become enthralled with an adolescent's new physical strength and agility—football, gymnastics, soccer, ballet: adults take pleasure in watching younger, stronger bodies exercising grace, skill, and strength. As we age, our need grows to enjoy vicariously the beauty and prowess of youth.

The award-winning film *Breaking Away* reveals, with warmth and humor, some of the conflicts adolescents stir up in adults. Though the film's emphasis is on what young people go through, and its portrayal of parents is more caricature than character study, it shows how teenagers push and provoke parents into new behaviors, forcing them to deal in one way or another with their children's physical superiority, self-absorption, and growing autonomy. One scene condenses a crucial issue which all adults must confront when a new generation is "coming up from behind," so to speak. On his bicycle, the young hero is preparing for a race by speeding down an expressway. He comes up behind a truck; the truck driver, seeing him in his rearview mirror, begins to clock his speed and communicates to the boy via hand signals how fast he is going. Both the young racer and the truck driver become enthralled with the youth's speed. In fact, the boy going faster and faster passes the truck. Then, just when the vigor of youth surpasses the truck driver and his machine, a policeman stops the older man and gives him a speeding ticket. The scene flashes to the boy's happy face as he speeds on, so full of himself that he has probably forgotten anyone helped him break his own speed record; then it flashes to the tired, rough-shaven truck driver receiving the ticket.

Just as our children's bodies reach the heights of physical strength and ability, the aging process forces us to slow down; if we don't, life hands us a speeding ticket in the form of fatigue, less stamina, bad knees, and so on. Adolescence is the body's prime time; it is also a reminder to those of us who are older of the body's inevitable decline.

On a subliminal, symbolic level, the father must grant his son not only physical prowess, but victory. The mother must give her daughter permission to become more beautiful, to experience her sexuality, and eventually share in her power to reproduce the species. During adolescence we allow our children to win. Though it may seem that we have little choice in the matter, if we do not affirm their physical maturation, give them permission to be stronger and more beautiful than ourselves, a terrible failure can occur, affecting both generations. Excessive guilt, rage, competitive feelings, and rebellion can consume the energies of adolescents, keeping them tied to the previous generation in an unhealthy way. Parents can retard their own development by refusing to face and accept the aging process and the ultimate succession of their children.

Feelings of envy and competition inevitably emerge at this time. Harriet, an attractive, forty-six-year-old marketing analyst, was candid about the conflicting emotions her adolescent daughter aroused in her. Though Harriet's beauty is far from fading, her sixteen-year-old, Julie, is clearly ravishing. Meeting me for lunch, Harriet brought photographs. "Just look at this kid," she said. "Can you believe it? Last year, I swear, she was so gawky. She looked like a bean pole. Now look at her!" Lighting a cigarette, Harriet explained what it was like for her when Julie suddenly grew up:

> • I think it was last March I realized my daughter was much more beautiful than I was. I mean this girl can't walk down the street without men whistling. They used to whistle at me. Now they don't even glance my way. Of course, she has no idea she's so stunning. Sometimes I feel like the wicked queen in *Snow White*. I don't know which is worse: feeling competitive with your own daughter or coming out the loser.

Despite feelings of competition, many mothers thoroughly enjoy their daughters' blossoming into adulthood. Interviewing Bettina in her living room, she showed me photographs of her daughter's senior prom and compared them with pictures of herself when she was in high school. The resemblance between Bettina and her only child was striking. A widow now, forty-eight-year-old Bettina works as a legal secretary. Last year she became a grandmother. But memories of her daughter's adolescence continue to be vivid:

> • I was thrilled by how my daughter was developing into a beautiful woman and how carefree she was. It brought everything back, all the fun I had in high school—my first prom, my first kiss, the first time I "went steady" with a boy . . .

Some mothers feel a deep sense of accomplishment when their children are adolescents and trust that the teenagers will do fine on their own. Susan, a high achiever who teaches history at a prestigious university, said that though it was hard "to let them grow up," she always felt confident as a mother:

> • When my son and daughter got to be teenagers, I drilled them in birth control and set them loose. But I trusted them—they've always been smart, responsible kids and I just didn't worry that much. In fact, I felt enormous relief. Like I'd done it—gotten them to the point where they could take care of themselves and I could devote more time to researching my next book.

The adolescent's new feelings of self-reliance and independence allow some mothers a feeling of completion, making it easy for them to involve themselves with fewer distractions in the careers that they had before maternity.

According to marriage and family counselor Lyn Ballard, some mothers seem to have more difficulty than their husbands at this stage because they are more sensitive to the aging process:

> *Older men are considered "distinguished looking" in our society. Unfortunately, some older women feel as though they've lost the power to attract men. It's hard for them not to feel vulnerable. How can you help but feel envious when you have some nubile teen queen reminding you every day that you're over the hill? It's normal*

for daughters to get real competitive with their mothers at this stage and it's difficult for mothers not to feel like they're the ones who are losing.

Adolescents have a need to see things and people in stark terms—as either all black or all white. To ease the process of separation, teenagers will often idealize one parent (or a teacher, friend, or rock star) and criticize the other parent. As clinical psychologist Dr. Christina Wendel put it:

Adolescents feel temporarily out of control when their bodies start growing, doing all these strange new things: menstruation, erections, ejaculations, orgasms. These tremendous physiological changes make teenagers self-absorbed and often they regress to an earlier mode of thinking—making one parent all-good, the other, all-bad, for instance. It's quite common to see them "splitting"— idealizing a teacher (or actor or football player) and devaluing the parents. This helps them separate from people they've been so dependent upon all their lives and are still deeply attached to. Most often the mother becomes a target for their aggressions. She's usually the one who's taken care of them all these years, the one they want to run back to when things get tough and away from when things are fun and exciting. Consequently they have to build up defenses against feelings of dependence they still have on her.

A recently divorced mother told me of her adolescent stepdaughter's tendency to romanticize and devalue—"split" the world into good and bad—and of the father who was seduced by his daughter's idealization of him. Unfortunately this father's inability to understand what was going on had unfavorable consequences for the entire family. Ellen, a forty-eight-year-old woman who sells real estate for a living, said her life fell apart after her sixteen-year-old stepdaughter came to live with her and her ex-husband:

· What broke my husband and I up was watching him be completely taken in by this kid. Here I'd welcomed her with open arms. I'd always thought her real mother was a complete nut case. At first it all seemed like the best thing I could do, take this kid into my home, help her out, encourage a wholesome relationship with her father. But then pretty soon she could do no wrong in his eyes—she adored him, worshipped him, and he's never been able to resist that kind of flattery.

Well, they began to spend more and more time together. Pretty soon it was clear he'd rather take long walks with her instead of me. It wasn't long before I became the witch to her and the bitchy wife to him. Imagine watching your husband being seduced by a gorgeous teenager who fawns all over him and thinks he's God! I suddenly became the one who's been dragging him down all these years. It all hurt so much, I don't think I will ever forgive him. And it's only made his daughter more neurotic than ever.

As children grow into their adult bodies, they can wreak havoc in families. Because of those early years of dependency on the primary care-giver, it's usually the mother (or stepmother) whom adolescents temporarily "trash." Yet there is a danger now of the nubile daughter replacing the mother in the father's affections (or the son replacing the father in the mother's affections) without anyone being conscious of what's happening.

Forewarnings of Loss

To grasp fully the emotional realities of parenting adolescents we must take into consideration our deep longings for family and children which persist despite the high divorce rate, the stresses inherent in the nuclear family, and the growing dissolution of traditional kinship ties. Perhaps we hunger most for what we are about to lose. In our society, when our children become adolescents, they begin preparing to leave us—to eventually establish their own families. Hopefully, after they go, they will remain closely connected to us. But we know it will be on different terms. When they return, they will be adults, our equals.

More subtle and traumatic for some mothers than the arousal of envious and competitive feelings is the loss, during adolescence, of the devotion and dependence of our children. When a young child relies on us, we are given respite from our ultimate aloneness, which during the second half of life is confirmed by intimations of our mortality. Few things lessen this feeling more than the care of young children. Their innocent love and need to idealize us; their need for physical and emotional closeness—in no other relationship do we experience such intimacy. Unlike schoolage children, who are still dependent on us, adolescents want less and less to do with us. It is not unusual for parents to have irrational feelings of loss at this time.

Elizabeth stayed home to raise her three sons until the youngest was five. She then worked part-time as a social worker. Now, at forty-three, her last child a freshman in high school, Elizabeth feels she can work the long hours that her new full-time job demands. Sitting on a city park bench, eating lunch, I was struck at first by her coolness and self-sufficiency. Later in the conversation, as Elizabeth opened up about her feelings, tears came to her eyes as she movingly described her reaction to her youngest son's entrance into prepubescence:

• Ever since he was about two, Larry, my "baby," has loved to play with toy trucks, cars, electric trains. He knows how to make these incredible noises with his mouth that sound just like an engine. For years I'd listened to these wonderful noises he makes when he's engrossed in his play. But then one day—he was around eleven or twelve—I went by his room and didn't hear the noises. He wasn't playing. He was staring into space, listening to rock and roll. The same thing had happened with my older son, only he was more social—didn't play by himself so much. Suddenly, overnight it seemed, around the same age, he started sitting in his room listening to rock and roll. It was more dramatic for me when my youngest started staring into space instead of making his motor noises. It meant he was gone—well, not physically—not for several more years; but it meant he was no longer my little boy. I felt this awful pang—almost a panicky feeling . . .

Other mothers feel unbearable rejection at this time. Barbara, who worked as a teacher's aide in her only child's school, said that when her daughter went into the seventh grade, she became nasty and insolent. Unable to have more children, thirty-three-year-old Barbara said her daughter had been the center of her life. "Until the age of thirteen, she had the sunniest disposition. She was the sweetest kid you could imagine." During seventh and eighth grades, however, everything changed:

• First she began acting like she was embarrassed by me—by everything I did and said. But everyone told me that was just normal. But then she got real snotty. And she began giving me dirty looks, all the time it seemed, and I had the feeling she was saying awful things about me to her best friend. Then she started locking the door of her room and when I knocked she began telling me to go away. I felt like an outcast in my own house! It was terrible—my own daughter acted like she hated my guts.

Because of such deliberate, hostile, often blatant distancing, some mothers feel their teenage children have turned against them. But the emotional realities of child rearing at this time are, fortunately, more complex than they seem. The loosening of close ties between mothers and their children during adolescence is a delicate, intricate process, which seems to have its own imperatives. In her short story "O Yes," Tillie Olsen describes the pain and confusion that lie beneath the surface when the body first begins that final revolution into adulthood.

The growing distance between a young white girl, Carol, and her black friend, Parialee, parallels what happens to mother and child during adolescence. At the beginning of the story, the black and white girls are still friends and both are still deeply tied to their mothers. At one point, their mothers, also friends, are watching them through the window, playing together. Up until now, the amazing energy of the young girls has been channeled, managed, tamed by pogo sticks, jump rope, tag, the countless rhythmic games, all the "leaping, bouncing, ballooning, bounding" that keep children within the safe protective reach of parents yet allow the rigorous freedom of movement they crave. As long as they play in their "old synchronized understanding," both daughters will remain inside the mothers' realm of control. But soon adolescence will pull both girls away from the safe, innocent world of childhood, which can bridge worlds much further apart than black and white, rich and poor.

Olsen reveals the tendency of mothers to deny at first the painful knowledge of the inevitable separation as well as the awful realities into which they are sending their children. The mother in this story is portrayed as naive and idealistic. An older daughter must initiate or "baptize" the mother into the truth. Carol's peer group will soon replace her mother. Carol's teenage sister must educate her mother about the ruthless white prejudice, which will eventually trap and hold Carol firmly in its grip. The mother resists knowing, for it means, among other things, she now has little control over her daughter's inner life as well as external reality.

Carol has noticed the white girls who are becoming her friends snubbing her black friend. Almost against her own will, Carol finds herself more and more under the influence of this white peer group because it offers her more autonomy from her mother and more control over her body's turmoil.

The story ends with the white mother holding her daughter, who sobs convulsively. Carol realizes she is being absorbed into the white culture. Unwittingly, she is being pulled into white prejudice as well. How does one bring up children in a world so painful and ugly that sometimes to feel is to be overwhelmed? At the end of the story, the mother must "shelter her daughter close," while at the same time "mourn the illusion of the embrace." For the daughter is about to be set loose in a cruel and frightening world. Carol's feelings of guilt and betrayal toward both her black friend and her mother will be assuaged to some extent by her peer group, which is now beginning to take the mother's place in her life.

It is often the peer group—rather, the feeling of strength or fortification that comes from being a part of the group—which helps the adolescent break away from the intense attachment to the mother.

Defenses Against Attachment

Adolescents develop strong defenses against their own dependency as well as against those they love. One of these defenses is the refusal to empathize with the adult world that has spawned them. Compassion threatens to make adolescents feel too much guilt for abandoning their parents or any of the adults who have helped them along the way. Their task (and it is not an easy one) is to leave behind those they love most and to whom they are closest—to assume the pleasures, responsibilities, and burdens of the adult world. Adolescents cannot do this if they are too sympathetic with the pain and problems of those who nurtured them. Later perhaps this will be possible, but the coldheartedness of youth has an important function: it helps them break away from loving parents whom they will always, on some level, long for.

Some teenagers act so brash, insensitive, critical, or rebellious that they provoke anger in adults. Several parents said they couldn't wait until their children left home. Others expressed anger and disappointment—almost disillusionment—at how their adolescents were turning out and how selfishly they behaved.

Another story by Tillie Olsen touches upon this aspect of adolescence. In "Hey Sailor" she juxtaposes an alcoholic sailor's longing for family with the coldheartedness of an adolescent who refuses to sympathize with any member of the adult world that threatens her new and tenuous autonomy. When the story begins, the sailor (for whom a family of his own has become an "unattainable . . . lost country") manages to get to the home of his old friends, the only people in the world who still care for him. As the parents help him through his painful withdrawal from alcohol, he is confronted by each of their children and the reader gets a double view: the child's reaction to the drunk, and the broken man's reaction to children of different ages. The younger children react with the same affection, openness, and trust that they feel toward anyone (drunk or sober) whom they have come to love. The adolescent daughter responds with intolerance and condemnation. The youngest child spontaneously cuddles next to him for reassurance after a bad dream. But when he reminds the adolescent of the time she crawled into bed with him and announced they were married, the teenage girl insults him mercilessly. Her deep, long-standing love for him can no longer be filtered through the innocent light of childhood. Like all adolescents, she must rigorously repress any feelings toward any parental figure that have the slightest sexual overtones. She is both embarrassed by her past intimate behavior with him and disillusioned by his visible disintegration. Able to see faults and flaws in adults clearly for the first time, adolescents are harsh in their judgments. What the sailor remembers is "the toys I mended and made, the questions answered, the care for you, the pride in you . . . the love . . . worship offered."

Adolescents have strong defenses against the devotion as well as the frailties that they begin to perceive in people close to them. Adults often suffer from uncomfortable feelings of exposure. Though the mother in this story tries to educate and humanize her daughter into a more tolerant attitude, the child is not yet equipped to feel compassion.

Unrequited Love

Children become a part of our lives that is difficult to relinquish. Before adolescence, they give us a sense of purpose, providing meaning and order, which the confusion of life always threatens to dissolve. Their loss or absence can produce states of disequilibrium.

In her novel *The Golden Notebook*, Doris Lessing gives us an example of one of the complex ways in which adults can become dependent on their children. Lessing describes her liberated heroine, Anna, ultimately clinging to the discipline of mothering to give her own chaotic life order and routine. Anna's daughter becomes a conventional, conservative child who uses the security of rules, school uniforms, and regulations to give herself a feeling of safety in a world of broken marriages and rapidly shifting values and norms. Anna finds that whenever she provides her daughter with the safe structured world a child needs, she as a *mother* is able to fend off overwhelming feelings of internal and external chaos.

There are so many ways and reasons we become and remain attached to our children; giving them up can be acutely painful as well as disorienting. Dorothy, a successful interior designer from Monterey, purposely spent her son and daughter's high school years studying so that she would have a full-fledged career to go into when they left for college. "Children let you know when you've become obsolete," she said.

• Both my kids became very independent during high school. I never had to worry about them the way so many other mothers I knew did. But it was hard for me in other ways. They were into everything after school—sports, drama. Sometimes I wouldn't see them all day until dinner time. I missed them terribly.

By the time her oldest graduated from high school, forty-one-year-old Dorothy had thrown herself into her career and started a lucrative business. Despite a successful reentry into society and work she thoroughly enjoyed, Dorothy had difficulties:

• After I drove my son to college his freshman year, I came home and cried so hard it took me days to recover. But eventually I got up, went back to work, and got over it. But then two years later, one month after I took my daughter to college, I discovered I was pregnant.

Of course I had mixed feelings about having a baby at forty, but basically I became ecstatic and more or less forgot about my daughter's going away to college. My husband nearly went through the ceiling when I told him I was pregnant. But I couldn't bring myself to have an abortion. Then a horrible thing happened—when I went to have the amnio, they discovered the baby had died. Suddenly it hit me—my daughter had grown up. Both my children had grown up and unless I had another child, I was in another phase of life—one I really didn't want to be in. Getting pregnant was the only way of enduring the pain of it . . .

During their children's adolescence, some parents temporarily experience feelings of extreme emotional impoverishment, states of emptiness that many strive to fill by any means. Some mothers respond as though they were unrequited lovers whose affection has been given but will never be returned. Understandably many women begin to hunger for relationships that have the same intensity as those they had with their children. In some marriages an erotic awakening occurs—a sense of sexual renewal. In other cases the desire to replace the lost love of the adolescent with someone unknown, outside the marriage, proves irresistible. Several mothers told me they had become involved in passionate, surreptitious affairs that had an adolescent flavor to them. Many of these intense liaisons happened at the same time that their own teenage children were falling passionately in love.

Sometimes the parents respond unconsciously to the highly charged sexual behavior of their nubile children, carrying on covert sexual competition with them. Others feel they are missing out on something or want to recapture the intense sexuality of adolescence. Many, however, are reacting to the loss of a close and gratifying relationship which the increasing maturity of children irrevocably alters.

Relinquishment

Can we forgive our children for breaking away from us? Let them go after we have given them so much? Is it possible to care for someone who gives little in return and walks away from us as soon as she can? The issue of separation—the giving up and letting go of the bodies and souls of our children—becomes clearest during adolescence.

Unlike other cultures or earlier times, children in our society are not usually required to work for their parents or take care of them in their old age. Most of us assume our children will not be around to help us till the fields in our old age, or take care of us emotionally or financially until we die. Though we may hope for a Cordelia, many of us take it for granted that our children will go their separate ways. In the present age, we do not consciously ask much of our children in return for caring for them. This puts our altruism to the test, especially when the child takes major steps toward independence and individuation.

Toward the end of their children's adolescence, mothers and fathers are thrown back upon their own resources, sometimes with a vengeance, sometimes as an effortless and welcome transition. Children and their demands take up psychic space and energy, filling up a parent's life so that some inner resources and deficits never have a chance to surface. Thus the end of childhood can be a time of tremendous inner turmoil and growth. Some parents must experience and work through flaws in their characters for the first time. Many discover unknown potentialities in themselves and begin to develop new gifts and talents.

Several mothers claimed they had to endure an excruciating period of adjustment after their youngest child left home, and that for a time they felt dead. Fifty-eight-year-old Judith, a librarian whose four children were all married, said:

· It was awful at first, not having young people around to keep my husband and me young. We went into a state of withdrawal and became very stodgy after the youngest left—got kind of depressed, ingrown. They might drive you nuts, but kids have so much life, so much energy and enthusiasm. It's hard not to feel a little dead when they leave. But now that we finally have a grandchild, and another one on the way, things have changed. I feel we've been given a whole new lease on life . . .

Marriage and childbirth, which create more children and make parents grandparents, are now being postponed by many men and women; some are forfeiting them altogether. As a result, the feelings of deadness which parents experience after their children leave home may have to do with the fact that the period of time we call adolescence has been extended—our grown-up children don't begin having children of their own for a long, long time.

Most men and women have friends, interests, meaningful work, a community or group to help soothe or diminish the sense of loss. This is especially true of people who have children later in life or have only one or two children and establish a separate adult identity.

Yet the emotional tasks of adults during this time are certainly as complex as the adolescent's.

Is it possible to "let go" of our children without becoming alienated from them? Can we remain connected to our children in a positive, life-enhancing way despite the fact they have left us? Relinquish control over them yet still remain lovingly attached?

Separation, as defined in Webster's dictionary, means "a space . . . that separates." Reality encourages us to experience and explore that "space" between ourselves and our children in order to realize fully that those we've raised and so closely identified with are not ourselves. Our children must create their own families, which, given the norms of our culture, we may or may not be a part of. The separation between ourselves and our children evokes in us profound emotional responses—sadness, longing, resentment, emptiness— which we deny at great cost to ourselves and our children. Until we integrate these feelings, we cannot really know who we are, our true mettle; nor can we become fully human.

Consciousness of our ambivalences and the ability to achieve a more authentic, profound form of love seem to be the ultimate test of our humanity—a test that at present we seem to be failing, as evidenced by our compulsion to pollute and destroy the earth. The grim and tragic features of our society are enough to make us wonder if we are in covert, unconscious ways trying to get back from our children what we have given—or trying to get back *at* them for their lack of reciprocity. Considering the wanton destruction of our natural resources, the massive nationwide manipulation and exploitation of children through advertisement, the proliferation of nuclear weapons—we seem to be saying to our children through our actions, "If we cannot be alive to share it with you, we don't want you to have anything." Let us hope this is a temporary phase in the history of human development.

In his poem "Dutch Graves in Bucks County," Wallace Stevens describes as "the pit of torment" the ambivalence we feel toward those who will inherit the earth from us after we die:

. . . mobs of birth
Avoid our stale perfections, seeking out
Their own, waiting until we go
To picnic in the ruins that we leave . . .

Perhaps to be fully human, beyond the achievement of compassion, tolerance, and mercy, we must accept the fact that we are going to die alone. Perhaps to be fully human means to know this and still to want others to live on after us, even though they will surely "picnic in the ruins that we leave." But imagine a world in which no young bodies were sent off to be killed in war but were kept home to be competed with, lost, and later regained as soulmates, people we love and will live alongside until we die.

Acceptance and integration of our ambivalent feelings—the ultimate process of humanization—has become a survival issue. The knowledge that we love and hate the same people, that we sometimes harbor destructive wishes toward those we love most on earth, is knowledge we can no longer avoid or deny. This knowledge comes to us when we begin to accept the separateness of our children, especially during adolescence and at the end of their childhood.

Part Four

FROM

MATERNAL FAILURE TO TRANSFORMATION

Chapter Eight

THE MEANING OF MATERNAL FAILURE: MATERNAL ANGUISH

No woman is considered "special" because she carries out her responsibilities as a parent; not to do so is considered a social crime.

—Adrienne Rich,
Of Woman Born

It is madness to suppose one owes something to one's mother . . . Hardly. She casts us into a world beset with dangers, and once in it, 'tis for us to manage as best we can . . .

—Marquis de Sade,
180 Days of Sodom

There is something else which has the power to awaken us to the truth. It is the works of writers of genius . . . They give us, in the guise of fiction, something equivalent to the actual density of the real, that density which life offers us every day but which we are unable to grasp because we are amusing ourselves with lies.

—Simone Weil,
"Morality and Literature"

Notes from Interviews

• *I'll never forget the time I literally had to crawl up the stairs. My youngest was eight months old, my second was three and a half, and the oldest was four. I'd had to leave for work at six that morning and when I got home all three of them were screaming. By nine o'clock all I knew was that if I wanted to make it to my bed, I'd have to get on all fours and drag myself up those damn stairs otherwise I'd have passed out on the floor. (Bonnie, fifty-one, mother of three)*

• *It's simply too painful to remember what it was like, having all four of them in diapers at the same time. I don't like to think about it. I don't like to talk about it. I don't like hearing other women talking about their children. It reminds me of the most awful years of my life. (Honor, forty-eight, mother of four)*

• *Amnesia is not the exception, it's the norm. No mother wants to remember how physically draining it is, how ghastly it can be on the psyche, all that giving, giving—those days when the kids are cranky and the baby never stops crying, no matter what you do. It's such a difficult job. Most women aren't trained or prepared or given any help whatsoever. It's like asking half the population to do brain surgery without sending them to medical school. (Parent-educator)*

For an infant to be loved and nurtured by its mother, the mother must be held and nurtured by her environment. No matter how self-reliant a woman is, the birth and care of an infant make her more dependent on others.

The stresses of child care during the first years of life are so arduous that most women cannot sustain this kind of intensive care giving without a great deal of encouragement. Societies either support a mother's activities as a care-giver, or they make the experience of mothering difficult. Without tremendous support for mothers to form a close bond with their infants, the crucial task of mothering becomes formidable. As a society, we expect that all mothers will be able to take care of their infants without needing to be taken care of themselves. This superhuman feat is beyond the resources of most women.

Usually, a society helps the mother to meet all of the rigorous demands of child care, at the very least during the first year of her baby's life. Social customs, traditions, extended families, special members of the tribe—a culture provides a protective environment for the mother as she cares for her child. Our society often does just the opposite: mothers are isolated from others, and they are under financial pressure to go back to work soon after childbirth or under emotional pressure to acheive in a more socially prestigious role than that of care-giver.

It is as though we have been looking in the wrong places, asking the wrong questions. Instead of inquiring how we should take care of our children, we should be examining how best to take care of our care-givers. Because the emotional soil of our society is lacking in nutrients, the process of maturation has become precarious for both parents and children. In too many cases, this country's treatment of children and mothers is at best haphazard, at worst reprehensible. The refusal of most work places to allow the mother time off to establish that crucial bond with her baby without putting her job in jeopardy and the refusal of both business and government to provide highly qualified care for infants and toddlers of mothers who must work have had a disastrous effect on mother and child.

Fifty-two percent of the work force in the United States is now composed of women. Half of the mothers who work outside the home have infants under a year old. Few work places have day-care facilities; in most businesses, maternity leave is brief (and still subsumed under "sick leave"). Too many mothers are unable to give to their children what those children truly need. It is not surprising that as a culture we have desensitized ourselves to the suffering this causes both mothers and children.

Much information now available about the realities of child care and the tremendous stresses mothers and their children experience each day is frightening to contemplate. According to psychiatrist Robert Jay Lifton, psychic numbing in humans is equivalent to "an animal freezing or being stunned when it is attacked or frightened." What happens on a daily basis to many mothers and their children is too overwhelming for our society to grasp fully and talk about openly. For this reason we have anesthetized ourselves to the anguish so many mothers feel.

Sometimes through artistic expression we can identify and empathize with what, in ordinary life, might be too horrifying to acknowledge. When we look at the work of writers such as Doris Lessing, Tillie Olsen, and Grace Paley, who transfigure in their fiction the anguish some mothers feel, we are able to recognize for the first time many things our culture has suppressed. Recurrent themes in their work—loss of understanding between the generations, the ways in which destructive patterns of child rearing get passed down from generation to generation, how emotional starvation can hamper our capacity to love our children—describe the growing difficulties many mothers face.

We must now find the courage to look into the darkest corners of maternal experience. I am not speaking here of child abuse or neglect, which are symptoms, the result of maternal pain and deprivation. To understand how to change conditions so that child abuse and neglect will not exist, we must look directly at the nature and causes of maternal failure. By filtering the more tragic emotional realities of child rearing through the luminosity of art, we can approach and understand what too many care-givers in this country must suffer, and begin the problem solving to alleviate that suffering.

The Failure of Generation

After the birth of a child, parents have tremendous need for a strong support system, others who will break up the intensity of ambivalent feelings and provide practical relief from the exhausting tasks of protecting and limit setting. Grandparents and extended family often live too far away to help with child care.

One mother I interviewed said that if her husband had not been transferred to California from their home in Tulsa, she would have had no problem finding loving, consistent care for her three-year-old daughter when she went back to work. Visibly distressed by her failure to find someone trustworthy, Margaret said her mother would have been overjoyed to be the full-time care-giver of her granddaughter:

• I can't tell you how long I looked just to find someone halfway decent. The first three day-care mothers were heartless and the places were overcrowded by all these runny-nosed kids. I got so desperate I begged my mother to move here. But that would have been awful for my parents—they've lived in Tulsa all their lives. I finally settled on the best situation I could find. I can't tell you how horrible it is to hear my daughter screaming every morning when I leave her with this woman I'd feel uncomfortable leaving my dog with. But by that time I just didn't have a choice. I had to start work or lose my job.

Unlike Margaret's parents, who were willing (if not able) to care for their grandchildren, Vickie's parents showed no interest in spending time with their granddaughter. Vickie said that at first she thought this was because they lived just far enough away to make visits inconvenient. But whenever she took her daughter to see them, she was forced to realize that her parents had no desire to be a part of their grandchild's life.

> • I think it was the biggest blow I've ever had. I somehow ex-
> pected Mom and Dad to be so delighted with her (and with me,
> for having a baby! I mean I was giving them a grandchild!) I was
> sure they'd want to be with her. But they couldn't have cared less.
> They just had no interest in spending any time with her. I felt so
> hurt, like it was me they were rejecting as well as my daughter.

Sometimes differing value systems make conflict inevitable between childbearing couples and their own parents, causing bitterness and in some cases permanent estrangement between the generations. Because of our society's extreme mobility (upward mobility as well as geographical mobility), there are no traditional methods of nurturing to which everyone adheres. Some mothers feel compelled to do something different with their children, to try to compensate for what was done to them.

Angela made a conscious decision to raise her two sons differently from the way she'd been raised. She said her mother had brought her up to succeed in a competitive world. Though Angela became a highly paid expert in her field, she felt she had paid too high a price for this, in terms of what she called "neurotic anxiety." What was important to Angela was her children's emotional well-being. Teaching them to "know themselves" rather than to "try to please," Angela wanted her sons to feel loved and accepted and purposely did not stress performance and high achievement.

This shift in parenting values created a sense of conflict and estrangement between Angela and her parents, who felt alienated by their grandchildren. Whenever they came to visit, they complained that the two boys were rude and spoiled. Angela would always end up feeling angry and criticized. Eventually the visits stopped. Only later did Angela begin having regrets and developing feelings of loss:

- I think my parents got totally threatened. I mean here I was doing the opposite of what they did with me and I think it just freaked them out. For a while I didn't care. I was so certain I was doing the right thing and they'd done the wrong thing. They brought me up to be successful, but I'm so driven it's hard for me to enjoy anything. But now that I hardly see them anymore, I feel a tremendous loss, like I've broken my only link to the past. Sometimes I think my sons have suffered the most. They've never had the experience of involved, loving grandparents.

To think critically about how our parents raised us very often disrupts both generations, sometimes causing permanent rifts. Criticism of the previous generation can also arouse feelings of guilt and disloyalty in the next generation. Most of us are intensely attached to our parents no matter what they did or failed to do to us. In some instances, feelings of disloyalty impede understanding of how hurtful ways of relating get passed on from generation to generation.

Two short stories by Tillie Olsen and Grace Paley deal with the lack of compassion and understanding that can exist between the generations. Their mother-heroines desperately need an older generation to help them care for their children and transmit important truths that they can use and eventually hand down to their own children.

In Tillie Olsen's "Tell Me a Riddle," an old man suddenly reexperiences the extreme deprivations he has lived through but has not passed on to his children and grandchildren. Though parents often feel pride that they have provided for their children in ways they themselves were never provided for, many can't acknowledge "the bereavement and betrayal" accompanying such feelings of accomplishment. Olsen describes an elderly man, overcome by these painful feelings, as having a "ravening hunger or thirst":

> *Without warning, the bereavement and betrayal he had sheltered . . . hidden even from himself, revealed itself . . . "Lost, how much I lost." . . . Escaped to the grandchildren whose childhoods were childish, who had never hungered, who lived unravaged by disease in warm houses of many rooms, had all the school for which they cared, could walk on any street, stood a head taller than their grandparents, towered above—beautiful skins, straight backs, clear straightforward eyes. "Yes, you in Olshana," he said to the town of sixty years ago, "they would be nobility to you."*

The realization that your offspring have experienced the benefits of a material (or emotional) well-being that you didn't get will often bring up feelings of envy as well as pride and satisfaction, especially when you see your children acting as though they are entitled, like nobility, or unappreciative, taking for granted the gifts bestowed upon them. When parents give to their children what they have never received, it hurts. We hate to look at how much this altruism hurts because it requires reexperiencing the deprivations we have suffered.

The generation so generously raised by the old man in "Tell Me a Riddle" cannot imagine the deprivations he survived—just as he cannot comprehend their feelings of spiritual emptiness, cynicism, and lack of faith (which affluence does not eradicate or ward off). Profound differences in experiencing the world can create gaps in communication and understanding, gaps that sometimes cannot be bridged.

In her short story "Faith in the Afternoon," Grace Paley portrays an older generation that has suffered extreme physical hardships and financial desperation. These elderly parents find it difficult to comprehend pain that is not visible in the form of poverty, starvation, or illness; they have little to give their daughter and grandsons. The emotional conflicts of their daughter, a single parent who is trying to raise her two sons alone, are totally foreign to them. The elderly parents are so needy and lonely themselves, the most they have to offer their daughter Faith is a brief moment of recognition. "Ah . . . I see you have trouble," says Faith's father (who has presented her with a long list of his own grievances). "You picked yourself out a hard world to raise a family."

These fictional characters, like so many mothers in real life, feel compassion toward their parents, who seem to be floundering in darkness and confusion. The resourcefulness of the previous generation, which required different strengths, is lost on them. Mothers now must nurture their children in a world that gives them neither support, nor values and traditions that might help them with the tasks of child rearing. Both the old and new generations make constant demands. Caught in the middle, many mothers must struggle alone.

Starvation in the Midst of Plenty

The tasks of care giving intensify in *all* mothers the normal need for love, support, and stimulation, creating a kind of hunger that is hard both to admit and satisfy. The real problem for many mothers is how to survive emotionally in a world that may provide for them materially but in no other manner. Many must learn to live in a world that may provide jobs (in some cases, affluence) but gives them no help with the emotional stresses that the care of children constantly create.

Some mothers can't take feelings of emotional deprivation seriously in a world where such enormous numbers of people are threatened with starvation or malnutrition. Yet cumulative feelings of emotional deprivation evoke in mothers potentially destructive emotions such as rage, self-hatred, and the desire for revenge. The attitudes and behavior of affluent mothers illuminate the ways prosperity can and cannot help us nurture our children.

Immediately after the birth of a child, mothers are so dependent on others for nurturance and support, they become extremely vulnerable to external influence. Doris Lessing and Tillie Olsen describe mothers with breasts full of milk, watching their hungry, screaming infants, unable to suckle and gratify their children because of the advice of "experts." These women have been told by the medical profession to feed their babies only on a rigid schedule. They are somehow unable to defy authority. The narrator in Tillie Olsen's "I Stand Here Ironing" says:

> I did like the books then said. Though her cries battered me to trembling and my breasts ached with swollenness, I waited till the clock decreed.

There is no reason for anyone to be hungry in these stories. Food is plentiful. The suffering of these infants is caused by the mother's susceptibility to the advice of "experts"—doctors, nurses, books. Doris Lessing's novel *A Proper Marriage* suggests that these "experts" may be symbolic equivalents of the mother's own parents. Lessing's main character, Martha Quest (who cannot bring herself to feed her child), listens to her infant's cries as though paralyzed:

> Martha would hang over the crib, hands locked behind her back to prevent them from reaching out to the child, watching the scarlet little face moving open mouthed from side to side to find the breast, while her heart beat with anxious pity.

Lessing then tells us that Martha's mother is oddly relieved that her daughter and granddaughter continue this cycle of deprivation:

> Mrs. Quest looked at [the infant] with an odd little smile, and then remarked with the bright guilty laugh in which was the note of triumph which always stung Martha, "I suppose you've been starving her as I starved you."

Why does Lessing's heroine have so little resistance to destructive influences and "bad advice"? Does feeding the infant on demand (i.e., when the infant is hungry, rather than at a set time decreed by so-called experts) represent on a symbolic level gratifying the mother's own needs for nurturing? If so, why can't the mother fulfill those needs?

Why are mothers so vulnerable to pressures that reinforce agonizing mother-child relationships? One reason may be a new mother's fear of competitive feelings. If Martha Quest were to feed and soothe her hungry infant, she would be showing up her own mother by being a superior nurturer—competing with her and coming out ahead. Another reason might be unconscious protective feelings: by starving her baby, Martha Quest is doing to her child what was done to her and thereby sheilding her mother (and herself) from a full awareness of serious maternal flaws.

Also, there is a tendency in some mothers to exact revenge for the hunger they have suffered from their own mother's withholding of food and/or love. Hostility toward the depriving mother is transferred and placed on the infant: the baby becomes the object of unconscious resentment. In this case, Martha would be repeating the trauma in the next generation out of an unconscious desire to wreak vengeance. The acting out of vengeful feelings, though hurtful and destructive, may bring temporary relief from the pain of being deprived.

The inability of a mother to have compassion for herself and have her own needs for love met can have disastrous consequences for the next generation. An example of this can be seen in the case of Lucy, who moved to San Francisco from Detroit. Lucy gave birth to her daughter when she was twenty-five. From the very beginning, she could not feed her infant without unbearable feelings of anxiety and depression. When her daughter was two months old, Lucy's pediatrician was worried that the infant was seriously undernourished and recommended psychotherapeutic treatment for both mother and child.

Growing up in Grosse Pointe, a wealthy suburb of Detroit, Lucy had been given every material advantage. Though the Puritan work ethic had made it possible for Lucy's parents to rise socioeconomically, it had not made child rearing a pleasurable, spontaneous experience. Lucy and her three brothers were expected to be autonomous at an early age and to perform and achieve. Though she had done extremely well in the private school she had attended and in college, Lucy had always felt "nothing was ever enough" to satisfy her parents. She had been plagued with feelings of extreme futility and depression as a child but had never mentioned this to anyone.

During her pregnancy Lucy became terrified she would not be able to take care of her child. Though she wanted to spare her baby the suffering she had experienced when she was young, she feared this would be impossible. Immediately after her child, Carolyn, was born, Lucy lived in constant fear that her baby would starve and possibly die. Tormented by the idea that Carolyn was not getting enough to eat, Lucy tried to force her to drink milk from a bottle when the baby wasn't interested. Feedings became a miserable experience for both mother and infant. Eventually Carolyn turned her head away and refused to eat every time Lucy tried to feed her.

The birth of her child had made Lucy reexperience her own voracious hunger to be loved and nurtured. Confusing her daughter with herself, Lucy was not able to contain her own feelings of emotional starvation and projected them onto her child. However much Lucy tried to make her daughter eat, Lucy's own hunger for love was never fed.

Because of the baby's serious weight loss, Lucy's pediatrician recommended that she hire a surrogate care-giver to take over the feedings. It was not long before Carolyn began eating normally and gained weight. Only after Lucy was able to take in and accept her therapist's understanding could she gradually become more in tune with her infant's needs and feel more relaxed at the feedings. To become more sensitive to her daughter's needs, Lucy herself had to be cared for, empathized with, understood. Lucy could then allow her daughter to eat what she wanted and take time to enjoy her food. Eventually Lucy was able to take over the feeding of her baby. What was particularly painful in the final stages of her therapy was Lucy's realization that she was caring for her daughter in ways she had never been cared for herself.

Some mothers have trouble feeding their babies because, on an emotional level, they themselves have not been fed. An infant's hunger can come to represent feelings of inner impoverishment and starvation the mother feels. Such mothers have been educated or conditioned to ignore their own needs for love and to feel they do not deserve to be gratified in any way. Yet until a mother learns to have compassion for herself and to fulfill her own needs for nurturing, child rearing can be a painful experience for both child and mother—an experience that perpetuates itself in the next generation.

Images of Imprisonment

In this society most fathers are expected to leave their children every day to earn money, compete with other men, and prove themselves in some way other than by caring for children. A woman who is attuned to her children's needs often finds it difficult to leave them without experiencing guilt and anguish. Mothers are sometimes confined to houses, rooms, apartments, or playgrounds, surrounded by other mothers. They cannot escape without abandoning their children.

The last image in Grace Paley's short story "A Subject of Childhood" is of Faith, a single mother, rocking her young son in their small apartment after yelling at him: "I want you to get out of here . . . I need ten minutes alone . . . I might kill you if you stay up here." Yell and beg as she might, her son will not leave her, even for ten minutes, so that she can sort out the rage caused by her relationship with a man who flits in and out of her life giving little, nothing, or the wrong thing to her father-hungry boys. Her youngest son, Tonto, sensing her pain and loss, crawls up onto her lap and says, "I want to be a baby, and stay right next to you every minute." The image in the last paragraph suggests feelings so deep and mixed with both pain and gratification that most women cannot express them. Such emotions are usually cheapened by our secularized, saccharine versions of the "Madonna and Child" image projected by the media. Images of the "perfect mother" falsify the love mothers feel for their children by ignoring the ambivalence. Grace Paley refuses to do this in her work:

> I held him so and rocked him. I cradled him. I closed my eyes and leaned on his dark head. But the sun in its course emerged from among the towers of downtown office buildings and suddenly shone white and bright on me. Then through the short fat fingers of my son, interred forever, like a black and white barred king in Alcatraz, my heart lit up in stripes . . .

Grace Paley is one of the few writers who speak of the pleasures of mothering without diminishing the more complex aspects. Love for her children makes Faith's "Alcatraz" of mothering a place of intimacy and pleasure as well as frustration.

In one of Paley's most powerful and disturbing stories, "The Long Distance Runner," Faith, a white middle-class mother, seeks refuge in a slum apartment which is both shelter and prison for a black welfare mother (Mrs. Luddy) and her four small children. To protect herself from the immediate danger of street violence, Faith begs entrance into Mrs. Luddy's cramped, overcrowded apartment. Faith ends up staying several weeks, becomes attached to the four children, and tries to connect with the overburdened mother and understand her experiences.

Paley poses one of the most difficult questions of our time: Are there differences—social and economic, emotional, experiential— so great they cannot be bridged? Faith comes to love the children, dotes on the oldest, teaching him black history and encouraging him to write poetry. Because Faith's maternal instincts are at work, thinking what would be best for a boy his age, she suggests to the mother at one point, "He ought to be with kids his age more, I think." The black mother may be protecting her son the only way she can, by keeping him locked up with herself in the small apartment, only letting him out briefly to cash the welfare check and buy groceries.

Mrs. Luddy at some point tells Faith a story of "slave times," which has been passed down by her mother:

> My mama had stories to tell, she raised me on. Her mama was a little thing, no sense. Stand in the door of the cabin all day, sucking her thumb. It was slave times. One day a young field boy come storming along. He knock on the door of the first cabin hollering, Sister, come out, it's freedom. She come out. She say, Yeah? When? He say, Now! It's freedom now! Then he knock at the next door and say, Sister! It's freedom! Now! From one cabin he run to the next cabin, crying out, Sister, it's freedom now!

The story suggests a painful analogy. Faith is the field boy coming into the alien slum shouting, "Freedom! Freedom!" Shouting, "Food! Education! Poetry! Play with other children!" Announcing what is presumably every child's birthright—and every mother's birthright (at least in middle-class America): to be able to provide such things for your children.

By the time "freedom" comes along, Mrs. Luddy's grandmother is standing in the doorway sucking her thumb. Slavery has already destroyed her. Mrs. Luddy also may have lost too much in not being able to control the environment in which she must raise her children. The damage to her maternal pride and joy-in-one's-children—the terrible wound caused by not being able to protect one's children and give them what they need—is too devastating.

Who has the resources to provide for Mrs. Luddy and her children, desperately in need emotionally as well as socioeconomically? One of the most ironic twists in this story is Mrs. Luddy's eventual rejection of Faith's gifts of support and nurturing.

The emotional health and energy Faith brings to the son, baby daughters, and mother might be all they ever get from anyone. But it is too little, too late. Extreme forms of deprivation, emotional as well as economic, and the accompanying humiliation have made it impossible for Mrs. Luddy to accept too much. Sometimes the less a person has been given, the less, later on, they can receive.

Some impoverished mothers feel too threatened when others try to help them. They might feel dethroned from their position as caregiver and replaced by someone who has more to give. Some vulnerable mothers turn to their children rather than the adult world of other mothers, whose assessments and suggestions, sometimes thinly veiled criticisms, are too painful to hear.

Children can become a mother's sole source of emotional support. In our culture of single mothers and absent or emotionally unavailable fathers, the children often become companions, nurturers, support-system, raison d'être—the only real relationship a mother has. What is good for Mrs. Luddy's son, Donald—to go out and play instead of taking care of his mother and sisters—might not be good for Mrs. Luddy or his siblings, who desperately need him.

Some mothers have only their children to help them become financially independent. When I first met Etta, a welfare mother living in Buffalo, New York, she had left her six children in a tiny apartment under the care of her oldest son, Robert, who was nine years old. Wearing white gloves in the middle of winter, Etta had escaped for a few hours to attend her first class at the local teacher's college. When Etta had married and moved north, she left her large extended family in Mississippi. Out of necessity, Robert had become both baby-sitter and "man of the house."

Once Etta began having children, she said her husband got jealous of the babies and began "stepping out." Yet during the first two years of their marriage, Etta had been unable to conceive. Fearing she was barren, she said she used to take a doll to bed with her each night and pretend it was real.

By the time their sixth child was born, Etta's husband had become an occasional visitor. Until her attendance at the teacher's college, Etta had spent nine years essentially imprisoned in tiny apartments throughout drug-infested and crime-ridden areas of the city. Robert had frequently been her only escape—sometimes just to go out and buy groceries.

Unlike Mrs. Luddy in Grace Paley's story, Etta became financially independent. She obtained a scholarship the year I met her and eventually became a second-grade teacher who could support herself and her six children. Yet her education during the first several years was dependent on her son baby-sitting, and this required him to miss school himself, sometimes for weeks at a time. Only during the last two years of college could Etta find a day-care situation that was both affordable and did not require her to have a car.

Maternal Abandonment

After hearing stories about mothers like Etta and Mrs. Luddy, we might doubt that the *inner* torment that drives a woman to abandon her children could be worse than the terrible external conditions oppressing many welfare mothers. Nonetheless, some women can't mother without harming themselves and their children. Most of us are not sympathetic to a mother who leaves her child unless she is financially pressed to do so. Some mothers abandon their children because they are *emotionally* bankrupt, have nothing to give—or the wrong things. What are a mother's real responsibilities to her children when she cannot take care of them? Finding the right childcare center? The most loving surrogate when she cannot give that essential care?

In her early fiction, Doris Lessing creates a character who has everything materially speaking: plenty of money; servants to take over the drudgery of domestic tasks. In spite of her wealth, this mother-heroine feels she is so destructive to her daughter, she abandons her to the care of others.

Of all the fictional images of maternal imprisonment, the most oppressive is in Doris Lessing's novel *A Proper Marriage*. Rather than the prison of poverty, it is the *acts* of mothering that confine Lessing's heroine, Martha Quest, to the oppressive colonial African society and to a smothering closeness to her own withholding mother.

In *A Proper Marriage*, the experience of pregnancy, childbirth, and mothering pulls Martha Quest back into the torturous relationship she has with her depriving yet intrusive mother. Through the acts of nurturing her daughter, Martha loses the strength to differentiate herself from her own mother.

In the character of Martha Quest, Doris Lessing shows how mothering can become a dangerous occupation for some women. Martha, like many women, needs emotional distance from others to function skillfully in the world.

Whenever Martha is with her child, she sinks into feelings of helplessness, impotence, and dissolution. The only way she stops such frightening feelings (and the undermining influence of her mother) is by leaving her daughter and joining something larger than herself—in this instance, the Communist Party—that will give her strength. Though she cannot feed and care for her own child, she tries to do the same for others more emotionally distant. Until

Martha becomes totally disillusioned with the failures of communism, the Party allows her to express a less intimate way of caring for others and to break away temporarily from the excruciating feelings of emotional starvation and despair sustained in her relationship with her daughter and mother.

Some mothers who are able to care for others in important ways cannot bear the intimacy of the mother-infant relationship. In his novel *Bleak House*, Charles Dickens parodies these less intimate ways of giving in the character of Mrs. Jellyby, who feigns helping all the unfortunate of the world while completely neglecting her own children. During the early years when close bonding and connectedness are required, some mothers find it impossible to nurture their own children. Though we readily accept the fact that many men have difficulties with this kind of intimacy, we struggle with acknowledging that women can also have problems with the closeness young children need.

The Inability to Provide

Another torment to mothers is knowing what their children need and knowing their limitations in providing for those needs. In Tillie Olsen's "I Stand Here Ironing," the main character is locked in a prison of guilt and anguish for all the things she knows her daughter needs yet because of *financial* circumstances, she cannot give. Olsen reveals a new kind of honesty about the mother's suffering as well as the daughter's, which makes it almost unbearable to read.

A social worker calls the mother-heroine in this story and tells her that her daughter needs help. This sets off a long interior monologue within the mother. As she stands ironing, she examines her relationship with her daughter and what she feels are her failures as a mother.

Olsen's mother-heroine then describes the agony of watching her own child dwindle in possibility, of all the ways she feels she has not been able to give and thus has thwarted her child's growth and development:

> *She was a child of anxious, not proud love . . . I was a young mother, I was a distracted mother . . . My wisdom came too late. She has much to her and probably little will come of it . . . So all that is in her will not bloom . . .*

To make a living, the mother had to leave her child with strangers who did not care. The image of the "dress on the ironing board, helpless before the iron" suggests a flattening of affect, making yourself emotionally dead or insensitive so that you do not feel the horror of watching your offspring grow more and more unhappy. This mother (like so many single mothers) had to abandon her child each day to mediocre child care—often to cold, indifferent people, to institutions, teachers, "nurseries that are only parking places for children." Each place she sends her child is worse than the last. Each time the daughter returns she is more scarred, dwarfed, fearful, unable to get comfort from her mother. Yet the mother is as helpless and vulnerable as the child.

This story reminds me of a nineteenth-century painting in which ladies with hoop skirts and parasols and formally dressed gentlemen are strolling casually, chatting gaily. Beautifully dressed white children are playing. In the background a slave woman clutching her infant is being sold. We register alarm now because the suffering caused by slavery has been brought to the foreground. Yet for centuries many people looking at such a picture of life would not have noticed anything wrong. Too many mothers and children in the real world are desperate and hurting, yet melt into the background of American life, just as at one time the sale of women and their babies was background of the everyday routine.

The mother in "I Stand Here Ironing" is both victim and damaged survivor. Her child is also victim and damaged survivor. In the story, the mother asks for reparation: will society help, if not her, then her daughter—save her from being like a dress on an ironing board, flattened, rendered helpless. The mother also pleads for forgiveness, telling painfully why she fears she has ruined her daughter's life. We are not used to hearing a mother or father say, "I did what I could, but it was simply not enough; it was not the right thing. Please help my child by giving what I didn't or couldn't." Such admissions reveal a terrible vulnerability. Our society has no provisions for children on that essential emotional level that ultimately makes or breaks a human life.

Financial deprivation, severe emotional impoverishment, and the lack of adequate child care can damage a child with the mother looking on, like the slave mother watching her child being sold. In actual fact, we are all watching while many mothers, for financial or emotional reasons, are simply not able to provide adequate child care.

If we don't acknowledge, discuss, mirror back, and validate how painful and destructive these negative aspects of child rearing are, then mothers will continue to suffer. The refusal to examine the mother's feelings and experience is similar to the refusal to examine any victim: it is easier to blame them, to hate the sufferer, rather than to understand and empathize with them and to work for change.

One cannot separate the mother from the social matrix in which she is embedded. Both reflect each other, just as the mother and her baby mirror each other during infancy. Mothers who are overburdened, exhausted, and emotionally deprived cannot help but experience their children's normal demands for love and attention as overwhelming. Too many mothers, in order to survive, are having to fall out of love with their infants. The doting love of parents toward their offspring is being replaced by socioeconomic or emotionally induced abandonment.

We are fortunate to have writers courageous enough to explore some of the most painful conditions mothers must endure. Through their powerful descriptions of the mother's environment, her anguish and deprivation, and her survival strategies, Tillie Olsen, Grace Paley, and Doris Lessing articulate issues and concerns that have remained unspoken for too long. In revealing these aspects of maternal experience, they encourage us to address, finally, the possibility of solutions.

Chapter Nine

THE DOUBLE VISION OF ANNE SEXTON AND SYLVIA PLATH

The mother who is not good enough is not able to implement the infant's omnipotence, and so she repeatedly fails to meet the infant gesture; instead she substitutes her own gesture, which is to be given sense by the compliance of the infant. This compliance on the part of the infant is the earliest stage of the False Self, and belongs to the mother's inability to sense her infant's needs . . .

—D. W. Winnicott,
The Maturational Processes and the Facilitating Environment

In a search for the self the person concerned may have produced something valuable in terms of art, but a successful artist may be universally acclaimed and yet have failed to find the self that he or she is looking for. The self is not really to be found in what is made out of products of body or mind, however valuable these constructs may be in terms of beauty, skill, and impact

. . . The finished creation never heals the underlying lack of
sense of self.

—D. W. Winnicott,
Playing and Reality

Journal Entries, 1984–85

• *Just reread Plath's last poems before her suicide . . . Both Sylvia Plath and Anne Sexton were mothers of young children when they went mad, became suicidal. Why has no one considered the strain child rearing put on them? In their poetry they are open and articulate about feelings most mothers have but are reluctant to reveal. When they speak of their experiences as mothers, you begin to understand why few women dare to investigate this intimate part of themselves.*

Plath and Sexton felt too much, knew too much, saw too much. Was this what pushed them closer to the edge? Somehow they found the courage to write about their perceptions. Is it better to remain ignorant than live with the awful knowledge of all the harm you can do to your children? Or is it possible to use all the things we are finding out now about ourselves and our children in a positive, life-giving way?

• *What does it mean when a mother of young children kills herself? Is she protecting her children from the rage she feels toward them and their demands? Does it mean that her pain is so great she becomes as indifferent to their lives as she feels toward her own? Does she feel hatred or regret or simply relief at the thought of not feeling? . . . Children do not cause a mother to commit suicide, but they can be reminders of previous painful relationships, stirring up the unresolved, pulling one back and down into unbearable states of being, forcing one into the prison of personal history.*

———

Sylvia Plath and Anne Sexton had children, loved them passionately, yet could not mother them. Anne Sexton suffered severe mental breakdowns after the births of both her daughters and had to be hospitalized for psychiatric treatment. When Sylvia Plath's daughter was two and her son only a year old, she committed suicide. Because of or in spite of the fact that these women lived so close to the cutting edge of pain and mental illness, their poetry reveals much that has been unspoken and unwritten about the mother-child relationship. Both women wrote about what it is like to be the daughter of a troubled mother and what it is like to *be* a troubled mother. From this double vision, a new consciousness emerges of how easy it is for us to fail our children.

Every woman who loves her children has had the experience of not being able to give what she knows those children need—a more stable, loving environment perhaps, or a different kind of care than the mother is able to provide. Because of physical exhaustion, emotional depletion, transient states of dislocation, or mental illness, mothers can't always act on their knowledge of what is best for their child. This chapter is about the anguish mothers feel when they cannot meet their children's legitimate needs. Though Plath and Sexton are extreme cases, I am using their poetry to examine the complexities of maternal love when it is compounded by failures in nurturing.

Our society does not think well of mothers who desert their children. Yet few people blame Plath and Sexton for abandoning their children by going mad or killing themselves. On the contrary, they are honored, revered. Until recently, few people looked at what Plath and Sexton had to say about child rearing. Oddly, many critics have glossed over images Plath and Sexton give us in which they convey the complexities of their experiences *as mothers.*

Their sensational deaths have made their work highly visible and popular with a wide audience. There is the suspicion that if these women had not killed themselves, few would read their poetry. On a superficial level, their suicides have made Plath and Sexton seem garishly fictional. The media attention, which has glamorized their deaths, has obscured the more ordinary aspects of their lives: though clearly gifted artists, they were mothers who, unless they were dead or certifiably insane, had to take care of babies.

Plath and Sexton's poetry has tapped a nerve in the maternal collective unconscious. They dared to speak of things that many mothers experience yet cannot talk openly about—of feelings that have not yet been named. The courage and honesty of these two poets in exploring the torment of maternal failure shows how the intimacy and immediacy of young children, and the intensive care they must have, can stretch us to the breaking point. What drives most mothers only briefly or temporarily around the bend, however, drove Plath and Sexton permanently over the edge.

The poems these women wrote about the emotional realities of child rearing provoke disturbing questions: What are the worst things that can happen to a mother of infants? What does child rearing take from the mind and soul and emotional life of an individual? If Sylvia Plath had not been imprisoned in her small cold apartment by the neediness and care her two babies demanded and she could no longer give, she might have survived her last crippling depression. The poems Plath wrote before her death give us valuable insights about what it is like to nurture children while suffering severe mental anguish, alone, without a supportive holding environment to help her.

Anne Sexton wrote about what it felt like to abandon her daughters to the care of others and the effect she felt her desertion had on them. Sexton is so open and honest about both sides of the mother-daughter relationship, it is easy to understand why, in the poem dedicated to her daughter Joy, "A Little Uncomplicated Hymn," the narrator speaks of sailing "off into madness" shortly after her child was born. Historically madness and suicide have been two of the only ways troubled mothers had to escape the overwhelming responsibility for their children's well-being and to protect their children from their own destructive impulses.

Most women do not talk about the need to keep a child safe from one very serious threat—their own impulses to hurt that child. However temporary these urges are, women have enormous guilt about their vengeful feelings toward their children. Frequently mothers become depressed rather than face these feelings.

One overburdened mother, whose situation was similar to Sylvia Plath's, admitted that for weeks she hovered between suicidal despair and child abuse. Twenty-seven-year-old Adele, whose husband had abandoned her and her two small sons, somehow found the strength to have herself hospitalized when she felt anger breaking through her severe depression. Afraid she would abuse her children, Adele put her two sons in a children's shelter and herself in a psychiatric ward until she felt more in control.

· Do you have any idea what it's like to have two little babies dependent on you and know you're losing it? I wanted to die—literally die—not exist. It was a nightmare. The only reason I didn't kill myself was the fear there'd be no one to feed them in the morning. When you have kids you just have to keep giving and giving . . . And here my husband was off screwing another woman. The kids were just being kids, but I didn't have it together anymore. At one point I started spanking them. I knew that was wrong—you just don't spank a nineteen-month-old baby. It's not right. But they got so whiny and demanding. At one point I got terrified I'd really hurt both of them—I had no one I could turn to. My mother lives on the other coast. The friends I made here are friends of my husband's . . .

Because Adele was courageous enough to seek help, she was able to get through this crisis without hurting herself or her children. After three days on the psychiatric ward, Adele felt strong enough to resume care of her children. She was referred to a psychotherapist and immediately began treatment. Adele's relationship with the compassionate woman who became her therapist made it possible for her to survive this painful time and continue nurturing her sons.

Psychotherapy can be extremely beneficial to a mother—it is one of the few resources that can help her through a difficult time. The cases of Anne Sexton and Sylvia Plath, however, show us that insight can be problematic for mothers as well as therapeutic, especially when it is not accompanied by emotional support and practical help.

Insight: Blessing and Curse

Both Anne Sexton and Sylvia Plath underwent extensive psychiatric treatment—Plath after a nearly fatal suicide attempt ten years before her death and Sexton for many years after her first hospitalization. Using insights gleaned from immersion in the psychotherapeutic process, Plath and Sexton wrote poems about the relationships they had with their parents as well as their own experience as mothers.

Some of their poems describe painful connections that exist between overburdened mothers who live vicariously through their daughters; other poems depict how difficult it is to *be* a mother. The narrator of their poems is often a daughter who craves maternal nurturing and approval, and is at the same time aware of carrying within herself her own mother's strivings and potential destructiveness.

Much of the content of Plath's and Sexton's poetry is the result of the advent of psychotherapy. Their involvement in intensive psychotherapeutic relationships made them acutely aware of their ambivalent feelings toward their parents and the violent emotions that raged within them. Insight acquired *before* you have children can mean something very different from insight *after* the birth of a child. For example, in Plath's first volume, *The Colossus*, her poem "The Disquieting Muses" explores the thorny issue of well-meaning but misguided mothering. Though the poem expresses muted rage toward the mother, it contains profound insight into the "True Self" and "False Self" of every young child. Such a poem could only have been written before Plath had children, and it intimates the kind of problems she herself would have as a mother.

A child's "True Self" is that part of all of us which craves love and approval yet is furious, the part of us that wants to cry, scream, whine, *not* perform, *not* put on an act to please. This poem expresses the agony of children whose mothers see only the "False Self," the self that complies, tries to ingratiate by hiding the terror and pain of growing up. The mother in the poem is unable to acknowledge what is most real about her daughter's experience, denies the terror of childhood with Ovaltine and cookies. With happy chants and rhymes of witches who ". . . always, always got baked into gingerbread," this mother tries to cover up the look of fear on her children's faces when frightening things happen. But the reality of the narrator as a child and later as an adult is the experience of being haunted by terrifying witchlike muses,

> With heads like darning eggs to nod
> And nod and nod . . .
> Mouthless, eyeless, with stitched bald head.

Two stanzas describe embarrassing awkward moments and experiences—a dance recital when the narrator was so clumsy and shy she could not "lift a foot, in the twinkle dress"—yet it is the mother who cries over her daughter's failure. The mother floats off in a green balloon, leaving her daughter below forever, with the three terrible muses who day and night "stand their vigil in gowns of stone." The ominous last lines express the narrator's suppressed rage at the mother who will see only the "False Self," which will persist in the adult, continuing to comply and ingratiate:

> *And this is the kingdom you bore me to,*
> *Mother, mother. But no frown of mine*
> *Will betray the company I keep.*

Incorporated as self-hate, the mother lives on in the narrator as the tormented soul who cannot cry for help when she needs it, who will remain alone, forever, with her worst fears. This daughter does not expect help or validation to be seen and loved for whatever she truly is—fears, rage, unhappiness, and all. You do not let on—even if it means you are going to kill yourself. You do not reach out and ask for help because this part of your personality has never been accepted. Such things were not allowed and therefore remain forbidden.

The mother in this poem is familiar to us. A mother who cries when her child fails because the mother needs success; the mother who pretends her child is good at something when it actually is not, happy when it is sad, loving when it is feeling angry and vengeful. This may be smugness and arrogance on our part, yet we expect previous generations to be portrayed as blind in ways we can no longer be, responding to an idea of what their child *should* be and feel, not what the child truly feels and is. We even understand some of the reasons for this: the child's inner experience is denied because the mother's inner experience was denied when she was a child. Because the mother was never allowed to admit her own feelings of rage, fear, and neediness, she cannot bear to be reminded of such shameful emotions in her child.

Unlike the mother in "The Disquieting Muses" and their own mothers, Plath and Sexton were blessed and cursed by the knowledge of what their children needed, felt, went through. Even with that insight, they were incapable of being there emotionally for the children, in part because they had not received that kind of emotional care themselves. Because of the nature of intensive psychotherapy, Plath and Sexton could not remain *un*conscious of their children's true selves, nor could they be unconscious of the desperation that makes parents try to use their children to fulfill their own needs and desires. What is the effect of such awful knowledge on a mother? Can mothers give their children what they themselves have not been given? Can love and understanding be coupled with a failure to care for one's own children?

As we have become more conscious of how difficult and complex a job it is to raise a child, especially in the world we have created, an enormous shift has occurred, both on an emotional level and an intellectual level. While past generations saw in their children whatever they wanted or needed to see, recent generations see perhaps too much of what their children really are and need. Many parents do not have the emotional (or financial) capacity to act on what they know about their children's needs. Knowledge combined with emotional crippling makes for the excruciating helplessness of a Cassandra: knowing the truth, yet being unable to use it to change things for the better.

From Child as Victim to Mother as Victim

Our tendency to see the mother as responsible for her children's problems and unhappiness has its roots in the nineteenth century, with its exposés of exploited children. Writers like Charles Dickens brought to light the brutality toward children in factories and sweatshops. Dickens portrays many children as casualties of the Industrial Revolution, victims of cruel institutions or heartless parental surrogates.

Later in the century, writers begin to describe the child's *own* parents as cruel or indifferent. By the twentieth century, in books and films like *The Catcher in the Rye* and *The Graduate*, we instantly recognize the exaggerated treatment of insensitive parents. The portrayal of the cold, vapid mother in *Ordinary People* is no longer caricature, but a study in maternal malignancy.

In their grim depictions of children committing suicide because of the cold indifference of their parents, Flannery O'Connor (in "The River") and Joyce Carol Oates (in "How I Contemplated the World" and "In the Region of Ice") forecast the present astronomical rise in teenage suicide, diagnosing the cause. In these short stories, the children suffer because of the parents' refusal to acknowledge and care about each child's inner life. In the latter part of the twentieth century, this unwillingness to know a child in all of his or her fear, neediness, and rage, as well as devotion, is portrayed as a kind of child abuse.

But when a victim speaks of his or her victimization, that is one thing. When the victim describes honestly what happens when he or she is given power over others, a shift in consciousness occurs. In the eyes of the world, a girl-child whom we might consider a victim, a survivor of severe emotional injury, sheds this identity after she gives birth.

As a society we tend to expect all mothers to take good care of their infants and blame them if they do not. Plath and Sexton wrote about what it did to them to give birth and assume, however briefly, responsibility for the lives of their children. Acquiring absolute power over creatures so powerless and vulnerable, perhaps knowing the harm they could do to their children, clearly contributed to their precarious emotional states. Because of the deep love Plath and Sexton felt toward their children, as well as their acute sensitivity to their children's needs and uniqueness, their work also reveals the shift in consciousness which comes from the knowledge of how easy it is to pass on suffering and emotional deprivation from one generation to the next. In a subtle, almost imperceptible way, the poetry of these two women alters the reader's perceptions about the victimization of children by "bad mothers."

Plath: Mothering Under Adversity

Unlike Anne Sexton, Sylvia Plath immersed herself in the care of her two babies, loved them intensely, and for a time was able to enjoy nurturing them. Several poems give us exquisite images of the ordinary aspects of mothering children. Plath describes feelings and events that are commonplace to *all* mothers of infants: rocking and singing to a baby during the many nighttime vigils; the sometimes fruitless attempts to comfort a fretful child; rushes of protectiveness that come from well-founded fears of the world's encroaching meanness.

In her poem "Magi," Plath expresses how child care throws us back on what is fleshly, corporeal, *real*. When a mother confronts her infant's bodily demands day in and day out, she cannot help seeing the world of intellectual abstractions as lacking in substance as "boiled water" and "Loveless as the multiplication table." Above all else, a mother must rapidly learn to decipher and attend to her baby's urgent visceral messages. This poem confirms, if not glorifies, the immediacy of bodily experience over "papery" theories:

> . . . *the heavy notion of Evil*
>
> *Attending her cot is less than a belly ache,*
> *And Love the mother of milk, no theory.*

In "Balloons" Plath gives us vivid perceptions of her son: his exquisite otherness, how he sits, bites, contemplates the world in dazed wonder. Such a loving description comes from that passionate place where mothers feel both a deep identification with a child and also awe at the miracle of their Otherness. This was the second-to-last poem she wrote before her death:

. . . Brother is making
His balloon squeak like a cat.
Seeming to see
A funny pink world he might eat on the other
*   side of it.*
He bites,

Then sits
Back, fat jug
Contemplating a world clear as water,
A red
Shred in his little fist.

In the poem "The Night Dances," a mother watching her baby's comical antics guesses what her child might become:

And how will your night dances
Lose themselves. In mathematics?

Such pure leaps and spirals— . . .

In many of her poems, Plath describes the intense love and pride a mother feels for her children and at the same time how very trying it can be just meeting the normal demands of normal babies. In "Brasilia," she describes the effect of a teething baby's shrieks and its urges to bite anything to get relief from its sore gums. The mother does whatever she can to give her baby relief, even if it is hurtful to herself:

And my baby, a nail
Driven, driven in.
He shrieks in his grease

Bones, nosing for distances
And I, nearly extinct,

His three teeth cutting

themselves on my thumb. . .

Listening to an inconsolable infant cry is an unnerving experience that can drive a mother to distraction. Some of Plath's last poems document how overwhelming the responsibility of parenthood is when going through a rough time. All mothers who love their children want to protect them, not only from the dangers of the external world but also from the unhappiness the mother herself might be feeling. Some of the poems written before Plath's death express both profound love for her children and the anguish of trying to keep her own pain and desperation separate from them. In "Nick and the Candlestick," the narrator cries:

O, love, how did you get here?
. . . The blood blooms clean
In you, ruby.

The pain
You wake to is not yours.

The poem ends with a vision of her son as the infant Christ, a not unfamiliar sentiment for mothers of newborn sons:

You are the one
Solid the spaces lean on, envious.
You are the baby in the barn.

In "Child," a poem written a few months later, the narrator feels despair because she knows perfectly what would bring joy to her child. Because of her anguish, she cannot provide even the emotional stability her child needs:

Your clear eye is the one absolutely beautiful thing.
I want to fill it with color and ducks . . .

Not this troublous
Wringing of hands . . .

A mother is most vulnerable and dependent on her husband for support just after the birth of a child and during the first crucial years of a baby's life. Hormonal changes alone can make a new mother prone to depression; lactation and weaning generate both chemical and emotional turmoil in every woman. A mother of young children is more sensitive to abandonment than at any other time. It was at this time that Plath's husband left her and was having an affair with another woman.

Situations of extreme maternal duress have rarely been documented. Plath's final poems express what it is like to have total responsibility for two babies after estrangement from a husband who felt free enough from care of his children to leave them.

Some of Plath's poems combine what is universal in a mother's experience with what is most alarming and nightmarish. Two poems in particular, "Death & Co." and "Lesbos," are like roadmaps through perilous uncharted territory. Plath lights up the pitfalls of maternal love and failure with such a harsh glare, most people have turned away from what she has to tell us about the grimmer aspects of nurturing young children.

In the poem "Death & Co.," Plath reveals a tormenting fantasy in which a mother sees her children dead:

. . . in their hospital
Icebox, a simple
Frill at the neck . . .
Death-gowns
Then two little feet . . .

When a mother is depressed, exhausted, or experiencing emotional stress, such images pass quickly before her mind's eye. In most mothers of young children, these fantasies are fleeting, quickly forgotten, and often remain unspoken. They are not uncommon, often having to do with fatigue on the mother's part, always indicating the mother is in need of relief, time off from caring for her infant. Unfortunately, they have the opposite effect—of making her feel so frightened that she tends to hover around her children even more to protect them from the imagined harm, the imagined death. Plath wrote about the terrifying feelings that can cause overburdened mothers to become "overprotective."

In "Lesbos," Plath speaks of the guilt and rage that lacerate every mother when she feels herself responsible for everything that goes wrong with her children. The poem is about being out of control and yet having to be in control. It is a domestic scene more common than any of us want to believe: the overwhelmed, overburdened mother, desperate for relief, yet somehow forced to assume total responsibility for her children. The father/husband, "hugging his ball and chain," is able to "slump out." The mother remains, blaming herself for her daughter's tantrums, imagining her daughter is mad and that *she* (the mother) is the cause:

> *Little unstrung puppet, kicking to disappear . . .*
> *Why she is schizophrenic,*
> *Her face red and white, a panic . . .*
>
> *She'll cut her throat at ten if she's mad at two . . .*

In this poem, Plath describes the chaos toddlers often create when their wishes are thwarted, conveying the effect of the bloodcurdling screams, so typical of two-year-olds, on sensitive nerve endings. When a mother with delicate sensibilities who has been abandoned by her husband and has no immediate way of getting relief must live through a toddler's temper tantrums and watch limbs thrash pretty regularly while the baby ("fat snail") leaves a "trail of slime" on polished linoleum floor—sometimes there is nowhere the rage can go except inward.

The mother who commits suicide bears some resemblance to the mother who abuses her child. Tormented by extreme internal and external forces, both cease to care about the consequences of their acts. The suicide loses interest in all life, not just her own. The connection between the urge to hurt oneself and the impulse to hurt others is a close one. On a subliminal level, children can come to represent aspects of ourselves. When we lash out at them, we are sometimes lashing out at the needy, demanding parts of ourselves we have come to despise.

Suicide and child abuse also have much to do with revenge. Plath's suicide may have been motivated partly by the rage she felt toward her husband (also a poet) for deserting her and by a desire for vengeance. One troubled mother said she felt such rage toward her husband that she no longer cared about the feelings of hurt and fear she saw on her children's faces. Thirty-year-old Edith, the mother of a three-year-old daughter and a son of five, said she wanted vengeance—any relief from her murderous anger, even if it was momentary. Unlike her abusive husband, Edith's children did not frighten or intimidate her, and this, she admitted, made them targets for her wrath and desire for retaliation.

Eventually, Edith became so filled with shame, disgust, and self-hate that she made an unsuccessful suicide attempt. After months of psychotherapy in a hospital setting, Edith said she realized that this self-destructive gesture was her nearly fatal way of "crying for help." Mothering had not come easily to Edith, who had been trained as lawyer but had given up her profession to care for her children. Though she was a successful attorney, Edith had never known how to ask for assistance when she needed it. Nor had Edith ever learned to acknowledge her need for love and support, which increased "a hundredfold," she said, after the birth of her children.

According to A. Alvarez, Sylvia Plath put up a competent front during the last excruciating months of her life, barricading her inner torment behind the arduously cultivated "False Self" that had sought approval since childhood through the piling up of achievements. Unable to cry for help when she desperately needed it, Plath could express her anguish only through her exquisite poems, which no one read until after her death.

In her essay "On Sylvia Plath," Elizabeth Hardwick unwittingly summarizes the blindnesses of the age regarding mothers:

> . . . it is sentimental to keep insisting that the birth of her children unlocked her poetic powers. Why should that be? The birth of children opens up the energy for taking care of them and for loving. The common observation that one must be prepared to put off other work for a few years is strongly founded.

No woman can know beforehand what emotions will be unleashed by the birth and care of a baby or whether her energies will be expanded or reduced. Hardwick's thinking in this passage reinforces the myth that women are naturally, instinctively prepared for the tasks of rearing children; and she refuses to consider the many situations in which women do not have the emotional or financial resources to sustain a loving, caring relationship with their children during their early years.

It *was* after the birth of her children that Plath wrote her most powerful poems, however, many expressing what the stresses of nurturing unleashed in her. So much has been written about Plath's ambition, her perfectionism, her drive to perform and succeed. Few acknowledge her intensive efforts to provide loving care for her babies, the refusal of her husband to help and support her when she was most vulnerable, and the ways in which the labor of child rearing may have undermined her tenuous stability.

Sexton: The Fear of Maternal Intrusiveness

Unlike Plath, Anne Sexton lived to see her daughters grow into adolescence. Because of her many suicide attempts and hospitalizations, she experienced much of her children's development at a distance. What makes it impossible for a woman to nurture her children, despite the fact that she loves them dearly? In her poetry Sexton documents the reasons why she could not take pleasure in the care of her children and illuminates some of the causes of maternal failure.

In many of her poems, Sexton speaks explicitly of the limitless power a mother has over her young child and the fluidity of boundaries between mother and daughter. In her poem "Housewife," she distinguishes between mother-son and mother-daughter relationships:

> *Men enter by force, drawn back like Jonah*
> *into their fleshy mothers*
> *. . . A woman is her mother*
> *That's the main thing . . .*

The lack of sharp edges between mother and daughter does not have to be a damaging thing. Fluid borders may be necessary in order to achieve deeper compassion and understanding of another's experiences. But when a child's relationship with its mother is a painful or frightening one, boundary confusion can become overwhelming.

In some of her most powerful poems, Sexton writes intimately of the perils of intimacy—of that thin line between closeness and impingement. For Sexton, losing the borders of her identity was a very real danger. In the chronologically written *Live or Die,* each poem brings the narrator closer to the rage and longing she feels toward her mother. In this volume Sexton uses domestic words and images, traditionally employed to convey the reassuring presence of a loving mother, to describe the absolute failure of the maternal, domestic life gone sour. Homey words and phrases and images of a sweet, docile domesticity: curtains, wallpaper, sneakers, "sashes and puffs with collars and two-inch hems," are used almost as incantations, yet fail to protect the narrator from what she describes as unspeakable violations in the mother-daughter relationship. In the poem "Those Times . . . ," Sexton describes a terrible maternal intrusiveness, which demands of the daughter a crippling, humiliating submission:

> . . . *stuffing my heart into a shoebox*
> . . . *I waited out the day*
> *until my mother,*
> *The large one,*
> *came to force me to undress*

The mother's invasive behavior, which borders on the lurid, seems to paralyze the narrator into a terrible passivity:

> *I lay there silently . . .*

> *I did not question the bedtime ritual*
> *where, on the cold bathroom tiles,*
> *I was spread out daily*
> *and examined for flaws . . .*

This lethal overstepping of boundaries weakens a child's ability to establish and maintain an identity distinct from the mother's. Experiences like this can be so damaging, the child has recourse only to a violent, yet impotent rage. The ferocity of this rage itself can be overwhelming to children. For one thing, it makes them feel absolutely alone, as though they have actually destroyed the object of their fury, upon whom they are totally dependent. Unmitigated by consistent, loving care, such feelings of anger can make one cling to and merge with the mother, in order not to lose her. This clinging dependency can undermine the strength necessary to withstand many things, including the pain of separateness.

Sexton forces us to think about rage toward the mother as a requirement—something necessary, employed to preserve a tenuous sense of self. In some cases, this anger becomes a means of self-preservation that defends the individual against frightening feelings of dissolution. When hatred felt toward the impinging mother is too extreme and cannot be managed or resolved, one becomes vulnerable to depression, severe mental instability, and an inability to nurture may result.

Though submission to her mother later became rebellion, revealing itself in attempts at both domestic and literary subversion (Sexton revolted against social and familial convention as well as the stuffy, male-dominated literary world), she was unable to use her rage toward her mother to separate from the poisonous aspects of their relationship. Because Sexton was unable to break the cloying bond with her own mother, she could not lay claim to her right to enjoy her children.

Sometimes a woman is able to barricade a fragile sense of self behind a strong career identity (or perhaps an identity that seems the opposite of her mother's). This strategy often works until the woman becomes a mother, at which point she is drawn back into the destructive relationship she had with her own mother. As long as she is not a mother, she is safe. When she assumes the mother's role, severe problems hinder her attempts to nurture.

Growing up, becoming a woman with full sexual capacities for both marriage and childbirth, a daughter must be able to take the mother's place in the world. When we have children, we are competing with our mothers as well as joining them and the ranks of all the mothers who came before us. Thus every mother must somehow give her daughter permission to separate—ultimately, to supercede her.

Sexton's poem "Those Times . . ." expresses a profound affirmation of womanhood as well as joy and pride in her own body and what it could do:

> I did not know the woman I would be
> . . . nor that children,
> two monuments,
> would break from between my legs
> two cramped girls breathing carelessly,
> each asleep in her tiny beauty . . .

Yet for Sexton, separation from her own mother is described again and again as betrayal at best—at worst, as matricide. Whenever Sexton speaks of sexual pleasure, the enjoyment of children of one's own, the fulfillments of adult life, she immediately cancels out such positive visions with images riddled with guilt and violence. Thus, after the above description of the birth of her two daughters, the narrator of the poem says:

> I did not know that my life, in the end
> would run over my mother's like a truck . . .

In her poem "Christmas Eve," Sexton describes the narrator's mother as a "sharp diamond." The narrator's anger toward her mother melts into guilt and then into the need to merge. Because she can no longer differentiate herself from her mother—about whom she thinks "as one thinks of murder"—she *becomes* her. Separation from the "sharp diamond" is impossible when intense hatred and love for the mother cannot be resolved. These feelings consume, leading the child (and later the adult) back again and again to cling to the object that in fantasy she fears she has destroyed.

We are only beginning to discover ways to break up harmful patterns inherited from previous generations—a slow and tortuous process at best. The inability to separate from the mother, especially when the relationship is a destructive one, inevitably makes the next generation vulnerable. Sexton was acutely aware of both the damage she could do to her children and the problems and pain she caused by leaving them to the care of others. In her poem "A Little Uncomplicated Hymn," she laments the effect her abandonment had on her daughter:

> *Even here in your school portrait*
> *where you repeat the third grade,*
> *caught in the need not to grow . . .*
>
> *even here you keep up the barrier*
> *with a smile that dies afraid . . .*

Such poems as "Little Girl, My String Bean, My Lovely Woman" make it clear that Sexton did not want to hand down her emotional conflicts to her daughters. In this poem she compares her own experience of puberty to her daughter's and tells her what every adolescent daughter wants to hear and know—that it is truly okay to grow up, to become a woman, to enjoy one's changing body; that she has the mother's blessing:

> *. . . I remember that I heard nothing myself.*
> *I was alone.*
> *I waited like a target . . .*
>
> *Oh, darling, let your body in,*
> *let it tie you in,*
> *in comfort.*
> *. . . there is nothing in your body that lies.*
> *All that is new is telling the truth.*

This poem expresses deep understanding of the need adolescents have for maternal affirmation of their budding sexuality. Yet Sexton's own experience of adolescence was fraught with guilt, inhibitions, and humiliation. In her poem "Mother and Jack and the Rain," the narrator is unable to use adolescent sexuality to escape from her ruinous tie to her mother and the prison of daughterhood. The boyfriend (who should be making this teenage girl forget all about her parents) merely plays cards with the narrator instead of carrying her off to a world of sensual delights. The intense sexuality of adolescence—that last hatch through which we must all escape if we are to successfully separate from mother, father, the seductive world of childhood—is denied to the narrator in this poem. The flowering sexuality of youth, which should be reinforcing the process of separation, is truncated here by a prudish, puritanical relationship. In other poems, sexuality is described as something intrusive, violent, incestuous. Yet Sexton wrote lucidly of her desire to spare her own daughters the same pain, trauma, and frustration.

Double Vision

Poems which express maternal love and understanding, no matter how poignant and beautiful, do not take the place of actual child care. Most troubled mothers do not commit suicide or go mad but remain the caretakers of their children no matter how depressed or destructive they become. The courageous ones seek help—get into family counseling, undergo psychotherapy, take classes in parenting, call parental stress hotlines. Yet this takes tremendous strength. Insight into the causes of maternal failure often requires the kind of double vision Plath and Sexton achieved. From the failures in patience we all experience with our children to the more serious transgressions, becoming aware of the mistakes we make and the difficulties we have in nurturing is painful and hard-won. Though we admire the work of Plath and Sexton, our culture does not value or validate the kind of knowledge they give us about the complexities of mothering, despite the fact that it is just such insight that could help so many mothers and their children.

Plath and Sexton's inability to nurture their children raises crucial questions: What should a mother do in extreme cases, if she simply cannot give her children the care they need?

If a mother has difficulty separating herself emotionally from destructive early relationships, she will tend to repeat those patterns with her children. It takes strength and courage to know when one is doing something harmful to a child—and to let someone else take over for a while. Sometimes all a mother can do, at least in the short run, is allow her child or children to form good relationships with others, become attached to someone else, either part- or full-time, until she recovers. A great degree of maturity is necessary to give a child the opportunity to love someone else with all the passionate intensity of infancy and early childhood. Children can seem, from time to time, so much like parts of ourselves. To let them go can evoke feelings of profound loss—even when keeping them close may lead to child abuse.

The work of Anne Sexton and Sylvia Plath reflects the pain of early attachments that failed to give the crucial affirmation that allows someone to endure life. Because they could not secure a firm identity or strong enough "Real Self," Plath and Sexton had severe problems nurturing their children. Plath's lack of a loving, supportive holding environment to help her in the care of her babies made the tasks of child rearing unbearable. Fearing their inability to prevent some variation of what had been painful and destructive in their own early lives, both women could not persist in caring for their children.

Plath and Sexton lived and wrote about the torment of maternal failure. Before them, few serious women poets wrote about mothering, a topic considered too banal and easily sentimentalized. Yet after their deaths, a whole body of poems dealing with the complexities of child rearing became accepted into the literary canon. By uncovering the darker truths about maternal experience, Plath and Sexton paved the way for poets such as Maxine Kumin, Adrienne Rich, Alicia Ostriker, Sharon Olds, Alta, and others to celebrate the feelings of empowerment that can come from mothering. But before those other poets could write about the richness of connection and be heard, Plath and Sexton had to tell of the "troublous / Wringing of hands" and of their attempt to keep their torment separate from their children. Let us hope that their unveiling of the most painful aspects of mothering is a foreshadowing of a new kind of honesty that will help all care-givers of children.

POSSIBILITIES OF
TRANSFORMATION

Today, we are everywhere surrounded by the remarkable conspicuousness of consumption and affluence, established by the multiplication of objects, services, and material goods. This now constitutes a fundamental mutation in the ecology of the human species . . . men . . . are no longer surrounded by other human beings, as they have been in the past, but by *objects*. Their daily exchange is no longer with their fellows, but rather . . . with the acquisition and manipulation of goods and messages.

—Jean Baudrillard,
Selected Writings

Youth has always been the most sensitive indicator whenever "Something is rotten in the state of Denmark." The adolescent is telling us, by his maladaptive behavior, about the wanton disarrangement of societal functions . . . although he is unable to articulate either the real nature of its cause or the measures needed for societal regeneration.

—Peter Blos,
The Adolescent Passage

Journal Entries: 1985–87

· *So few people have mirrored back the mother's deepest feelings. This perhaps is our greatest sin—what we choose not to know. If there is no one to accept our deepest selves—the part of us that is most real—this can result in a "shut down." Feelings and events then come to seem random and meaningless, but they are not. Now that women are becoming more open about their experiences as mothers, we can see that many frightening things are not random and meaningless but have a terrible logic . . .*

· *Seldom do mothers deliberately hurt their children. Most often they are just trying to escape painful feelings of emotional deprivation. Can a child be happy if its mother is not? For a long time, the child is the mother; the mother, the child. If the mother has no compassion for herself, can she have any for her offspring? If so, it would be hard to sustain.*

· *How strange—that we seem to have at our fingertips all the information we need. Despite this knowledge, most people—children as well as adults—are kept unsatisfied in practically every respect. The emotional hunger that permeates our lives is hidden, cropping up under the guise of voracious consumerism, and this seems to be transferred, intact, from generation to generation. Has our feverish economy made it impossible to raise our children with the care and joy necessary to make them decent human beings?*

At the beginning of this book, I suggested the fictional character of Huckleberry Finn as a symbol of freedom, representing the desire in all of us to run from the mother toward liberation and autonomy. In Mark Twain's novel, the care-giver is an oppressive figure, someone who curbs and thwarts what many feel to be most precious—our independence—in exchange for care giving: the provision of warmth, shelter, food, safety. What I have explored in this book is the other side of this exchange: the experience of those who must take care of a child.

At present, most of us in this culture identify so closely with children, we forget that *we* are the adults who must provide constant care for them. Consequently, we have been reluctant to examine both our deepest feelings toward our offspring and the complex tasks involved in caring for them.

The fields of psychiatry, clinical psychology, and psychoanalysis, while opening up uncharted territory for exploration and providing tools for inquiry, may have unintentionally retarded insight into the emotional realities of child rearing. By describing the mother (and sometimes the father) as the villain in case study after case study, the mental health profession has reflected and strengthened myths and beliefs already firmly entrenched in society at large. While giving us crucial information about the psychodynamics of children and adults, many psychological theories tend to disregard the needs and feelings of care-givers, and our culture's gross devaluation of the mother.

The moment we become aware of the harm we can do to a child, parenting becomes imbued with moral overtones. For this reason, everything we do and feel when we are caring for children has acquired an ethical dimension. Hence, the widespread use of the terms: good mother, bad mother, good-enough mother. Since we naturally wish to think of ourselves as good parents, it is understandable that people might not want to look at the darker passions child rearing unleashes. Nor is it surprising that many avoid this arduous process of transformation or remain blind to what it has to teach us.

It grieves us to know how easy it is to hurt those as vulnerable and dear to us as our children. Yet when we care for them, we all become at times self-absorbed, depriving, intrusive, impatient. We cannot help but demand some form of submission. From time to time, we all use our children in some way to get our own needs met. The Myth of the Bad Mother would have us believe that it is only bad mothers who do such things.

During this century the media have contributed to this myth by presenting us with grossly distorted images of the mother. Showing care-givers as either loving and generous or selfish and abusive, books, films, television, and advertising have reinforced the most destructive beliefs a woman can have: that as a mother you are either good (or good enough) and have no serious problems, or bad and unable to learn from your mistakes; that care-givers are incapable of change; and that whatever harm you do to your children is irreparable.

Fortunately in recent years, rigid attitudes have slowly given way to a more humane and realistic assessment of our needs, mistakes, wishes, and failures—all the things we are and are not. Gradually it is becoming permissible for parents to talk more openly about the complexities of child rearing and seek help when they need it. Many couples become involved in family counseling or therapy for their children if they are troubled. Though some parents are still ashamed to admit when they are perplexed and disturbed by their children's behavior as well as their own reactions, it is becoming more acceptable for parents to examine their feelings, to understand and talk about mistakes they have made, and to make efforts to change.

Ideally child rearing leads to a more open and compassionate response to others. As one loving father said,

• Sometimes there is no other way you can learn than by seeing that look of fear or humiliation on your kid's face, knowing it's you who caused it—it's you who made him feel hurt—and wanting to right the wrong just by never doing it again.

We must learn to confront our errors, find the courage to experience the guilt and anxiety this might arouse, and use such feelings to transform our behavior.

Error and Insight

All parents make mistakes with their children. The question is: what happens after the mistakes? According to most mental health professionals, only through recognition of our errors can we effect change.

Crucial to our understanding of the emotional realities of child rearing are the implications from research that indicates *it is never too late*. Work done by Rutter (1979), Kagan (1984), Settlage et al. (1988), and others strongly suggests that there are infinite chances for a child to recover from losses, traumas, and deprivations experienced during the early years. In other words, insight on the parents' part and improvements in environmental conditions can lead to tremendous gains in later childhood, no matter what has occurred earlier.

Despite the widespread prevalence of mother blaming, there is a growing willingness to be conscious of our own part in how we all—men and women alike—fail or hurt our children, and how we can make reparation. Such heightened consciousness goes hand in hand with the awareness of the ways our own parents disappointed and failed us, and how easy it is for us to do the same thing with our own children. Whether this is a new kind of courage, the result of desperation at what the world has become, or the impoverishment in human relationships which drives us to look at painful areas of experience, we are finally becoming curious and willing to learn from our mistakes.

Both men and women told me how they gained and learned to use this kind of insight. Lytton, a forty-three-year-old investment banker from San Francisco, spent years working from six in the morning until eight or nine at night, seven days a week. Until his first child was born, Lytton never questioned this lifestyle. When I talked to him about his work, I could feel the high-powered intensity of this man, like a strong electric current.

When we began discussing his son, Lytton's voice dropped slightly and his tone changed. Lytton said he had had to learn "the hard way":

• This is how I was trained to live: you work hard, you never stop. I was taught that if you slowed down even for a minute, it wouldn't be long before you start losing. How was I to know I was hurting my kid? I didn't even know you could hurt a kid, for Christ sake. Where I grew up in New Jersey, people didn't think in those terms.

My son would take such a long time to do everything. It drove me crazy every time I was with him. I'd always be thinking of something else. Like who I had to meet with the next day. The closing of some lucrative deal. So I'd try to rush him through everything—even playing ball with him in the park—we'd have to do everything in a hurry so I could get back to work.

At first the fact that he had "problems" was an embarrassment. I couldn't really take it seriously. It literally took a shrink (at ninety-five dollars an hour) to tell me that if I wanted to help my son, I had to slow down, learn to enjoy myself, learn to enjoy him. Enjoy! It was basically that simple. I felt like I'd just discovered the wheel . . .

Because of strenuous efforts and pressures to succeed in areas outside the role of care-giver, most parents learn about child care "the hard way," by making mistakes. One mother told me it took her a long and frustrating year to realize that her toddler had an urgent need to stop and stare, sometimes touch the most ordinary things—a drainpipe, raindrops falling off a leaf, fireplugs, trees—that her task as a mother was somehow to find the patience and energy (or find someone else who had it) to allow her child the time to explore and experience his wonder at the world.

Richard, a thirty-two-year-old product development manager, was transferred from his hometown, twenty miles outside of Syracuse, to an ugly sprawling suburb of Los Angeles. Richard said he spent six months taking out his anger on his two children until it finally dawned on him how much harm he was doing to them:

> • It's so easy to yell at them. I mean it's safe—they're small. They don't fight back the way adults do. One day I found my daughter curled up, her little hands covering her face, sobbing because I'd been yelling at her for some damn thing. I started to wonder if I wasn't just a natural bully.

When Richard realized he was hurting his children, he began to search for ways to lessen the pressures and frustrations of his new life. When he spent time with his children, he learned to try things they all enjoyed so that he could nourish himself when he was with them. This seems to be an important thing all parents have to learn —how to enjoy their children.

For some women, the early nurturing process is difficult. Two mothers I interviewed had trouble caring for their children when they were small, yet were able to nurture quite well later on. Thirty-six-year-old Jill, who had rapidly climbed up the executive ladder of a large, intensely competitive insurance company, said that if she had stayed home to take care of her daughter during infancy, she would have remained in middle management. Jill has an air of kindness and genuine concern about her; she is an obviously talented and ambitious woman. When I asked how she would have felt working part-time when her daughter was small, she said:

> • If I hadn't worked full-time like I did, I would have been miserable, at least then. My career would have been finished. And it

wasn't the money I was after, though Lord knows, it's great to make a lot of money. But my husband makes plenty. I've just always wanted to be the best, go the farthest—it's the way I am. But I had no idea the kind of care babies need. Three out of the four women I'd hired to take care of my daughter during the first five years of her life were bad caretakers. I made lousy choices and I had no idea how much she suffered because of this.

I never really caught on until she started to school and began to have all these learning disability problems. Eventually I had her tested. It wasn't until she was in second grade and doing really poorly that I decided to take a year off. After that I've worked only part-time—she needs a mother and I realized I didn't want to entrust her to anyone else, even though by that time I'd found a special school. But I'm there for her when she gets out of school now, and I help her every night with her homework.

Though it is extremely painful for mothers and fathers to learn "the hard way," most feel relief that they finally see what is going on with their children and are able to correct or at least improve the situation. For some mothers, it takes a period of time before they can put the best interests of their children before their own. When her daughter was two and a half, Joanne said that she became extremely depressed. Because her work as a documentary filmmaker took her far from home, she had put her career temporarily "on hold." Her decision to devote herself to mothering began to have disastrous consequences for Joanne:

• At first I thought it was just restlessness and boredom—I mean, taking care of a kid that age is not exactly inspiring. I'd purposely stopped work, thinking it wouldn't be too great a sacrifice to take off a few years. But then it got so I couldn't sleep, I didn't want to eat, I lost a lot of weight. I kept feeling this horrible anxiety in the pit of my stomach. Finally I just split. This was when she was close to three. I told myself she didn't need me anymore. I began to feel like staying home taking care of this kid was making me crazy. So I just split. I wanted to find out who the hell I was. The problem was my daughter felt totally abandoned when I left. But by that point I didn't even care. I thought my husband would take care of her, but he just hired a housekeeper and was gone most of the day. He wasn't used to thinking of what children need.

I had no trouble finding work and traveled all over the world for about a year and a half. When I returned to the States, my daughter was a wreck. She'd lost the ability to sleep and used to rock back and forth all day long. It's been so hard to make it up to her and we've needed professional help. But things are getting better—slowly.

Several women who were unable to nurture their children when they were infants had to make some hard career decisions later on, rearranging priorities, so that they could spend more time with their children. One mother said, "I had to decide what was more important, my work or my kids."

Many mothers, for financial reasons, do not have this luxury; they are completely dependent on surrogate care-givers. They have the difficult task of finding others capable of nurturing who will form a loving attachment to their children. Many working mothers experience painful feelings of jealousy when they find their children preferring the caretakers to themselves.

Some mothers have the opposite problem: their children become their sole domain. Many said they felt extremely possessive and overprotective of their infants from birth on, and unwittingly made their husbands feel excluded and inadequate. One mother spoke of the jealousy she felt whenever her husband played or spent time with her son and daughter.

The Hollywood film *Shoot the Moon* dramatically captures the seriousness of this problem. The wife is portrayed as experiencing much more pleasure in her relationship with her children than in her relationship with her husband. Over the years her husband feels more and more excluded and estranged from the family. He has spent so little time with his children that he has not bothered to learn the skills involved in caring for them. Consequently, when he is with his children, he is impatient, frustrated, bored, ineffectual. Because he has not participated in child rearing, the father in this film becomes an emotional infant. By not becoming more involved as a parent, he remains immature and selfish—much like a child himself. This unfortunate but common pattern—which must be understood as an unconscious collusion between men and women—keeps some men from the humanization process. Many such marriages ultimately end in divorce.

Mothers who give themselves over completely to the mothering role have trouble later, when their children begin to separate. Thirty-two-year-old Grace, who grew up in the Deep South, said her problem was with enmeshment—the inability to keep her own needs and identity separate from her daughter's:

- For years I lived through my daughter, through her talents and accomplishments. Of course, I didn't realize it at the time. This would not have been considered unusual where I come from. Growing up in the family where I did, just outside of Mobile, women weren't given a lot of encouragement to accomplish things on their own. All the mothers I knew lived through their children.

What I did was push my daughter, without even knowing it. You don't know what I did so that she finally got a good part in the show *Annie*. I was thrilled. At first she loved it and had a lot of fun. Kids just naturally love to act. But then they took the show on the road and we began living out of a suitcase in dirty hotel rooms with these horrible stage mothers and their bratty kids. One day I found her hiding backstage playing with her dolls, when she was supposed to be getting ready for the show. She said, "I just want to go home so I can play with my dolls." Here I'd studied drama in college, always wanted to be an actress, had been in amateur productions, and now my daughter was fulfilling all my dreams, only it wasn't right, it was awful. We got on the next plane. So now I'm back getting my credentials (I'm planning to teach drama in the high schools) and she's back to leading a normal kid's life, which I guess is what she really wants.

Unwittingly children sometimes push us to develop in unexpected ways. Without knowing it, they give us opportunities to do things better the second time around. When Rita was "trying to grow up" in Cheyenne, Wyoming, she married her high school sweetheart right after graduation and got pregnant immediately. Rita said that at that time in her life, she had no maternal instincts whatsoever. Feeling trapped and unbearably miserable, Rita got a quick divorce, let her ex-husband have custody of her daughter, and bolted. Unable to be a mother to her own daughter, Rita was given "another chance" by her second husband's children, who had been abandoned by their mother:

> • When I gave birth to my daughter, I was seventeen. It meant nothing to me that my ex-husband's parents raised her. (This makes me cringe when I think about it now. They're horrible people.) But I just wanted out so bad it didn't matter to me then. That's the kind of person I was and I still feel bad when I think about it. Thank God I got a second chance. I devote myself to my husband's kids now (nine years later). And they really need a mother. His first wife completely neglected them. Thank God I could finally do something right—at least make something righter than it was.

Other parents in seemingly hopeless, destructive situations were able to correct them, though it took enormous effort on their part. Forty-four-year-old research biologist Lee said it took a serious illness to bring her ex-husband and herself to a deeper understanding of how they were hurting their son:

· My ex-husband and I used Joel as a battleground to get back at each other. It tore the boy apart. He was four and needed a father, but I couldn't see that then and hated the bastard so much I kept telling myself he was a lousy father. I just didn't want him to have the satisfaction of enjoying his son. Divorce brought out the worst in both of us, but it was Joel who suffered the most. I don't think it was until we almost lost him—he came down with spinal meningitis—that my ex and I finally put our petty shit aside and actually focused on the boy—his needs rather than our endless grievances with each other. Even after we saw the light, it's taken years to repair the damage. Now we both go to great lengths not to criticize the other in front of him, and do what we can to make Joel's time with the other as conflict-free as possible . . .

A child's behavior sometimes forces us out of ourselves, into a whole new awareness of things. One father, a Vietnam veteran who now works as an airline pilot, said he'd been brought up to think courage had to do with "macho" behavior, which to him was physical bravery. The hardest thing thirty-nine-year-old Robert said he had ever done in his life was to face his part in the deterioration of his fifteen-year marriage:

· My daughter was so much more loving than my wife, I had no idea I was being seductive. I thought I was being a good father, spending a lot of time with my kid. But then she started having all these problems at school, got involved with a bad crowd. It took a marriage and family counselor to point out that there was something wrong with the marriage and that my daughter was acting out our problems.

When a kid hits you with the truth by doing something awful to herself, you have to stop fooling yourself. (She'd gotten into drugs by the time I finally let it in.) Of course it took someone to point out I was using her to avoid our marriage. I didn't believe it until my wife and I started working on our relationship. It was like a miracle. My daughter's problems seemed to dissolve.

Robert said he and his wife are now trying to salvage their marriage and there are signs of hope. But it was not until his daughter, through her destructive behavior, sounded the alarm—drawing attention to the fact that there was something wrong within the family. Only then could Robert and his wife gain insight into their own actions.

As these examples suggest, we must learn never to dismiss the errors we make with our children until we have gleaned thorough knowledge of their meaning—and to come to terms with the feelings and circumstances that provoked the mistakes. Understanding of the deeper meanings of our failures in nurturing seems to be a two-fold gift—to our children and ultimately to ourselves. Learning from those mistakes seems to be an essential part of the humanization process.

The Effects of Deprivation

We have created for ourselves a society in which it is increasingly difficult to care for our children. Sensitivities to the needs of children are often numbed by the interference—if not the actual bombardment—of external stimuli (to use the words of Baudrillard, "the acquisition and manipulation of goods and messages"). Our capacities to nurture are constantly being undermined and fractured by pressures to produce and achieve that are antithetical to altruistic giving. Our energies are taken up and exhausted by trying to survive financially in a society that tantalizes its members to accumulate material goods. The values of the marketplace, which dominate all of our lives, often make children seem, if not exploitable, then irrelevant—almost a retreat from or impediment to "real" life. An alternative to this attitude is the realization that child rearing may be one of the few ways in which we can achieve greater insight and greater humanity.

Children let us know, sometimes cryptically, through their behavior—when something is wrong with *us*, our lives, and the society they must adapt to. Of course, children do not try to teach their parents. For their own natural, self-centered reasons, they want us to be loving and "together" so that they can simply grow—without having to worry about their parents at all.

When our behavior becomes truly destructive, our children let us know in glaring, tragic ways: the growing rise of teenage suicide, depression, violence, and the widespread use of illegal drugs in the schools—now even among children who are prepubescent. By exploring the implications of our children's behavior and the emotional realities of caring for them, we gain access to the deeper meanings of the maladies of our troubled age. One cause of the ills that afflict us is the disastrous effect of emotional deprivation on both mothers and children. Outside of those in the mental health professions, few people take it seriously. Yet it is the cumulative experiencing of emotional deprivation which inevitably leads to our most potentially destructive feelings: rage, envy, self-hate, greed, and the desire for revenge. Such feelings are the cause of child abuse and neglect. To ward off these destructive emotions, some parents disengage themselves from their children altogether. Feelings of emotional deprivation can cause massive numbers of people to withdraw their concern for the well-being of their children.

Because of our present power to destroy all life, a new kind of courage is needed to understand the dwindling concern for future generations. The reluctance to explore, understand, and make accessible to children and their care-givers what they both need to thrive is tied to lethal elements in our culture—tendencies that are threatening the future of civilization itself. The fear, hostility, and aggression that makes us prone to war may be related to the growing indifference to our children and their future.

The biggest problem we now face is the containment of our most destructive emotions so that they will not spill over onto the lives of our children. One of the most horrifying aspects of war is how easy it is to get our children to fight. Any religious or ethnic group, political system, family, or clan can induce its children to hate some enemy and thereby maintain feuds and wars for generations. One way we do this is the perpetuation of feelings of deprivation in children. This makes them vulnerable, extremely dependent, and filled with anger, which is then easy to manipulate and divert away from ourselves to some evil Other. It seems all too easy to get our children to fight our wars for us, to act out our feelings, to rob them of their subjectivity (their objectivity as well) rather than allow them the individuality we claim to be so important.

How do we induce our children to continue our warlike, destructive inclinations? We are beginning to explore this difficult question by the recognition and understanding of our capacities and failures to nurture our children. As a culture, many of our sins are those of omission, having to do with the kinds of issues and problems we neglect, avoid, or deny altogether. For instance, we pretend that child rearing is easy, women's work, even now when most mothers work outside the home and often have no one they can trust as reliable, loving, or competent to care for their children. We continue to evade a full awareness of the fact that, like physical starvation, emotional deprivation can destroy lives, generating overwhelming feelings of hatred and an obsession with revenge. Mothers, in their role as care-givers, are looked down upon, demeaned, and isolated from the centers of power; given total responsibility for their children yet no support for child rearing; and blamed when their children have problems. Beneath flimsy idealizations, we refuse to acknowledge the absolute importance of child care, the crucial need to involve fathers at the very center of it, and the irreparable damage that can be done to children by not providing them with loving and respected care-givers.

Radical Transformations

In a short story entitled "Conversations with my Father," Grace Paley describes a grossly pathological mother-son relationship in which a mother tries to maintain her "close friendship" with her son, a fifteen-year-old junkie, by becoming a heroin addict herself. Yet even in this extreme situation, Paley invites us to consider the possibility of learning from our children—and of transforming our basest metals into gold.

After his mother becomes an addict herself, the son leaves the city in disgust, cures himself of his heroin addiction, and refuses to see his mother again unless she also kicks the habit. The ex-junkie son becomes the role model for his mother. *He* shows her the way out of her heroin addiction, a symptom of her malady as well as his.

Unable to bear the emptiness of her life, this mother uses her child to ward off feelings of abandonment. The mother in the short story becomes *like* her son—doing whatever he does. (This is similar to the way children mimic their mothers whenever they feel abandoned, copying their mother's gestures and behavior to evoke the mother's presence, attempting to maintain the illusion that *they* are their mothers and thus are not alone.)

As this story suggests, parents tend to become like their children, especially after intense involvement in their daily care over many years. It seems to take enormous effort and strength of will not to become dependent on our children, not to adopt their childish characteristics when they are small, and their erratic, highly charged (in this case, highly destructive) behavior when they become adolescents.

Like Huck Finn, the fifteen-year-old son is trying to grow up, to escape his dependency on his mother (and hers on him), to flee his childhood. His raft, however, is not the wholesome, natural world of adventure, hightailing it out to "the Territory" with Jim, who is a slave also trying to get away. At first the raft is a debilitating illegal drug which obliterates feeling. (The mother starts taking it too because her life is so impoverished she cannot stand to be alone with herself.) Then the raft switches to rehabilitation, to emotional health. The raft becomes withdrawal from heroin, recovery, mental health. (We might speculate that Plath and Sexton tried to get on that raft—in their attempt to flee destructive internalized relationships—but they could not escape.)

In fact, drug addiction is often used as a substitute/compensation for earlier ties which have left the child emotionally crippled and dependent. Drugs blot out feelings of deprivation and longing which so many adolescents now find difficult to tolerate. Teenage violence and suicide are also prompted in part by the pain and rage caused by hurtful, impoverished relationships.

The mother in Paley's story learns from her son's exemplary behavior, becomes conscious of her destructive attempt to "keep" her son by becoming an addict herself. At the end of the story, the mother becomes a "receptionist in a storefront community clinic in the East Village" who helps people. After all, the mother is ". . . only about forty. She could be a hundred things in this world as time goes on—a teacher or a social worker; an ex-junkie! Sometimes it's better than having a masters in education."

This mother grows instead of shrinking; through the process of bonding and the tortuous relinquishment of that bond, she achieves a more mature and loving attitude toward herself and others. The story shows how our children sometimes offer us amazing possibilities for insight, transformation, and renewal.

Another wonderful example of a mother gaining insight from observing her child's behavior is described in the story "Faith in the Afternoon." Paley describes a young boy's indignation when he sees a peaceful demonstration against war being brutally and illegally dispersed by a policeman. This child does not consciously try to change his mother (a single, working parent who, during the intensive years of child rearing, has become prone to pettiness, and whose interests have dwindled to trying to find a man). Her son's behavior brings about a metamorphosis in the mother. She notices the outrage on her boy's face, notices his brave and compassionate defiance; she learns to direct her mind "out of that sexy playground" where she has raised her children. She begins to observe her child's "heartfelt brains," to take heed of his concerns and his future, which is precarious with the prospect of an endless, senseless war. This mother begins to mature, individuate, think "more and more every day about the world," for it is the world that becomes the holding environment into which we send our children.

What is it that we want for our children, now and in the future? We must think about these things every day. We must learn how to provide them with the most nurturing holding environment possible. But we must also explore the entire spectrum of our feelings toward our children. Only in this way can we ferret out whatever is destructive in us and hold it to the light. By illuminating these areas of darkness we will be able to confront the dangers facing the next generation.

Children are like windows that open onto the future as well as the past, the external world as well as our own private inner landscapes. We must find the courage to learn from all that they reveal to us.

The hope of a new generation, fed by the tenderness and care of an older generation, is threatened with extinction. The future of our children and grandchildren depends on our ability to explore the more dangerous aspects of parent-child relationships. What is most crucial to the fate of humanity is what, until recently, has been most hidden, suppressed, and denied in our culture. A thorough exploration of the emotional realities of child rearing has become a survival issue. We must persist in learning about this aspect of ourselves despite the fact that consciousness of our failures in nurturing naturally provokes feelings of shame and defensiveness.

We must learn to cherish each child from birth on and to honor and support every nurturer of children. Not to do so has become suicidal for the species. We can no longer afford to resist knowing what is involved in nurturing all children. We know now that we can repair, resolve, and heal our deepest wounds so that we will not pass them on to our children. Knowledge of the processes involved in the emotional life of care-givers can lead us to the problem solving we so urgently need, transforming destructive tendencies and distortions into positive ways of caring for ourselves and the world.

BIBLIOGRAPHY

Abelin, E. L., "Some Further Observations and Comments on the Earliest Role of the Father," *International Journal of Psychoanalysis* 56 (1975), 293–302.

Aries, Phillipe, *Centuries of Childhood, A Social History of Family Life*, New York: Vintage Books, 1962.

Badingter, Elizabeth, *Mother Love, Myth and Reality*, New York: Macmillan, 1980.

Balint, Alice, "Love for the Mother," *Primary Love and Psycho-Analytic Technique*, ed. Michael Balint, London: Tavistock Publications, 1939.

Benjamin, Jessica, *Bonds of Love*, New York: Pantheon Books, 1988.

_____, *Like Subjects, Love Objects*, New Haven: Yale University Press, 1995.

Bergman, Anni, "Considerations About the Development of the Girl During the Separation-Individuation Process," pp. 61–81 in *Early Female Development, Current Psychoanalytic Views*, ed. Dale Mendell, New York: Medical and Scientific Books, 1982.

Bernay, Toni, and Dorothy W. Cantor, *The Psychology of Today's Woman*, Hillsdale, N.J.: The Analytic Press, 1986.

Bettelheim, Bruno, *A Good Enough Parent*, New York: Vintage Books, 1987.

Bibring, Grete L., and Ralph J. Kahana, *Lectures in Medical Technology*, New York: International Universities Press, 1968.

Blos, Jr., Peter, "International Separation-Individuation: Treating the Mother-Infant Pair," *Psychoanalytic Study of the Child* 40 (1985), 41–57.

Bollas, Christopher, *The Shadow of the Object*, New York: Columbia University Press, 1987.

Bowlby, John, *Attachment and Loss: Vol. 1, Attachment*, New York: Basic Books, 1969.

———, *Attachment and Loss: Vol. 2, Separation, Anxiety and Anger*, New York: Basic Books, 1973.

Cahill, Susan, *Women and Fiction*, New York: Mentor, 1975.

Chasseguet-Smirgel, Janine, *Female Sexuality*, Ann Arbor: University of Michigan Press, 1970.

———, "The Femininity of the Analyst in Professional Practice," *International Journal of Psycho-Analysis* 65 (1984), 169–79.

Chayes, M., quoted in *Projection, Identification, Projective Identification*, ed. Joseph Sandler, Madison, Conn.: International Universities Press, 1987.

Chodorow, Nancy, *The Reproduction of Mothering*, Berkeley: University of California Press, 1978.

Chodorow, Nancy, and Susan Contratto, "The Fantasy of the Perfect Mother," in *Rethinking the Family*, New York and London: Longman, 1984.

Chopin, Kate, *The Awakening* (1899), Norton Critical Edition, New York: Norton, 1976.

Coontz, Stephanie, *The Way We Really Are*, New York: Basic Books, 1998.

Deutsch, Helene, *The Psychology of Women*, New York: Grune & Stratton, 1944.

———, *Confrontations with Myself*, New York: Norton, 1973.

Dinnerstein, Dorothy, *The Mermaid and the Minotaur*, New York: Harper and Row, 1976.

Emde, Robert N., "Development Terminable and Interminable: 1. Innate and Motivational Factors from Infancy," *The International Journal of Psychoanalysis*, V. 69 (1988).

Fraiberg, Selma H., *Every Child's Birthright, In Defense of Mothering*, New York: Basic Books, 1977.

———, "Ghosts in the Nursery," *Psychoanalytic Study of the Child*, New Haven: Yale University Press, 1983.

Frodi, A. M., and M. E. Lamb, "Sex Differences and Responsiveness to Infants," *Child Development* 49 (1978), 1182–88.

Furman, Edna, "Mothers Have to Be There to Be Left," *Psychoanalytic Study of the Child*, New Haven: Yale University Press, 1983.

Grubrich-Simitis, Ilse, "Extreme Traumatization as Cumulative Trauma," *Psychoanalytic Study of the Child*, New Haven: Yale University Press, 1981.

Harding, M. Esther, *The Way of All Women*, New York: Harper and Row, 1975 (originally published in 1970 by G. P. Putnam's Sons for the C. G. Jung Foundation).

Hardwick, Elizabeth, "On Sylvia Plath," in *Ariel Ascending*, ed. Paul Alexander, New York: Harper and Row, 1984.

Harris, Marvin, *Cultural Materialism*, New York: Vintage Books, 1980.

Hochschild, Arlie, *The Time Bind*, New York: Metropolitan Books, 1997.

500 Montezuma
Santa Fe NM 87501
505-954-4722

STORE: 0278   REG# 04/01 TRAN#: 0150
    5437957 CD T   15.99
GONE FROM DANGER
FULLY EMPOWERED
MYTH OF PERFECT MOTHER
MISS LEA'S BIBLE STORIES
WHEN THEY WERE KIDS
    5351210 OP T   14.95
TREASURY WOMENS QUOT
    4923549 IR T   4.99
AMEN
    4865484 IR T   3.98
EVERYTHING IS SOMEWHERE
    AUTH: 5278HM

THANK YOU FOR SHOPPING AT BORDERS
PLEASE ASK ABOUT OUR SPECIAL EVENTS

BORDERS
BOOKS AND MUSIC
500 Montezuma
Santa Fe NM 87501
505-954-4722

STORE: 0278   REG: 04/01   TRAN#: 0150
SALE   09/26/1998   EMP: 00022

SCOTCH HUMOUR-AYRES FOR VLN/GR
        5437957 CD T   15.99
GONE FROM DANGER
        4925382 CD T   15.99
FULLY EMPOWERED
        0900648 QP T   10.95
MYTH OF PERFECT MOTHER
        5308502 QP T   14.95
MISS LEA'S BIBLE STORIES
        5200060 IR T   4.99
WHEN THEY WERE KIDS
        5351210 QP T   14.95
TREASURY WOMENS QUOT
        4923349 IR T   4.99
AMEN
        4865486 IR T   3.98
EVERYTHING IS SOMEWHERE
        5349887 IR T   2.99

        Subtotal   89.78
        NM 6.25%   5.61
        Total   95.39
        PERS CHK   95.39
ACCT #   866413

            AUTH: 5278HM

        09/26/1998 03:13PM

THANK YOU FOR SHOPPING AT BORDERS
PLEASE ASK ABOUT OUR SPECIAL EVENTS

James, A. E., and T. Benedek, *Parenthood, Its Psychology and Psychopathology,* Boston: Little, Brown, 1970.

Kagan, J., *The Nature of the Child,* New York: Basic Books, 1984.

Klein, Melanie, *Love, Guilt and Reparation and Other Works 1921–45,* New York: Dell, 1975.

Kotelchuck, M., "The Infant's Relationship to the Father," in *The Role of the Father in Child Development,* ed. M. E. Lamb, New York: Wiley, 1976, 329–44.

Lasch, Christopher, *Women and the Common Life,* New York: Norton, 1997.

Lazarre, Jane, *The Mother Knot,* New York: Dell, 1976.

Lessing, Doris, *A Proper Marriage,* London: Michael Joseph, 1954.

Loewald, Elizabeth, "The Baby in Mother's Therapy," *The Psychoanalytic Study of the Child,* New Haven: Yale University Press, 1983.

Mahler, Margaret, and B. Gosliner, "On Symbiotic Psychosis," *The Psychoanalytic Study of the Child,* New Haven: Yale University Press, 1955.

Mahler, Margaret, Fred Pine, and Anni Bergman, *The Psychological Birth of the Human Infant,* New York: Basic Books, 1975.

McBride, Angela Baron, *The Growth and Development of Mothers,* New York: Harper and Row, 1973.

Mitscherlich, Alexander, *Society Without the Father,* New York: Schocken Books, 1963.

Ogden, Thomas H., "On Potential Space," *The International Journal of Psycho-Analysis,* vol. 66, 1985, 129–43.

———, *The Matrix of the Mind,* Northvale, N.J.: Jason Aronson, 1986.

Olds, Sharon, *The Gold Cell,* New York: Knopf, 1987.

Olsen, Tillie, *Tell Me a Riddle,* New York: Dell, 1960.

Ostriker, Alicia S., *The Mother-Child Papers,* Boston: Beacon Press, 1986.

———, *Stealing the Language,* Boston: Beacon Press, 1986.

Paley, Grace, *The Little Disturbances of Man,* New York: Viking, 1956.

———, *Enormous Changes at the Last Minute,* New York: Farrar, Straus, Giroux, 1960.

Parke, R., "Perspectives in Father-Infant Interactions," in *Handbook of Infant Development,* ed. J. D. Osofsky, New York: Wiley, 1979, pp. 110–30.

Parke, R., and D. B. Sawin, "The Family in Early Infancy," in *The Father-Infant Relationship,* ed. F. A. Pedersen, New York: Praeger, 1980, pp. 44–70.

Pedersen, F. A., B. Anderson, and R. Kain, "Parent-Infant and Husband-Wife Interactions Observed at Five Months," in *The Father-Infant Relationship,* ed. F. A. Pedersen, New York: Praeger, 1980, pp. 65–91.

Plath, Sylvia, *The Collected Poems,* New York: Harper and Row, 1960.

Pruett, Kyle D., "Infants of Primary Nurturing Fathers," in *Psychoanalytic Study of the Child,* New Haven: Yale University Press, 1983.

———, "Oedipal Configurations in Young Father-Raised Children," in *Psychoanalytic Study of the Child,* New Haven: Yale University Press, 1985.

Rich, Adrienne, *Of Woman Born*, New York: Norton, 1976.

Ruddick, Sara, *Maternal Thinking*, Boston: Beacon Press, 1989.

Rutter, M., "Maternal Deprivation, 1972–1978: New Findings, New Concepts, New Approaches," *Child Development*, 50 (1979), 283–305.

Seligman, Stephen, Special Issues in Child Abuse Cases. Presentation at the Biennial Training Institute of the National Center for Clinical Infant Programs, Washington, D.C., December 1985.

_____, "Concepts in Infant Mental Health: Implications for Work with the Developmentally Disabled," *Infants and Young Children*, (1988), 1:41–51.

_____, The effect of intervention relationships on parent-infant relationships: Perspectives from infant observation research and psychoanalysis. Presentation at the Reginald S. Lourie Scientific Forum, Washington, D.C., May 1989.

_____, "Applying Psychoanalysis in an Unusual Context: Adapting Infant-Parent Psychotherapy to a Changing Population," in *Psychoanalytic Study of the Child*, (1994), 49, pp. 481–501.

Seligman, S., and J. Pawl, "Impediments to the Formation of the Working Alliance in Infant-Parent Psychotherapy," in *Frontiers of Infant Psychiatry*, vol. 2, ed. J. D. Call, E. Galenson, and R. Tyson, New York: Basic Books, 1984.

Settlage, C. F., J. Curtiss, Marjorie Lozoff, Milton Lozoff, G. Silverschatz, and E. J. Simburg, "Conceptualizing Adult Development," *Journal of the American Psychoanalytic Association*, 36:2 (1988).

Sexton, Anne, *All My Pretty Ones*, Boston: Houghton Mifflin, 1961.

_____, *Live or Die*, Boston: Houghton Mifflin, 1966.

Slade, Arietta, and Lisa J. Cohen, "The Process of Parenting and the Remembrance of Things Past," *Infant Mental Health Journal*, vol. 17(3), 1996, 217–38.

Stern, Daniel, *The Interpersonal World of the Infant*, New York: Basic Books, 1985.

_____, *The Motherhood Constellation*, New York: Basic Books, 1995.

Winnicott, D. W., *The Maturational Processes and the Facilitating Environment*, Madison, Conn.: International Universities Press, 1965.

_____, *Playing and Reality*, London: Tavistock Publications, 1971.

Zak de Goldstein, Raquel, "The Dark Continent and Its Enigmas," *The International Journal of Psycho-Analysis*, 65 (1984).